Negativity and Revolution

Negativity and Revolution

Adorno and Political Activism

Edited by
JOHN HOLLOWAY,
FERNANDO MATAMOROS
and SERGIO TISCHLER

"ALFONSO VÉLEZ PLIEGO"

Instituto de Ciencias Sociales y Humanidades
Benemérita Universidad Autónoma de Puebla

PLUTO PRESS
www.plutobooks.com

First published 2009 by Pluto Press
345 Archway Road, London N6 5AA

www.plutobooks.com

British Library Cataloguing in Publication Data
A catalogue record for this book is available from the British Library

ISBN   978 0 7453 2837 9   Hardback
ISBN   978 0 7453 2836 2   Paperback

Library of Congress Cataloging in Publication Data applied for

10   9   8   7   6   5   4   3   2   1

Designed and produced for Pluto Press by
Chase Publishing Services Ltd, Sidmouth, EX10 9QG, England
Typeset from disk by Stanford DTP Services, Northampton
Printed and bound in the European Union by
CPI Antony Rowe, Chippenham and Eastbourne

CONTENTS

ACKNOWLEDGEMENTS

This book is the outcome of our collaboration in the permanent seminar on Subjectivity and Critical Theory in the postgraduate programme of sociology in the Instituto de Ciencias Sociales y Humanidades Alfonso Vélez Pliego of the Benemérita Universidad Autónoma de Puebla, which has been meeting fortnightly now for almost nine years. Without this constant stimulus the book would not have been possible. To all those who have participated in the seminar over the years, and especially those who participated in the sessions of the winter of 2006–07, which were devoted to discussing the draft chapters which now make up this book, our warmest thanks.

We wish also to thank Dr. Agustin Grajales, the Director of the Institute, for his work in making the Institute such a stimulating and agreeable place to work, and for his support for the publication of this English edition of the book.

To Yerson Rojas our thanks for the constant support and practical assistance that he provides us in dealing with the world of administration. To Anna-Maeve Holloway our warmest gratitude for the care and skill with which she has translated the texts that were written in Spanish and her preparation of the final manuscript of the book. And to Néstor López, Carlos Cuellar and all at Herramienta (Buenos Aires), our thanks for their help and support in the original publication of this book in Spanish.

An earlier version of Chapter 3 ('Pied Pipers and Polymaths: Adorno's Critique of Praxisism' by Adrian Wilding) appeared in Stefano Giacchetti Ludovisi (ed.), *Nostalgia For a Redeemed Future: Critical Theory* (Rome: John Cabot University Press, 2008). It is reproduced here by permission of the original publishers.

John Holloway, Fernando Matamoros and Sergio Tischler

I

Introduction to the Issues

1

NEGATIVITY AND REVOLUTION: ADORNO AND POLITICAL ACTIVISM

John Holloway, Fernando Matamoros, Sergio Tischler

I

This is not a book about Adorno; nor is it written by specialists in Adorno or set out to give a full and active portrayal of Adorno and his work. It is written, rather, by a number of people who consider it important for the development of anti-capitalist thought to read Adorno and particularly to develop his idea of negative dialectics. It starts from a simple question: why, in spite of everything, do we consider it important to develop Adorno's ideas? The "in spite of everything" refers to the difficulty of Adorno's language, but above all to the fact that he called in the police when students occupied the Institute of Social Research in January 1969.

II

This book takes sides in a political-theoretical controversy. This is a controversy that grows out of the collapse of the USSR and of the Leninist conception of revolution. The debate has to do with the meaning of dialectics and its role in revolutionary thought.

It has become common in recent years to denounce dialectics and argue that the anti-capitalist movement should abandon the concept. This rejection grows out of an identification of dialectics with the "dialectical materialism" proclaimed by the USSR and the Communist Parties, and it is particularly strong in those countries in which the Communist Parties were highly influential, politically and intellectually, especially France and Italy. The authors who take this position – Althusser, Deleuze, Guattari, Foucault, Derrida, Macherey, and more recently Hardt, Negri and Virno, among many others – see "dialectical materialism" as rooted in Hegel's dialectic, and their criticism of Communist Party politics takes the form of a repudiation of Hegel and a declared preference for Spinoza.

The rejection of dialectics focuses principally on two related points. It is argued that dialectical thought leads to closure rather than openness. The typical Hegelian triad of thesis–antithesis–synthesis ends in a closing synthesis, which provides the basis of a view of history as a series of stages or steps. The synthesis is a reconciliation of opposites, the establishment, in other words, of a new *modus vivendi* between labour and capital. A recent article by Hardt and Colectivo Situaciones states the charge clearly:

> The dialectical operation consists in putting an end to that which has none, giving a defined orientation to that which has no finality, taking (overcoming) the previous moments by rescuing what is useful (preserving) in the service of a new affirmation, prohibiting every consciousness of an irreducible diversity, of an excess which is not retaken… As final moment, this idea of the dialectic concludes open processes, synthesises in a final unity multiplicities without relations that are *a priori* determinable. (Hardt and Colectivo Situaciones 2007)

Related to this is the charge that the dialectical notion of contradiction means the suppression of differences, the reduction of a multi-coloured multiplicity of varied lives and struggles to the single contradiction of labour against capital. "The Hegelian dialectic destroys difference in two distinct moments: first it pushes all the differences to the point of contradiction, masking their specificities; and, precisely because the differences are emptied, as terms of a contradiction, it is possible to subsume them in a unity" (Hardt and Colectivo Situaciones 2007). The world is seen as a multiplicity of differences or singularities. The problem with the Hegelian dialectic is twofold: it pushes this great multiplicity into a single contradiction, and, because this contradiction is then devoid of content, it is easy to subsume it within a unitary synthesis. In the practice of the Communist Parties, the rich variety of struggles was subordinated to a concept of the working class (labour as contradiction of capital), and this working class, a concept largely devoid of meaning since it had been abstracted from the richness of real struggles and subordinated to the discipline of the Party, could then be easily integrated into a new capitalist synthesis (a welfare state, for example).

Those who argue against dialectics do so, then, in order to reject the synthetic closure associated with Hegelian dialectics and to emphasise the richness of social struggle, which they see as a multiplicity of differences rather than a single contradiction.

The emphasis on difference rather than contradiction has had a considerable influence. Whereas contradiction appeared to fit easily with forms of organisation that pitted (or seemed to pit) the working class against capital, the concept of difference is accommodated more easily to an organisation of struggle that takes the form of a multiplicity of groups emphasising their specific identities as homosexuals, indigenous, women, blacks, and so on. For such struggles, the attraction of the concept of multitude is clear: multitude refers to the loose alliance of struggles against the existing form of oppression (capitalism, neo-liberalism, postmodernism, whatever one likes to call it).

In spite of the attractions of this approach, there are problems, however, connected principally with the questions of negation and contradiction.

In the extension of the rejection of the Hegelian synthesis to the rejection of dialectics altogether, there is a throwing the baby out with the bathwater. It is not only synthesis that is abandoned, but also the central notion of movement through negation. "In the radical philosophy of immanence it is not life that is absent but negativity, contradiction as the model of movement" (Hardt and Colectivo Situaciones 2007). Life becomes a positive concept rather than the struggle against the negation of life. There is in general a positivisation of thought. Struggles are seen as struggles for, rather than being principally struggles against. The centrality of crisis (a negative concept) is lost and replaced by an emphasis on restructuring (a positive concept). Refusal is marginalised (though not denied) in the movement from the origins of autonomism (Tronti and his seminal article on "The Strategy of Refusal") to the post-autonomism of recent years (represented in particular by Hardt and Negri). Irony of ironies, a theory of stages makes its reappearance in the form of changing "paradigms": the world is to be understood at any particular moment in terms of the prevalent paradigm of domination. The rejection of dialectics, because it includes the rejection of negation, leads precisely to synthetic thought, a thinking that seeks to fit everything in place within the scheme of the dominant paradigm. This has not only theoretical but also political consequences: it can lead to a blurring of the distinction between negation and synthesis, between refusal and reconciliation, between an uprising and the reconciling government that follows the uprising.

The second problem is the abandonment of the idea of contradiction. The argument, as we have seen, is that the idea of contradiction operates like a straitjacket, forcing the infinite richness of life and struggle into a binary antagonism. The question, however, is whether this is the result of dialectical thought, or whether dialectics is simply reporting a process of antagonistic binarism that is actually taking place in the world. Capital is the name given to this process of antagonistic binarisation. Capital is not a thing but a social relation, a forced transformation of people's activity into labour: an alien activity shaped by the requirements of producing profit. It is not dialectics but capital that is the name of the straitjacket that forces our multiple differences into the binary antagonism of exploited labour. The immense and multicoloured richness of useful-creative doing (useful labour, as Marx calls it) is forcefully reduced to abstract, value-producing labour: that is what capital means. Difference is reduced by capital to contradiction, to an antagonism against its own suppression. In all our variety and difference we are put in prison, the prison of capitalism. Dialectics is, then, the escape plan, the thinking-against-the-prison, thinking-against-the-wrong-world, a thinking that would no longer make sense if we were outside the prison of the wrong world – but we are not. To put aside the dialectical awareness (not creation) of contradiction is to forget that we are in a prison, that we are living in a form of social organisation that daily reduces our infinite creativity to the monotonous process of producing profit. And that is in fact what happens with this line of thought: the concept of capital and capitalism fades into the background and the struggle is seen primarily not as one against capital but as a struggle for "real democracy." This leaves out of sight the central issue of any struggle for change: the organisation of our daily doing, the struggle of doing against labour. Our doing pushes towards difference, yearns for a world free of contradiction, but for the moment it is entrapped within contradiction, within a world of coercion enforced by money. To assert difference, then, is to make an assertion against, but the possibilities and movement of this assertion against can be understood only if we understand it as the movement of a contradiction.

This book shares many of the concerns mentioned above – the use of dialectical thought to impose closure and impose uniformity on struggle – but insists that it is nevertheless important to defend and develop the concept of dialectics. What we need is not to reject dialectics as such, but only the synthetic understanding of it: to insist, in other words, on a *negative* dialectics, a restless movement of negation that does not lead necessarily to a happy ending. History is seen not as a series of stages, but as the movement of endless revolt.

Adorno's importance, then, lies in the fact that it is he who develops the notion of a negative dialectic most directly, in his book of the same name. The opening words of the Preface declare his aim to be the freeing of dialectics from its positive heritage: "*Negative Dialectics* is a phrase that flouts tradition. As early as Plato, dialectics meant to achieve something positive by means of negation: the thought figure of a 'negation of negation' later became the succinct term. This book seeks to free dialectics from such affirmative traits without reducing its determinacy" (1990: xix). For Adorno, as for all the authors we have mentioned, the starting point is the political-theoretical failure of orthodox Marxism: he writes "after the attempt to change the world miscarried", after the "moment to realise [philosophy] was missed" (1990: 3). After Stalin, Auschwitz and Hiroshima there are no certainties, above all no guarantee of a happy ending. That is why it is necessary to abandon the notion of dialectics as a process of negation leading to a synthesis, a negation of negation leading to a positive ending. The only way in which we can now conceive dialectics is negatively, as a movement of negation rather than of synthesis, as a negative dialectics.

Why dialectics at all, then? Simply because it is the only form of thought adequate to a wrong world. Dialectics exists because we are in the wrong place, in the wrong sort of society: "dialectics is the ontology of the wrong state of things. The right state of things would be free of it: neither a system nor a contradiction" (1990: 11). It is the wrongness of the world that makes dialectics or negative thought necessary. The wrongness of the world means that right-thinking and right-doing are necessarily negative, thinking against and doing against. If the world is wrong, then we are negative beings; our very existence is a movement against. For Adorno, the central category is non-identity, the movement against identity, against that which is. "The name of dialectics says no more, to begin with, than that objects do not go into their concepts without leaving a remainder ... Contradiction ... indicates the untruth of identity, the fact that the concept does not exhaust the thing conceived" (1990: 5). Non-identity is the subterranean movement of the refusal of identity, of that which is: "contradiction is non-identity under the aspect of identity" (1990: 5). Dialectics is sensibility to the movement of this refusal: "dialectics is the consistent sense of non-identity."

Dialectics understood in this way is a movement of breaking and opening. Non-identity breaks identity and opens the way to the creation of something new. The movement of non-identity is the movement of creativity. Non-identity is an overflowing beyond what is, it is change and self-change, creation and self-creation. To put non-identity at the centre of philosophy is to put negation-creation at the centre.

Dialectics, so understood, is a long way from the dialectics rejected by Deleuze, Guattari, Hardt, Negri and others. Hardt and Colectivo Situaciones have recently recognised the danger of identifying all dialectics with the synthetic, Hegelian dialectics and, quoting Macherey, they suggest the need for an open dialectic: "What is a dialectic like here and now that functions in the absence of all guarantee ... without the promise that all contradictions on which it embarks will be resolved by right, because they carry in themselves the conditions of their resolution?" (Hardt and Colectivo Situaciones 2007). This is essentially the question asked by Adorno and the other members of the so-called Frankfurt School. The answer, Adorno suggests, can be conceived only in terms of a firmly negative dialectic.

III

This book is a series of reflections on the challenge posed by the idea of a negative dialectic.

The short opening chapter by John Holloway asks why we should read Adorno and suggests that an answer can be found by confronting him with Tronti and the autonomist tradition from which he is so different but with which he nevertheless shares the starting point of negation/refusal. The most striking difference between Adorno and the theorists of the autonomist tradition is, of course, that they immersed themselves in direct political action (and many of them were imprisoned as a result), whereas Adorno held himself aloof from the student movement of the late 1960s. And yet ...? Adrian Wilding, through an examination of Adorno's last lectures, discusses the complex relation between Adorno and the student movement in terms of Adorno's warning of the dangers of "thought bowing irrationally to the primacy of practice" and his fear of being pushed into the role of guru or, worse, Pied Piper of the movement. Wilding warns against coming to simplistic conclusions and emphasises Marcuse's strong defence of Adorno's political importance, despite the fact that Marcuse himself took a very different position in relation to the student movement.

In the second part of the book we focus specifically on the central theme of negative dialectics as a critique of neo-structuralism. In his chapter on "Antagonism and Difference," Alberto Bonnet centres his argument on the contrast between Adorno's emphasis on contradiction and the rejection by Deleuze and others of the notion of contradiction in favour of difference. He argues that the distinction has important political implications and that the emphasis on difference can easily lead to the theory and politics of liberalism. Darij Zadnikar takes up the same issue of the political implications of the rejection of dialectics and suggests that it is connected to the growth of a new "post-vanguardism" in the global movement against capitalism. A second short contribution by Holloway develops a similar point in terms of a contrast between positive and negative autonomism.

The third part of the book develops some of the key elements of the critique of mainstream revolutionary theory. Sergio Tischler focuses on the importance of Adorno's critique of totality and his insistence on the importance of particularity. The crisis of totality is the crisis of a whole mode of understanding and organising class struggle – in short, the crisis of party-Marxism which received its highest theoretical expression in the work of Lukács. The movement of particularity (or of non-identity) is the driving principle of an emerging new constellation of class struggle. Werner Bonefeld addresses the question of the political richness of Adorno through a discussion of Adorno's concept of the concept. The "constitutive character of the non-conceptual in the concept" (Adorno 1973: 12) unlocks the door to a critical understanding of class struggle as "permanent revolution", the ceaseless movement of determinate negation. This movement breaks through the pessimism that gives the tone to much of Adorno's work.

The book concludes with three chapters devoted to the themes of sexuality, art and metaphysics. Marcel Stoetzler opens up new directions with his exploration of the implications of Adorno's concept of non-identity for the politics of sexuality, linking Adorno with discussions in feminist and gay theory and the critique of the idea that sex can be understood in terms of a simple binary division into male and female. Sexual dimorphism is, he argues, an aspect or expression of the increasingly genital organisation of sexuality and the sublimation of Eros in the service of modern capitalism. Fernando Matamoros takes us in a rather different direction with his incursion into the realm of metaphysics as a starting point for the necessary criticism of the reified and repetitive world. He asks about Adorno's relation to metaphysics and the connection between his work and that of Benjamin and Bloch, and argues that the force of metaphysics is the critical utopia that can be found at the centre of the "dialectical carnivals of the everyday." José Manuel Martínez closes the book with a discussion of Adorno's aesthetic theory and its political relevance. He underlines the importance of seeing the "Aesthetic Theory" and the "Negative Dialectics" as a single project and suggests that they formed the basis for a richer understanding of social struggle in contemporary capitalism.

IV

This book is both an argument and an exploration. It argues that it is theoretically and politically important to develop the notion of a negative dialectic. But the argument is a challenge and an exploration. The movement of negation is a movement that detonates concepts, detonates power, detonates identity, detonates all that is familiar to us. It opens up a frightening, vertiginous, exciting world in which we are forced to question everything around us. The argument is a treading on unsafe ground, a feeling our way forward, an exploration of the world that opens up before us, theoretically and practically. Our argument is not the dogmatic one of certainty, but an argument that seeks to open, at times by provocation. We write in a context in which Zapatistas have made "*preguntando caminamos*" (asking we walk) a central principle of both political practice and scientific thought. That is the tone, then, of our argument and our exploration: *preguntando caminamos*, asking we walk.

REFERENCES

Adorno, T. W. (1990), *Negative Dialectics*. London, Routledge.
Hardt, M. and Colectivo Situaciones (2007) "Leer a Macherey," in P. Macherey, *Hegel o Spinoza*. Buenos Aires, Tinta Limón.
Tronti, M. (1979) "The Strategy of Refusal," in Red Notes, *Working Class Autonomy and the Crisis*. London, Red Notes.

2

WHY ADORNO?

John Holloway

Why Adorno? Adorno is difficult to read. Even worse, Adorno called in the police in 1969 when the Institute of Social Research in Frankfurt was occupied by students. So why turn to him now when our aim is not to become experts on Adorno or the Frankfurt School, but to sharpen our critique of capitalism?

Rupture and revolt and fragility and uncertainty and openness and pain are at the centre of Adorno's thought: that is why he is so exciting.

The starting point, for him as for us, is the political-theoretical failure of orthodox Marxism: "after the attempt to change the world miscarried," after the "moment to realise [philosophy] was missed," as he puts it in the opening lines of *Negative Dialectics* (1990: 3). After Stalin, Auschwitz and Hiroshima there are no certainties, above all no guarantee of a happy ending. That is why it is necessary to abandon the notion of dialectics as a process of negation leading to a synthesis, a negation of negation leading to a positive ending. The only way in which we can now conceive dialectics is negatively, as a movement of negation rather than of synthesis, as a negative dialectics.

But why bother with dialectics at all when orthodox "dialectical materialism" had "degenerated into a dogma" (1990: 7)? Others (Negri, for example, but also the whole poststructuralist current – Foucault, Deleuze, Guattari, Virno, and so on – that is currently so influential in anti-capitalist thought) took the opposite route and decided to reject dialectics and emphasise materialism. To focus on Adorno is to question the poststructuralist route taken by those authors.

Why dialectics, then? Adorno's reply is that dialectics is not a standpoint. It expresses, rather, the inevitable insufficiency of thought, the disjointed relation between thought and the objects of thought. "The name of dialectics says no more, to begin with, than that objects do not go into their concepts without leaving a remainder ... Contradiction ... indicates the untruth of identity, the fact that the concept does not exhaust the thing conceived" (1990: 5). Thought identifies ("to think is to identify"), but that which is thought overflows the thought itself. Dialectics is thought's awareness of its own inadequacy, of the non-identity which is contained within, bursts from and overflows the identity which thought would impose. "Contradiction is non-identity under the aspect of identity" and "dialectics is the consistent sense of non-identity."

That is the central theme of Adorno's thought: dialectics as the consistent sense of non-identity, of that which does not fit. It is both libertarian and revolutionary. It is libertarian because its pivot and driving force is the misfit, irreducible particularity, the non-identity that cannot be contained, the rebel who will not submit to party discipline. It is revolutionary because it is explosive, volcanic. If there is no identity other than the identity that is undermined by non-identity, then there is no possibility of stability. All identity is false, contradictory, resting on the negation of the non-identity which it suppresses, which it seeks to contain but cannot. And it cannot contain it, not just for some contingent reason, such as the inefficiency of the police, but because identification always runs behind the flow of non-identity, is never able to pin it down and hold it still.

It is clear that non-identity is the hero, the centre, the moving force of the world as Adorno presents it. But what do we understand by non-identity? Is it just a philosophical concept, or is it the conceptualisation of a social force? The answer, surely, is that *we* are non-identity. The force that does not fit, the force that contradicts all identification, the force that overflows is subjectivity, *we*. And who are *we*? We are the subject, uncontainable within any definition. We can say that we are the working class, but that makes sense only if we understand "working class" as a concept that explodes against itself, a concept that bursts its own bounds.

Does Adorno actually say that *we* are non-identity? Not as far as I know. Perhaps I am reading him in a non-identitarian way, against and beyond Adorno. But how else can we understand non-identity? Non-identity can only be a force that changes itself, that drives beyond itself, that creates and creates itself. And where do we find a creative and self-creative force? Not animals, not god, not nature, only humans, we. Not an identitarian we, but a disjointed, ill-fitting, creative we.

This is not a liberal-humanist we, but an antagonistic, self-antagonistic we. We are part of an antagonistic entirety in which the "subject [is] the subject's foe" (1990: 10). Dialectics exists because we are in the wrong place, in the wrong sort of society: "dialectics is the ontology of the wrong state of things. The right state of things would be free of it: neither a system nor a contradiction." The dialectical *we* is the contradictory *we* who live in-and-against capitalist society, a non-identitarian class *we*.

II

Adorno Meets Tronti. In his seminal article "Lenin in England" (published in 1964, two years before Adorno's *Negative Dialectics*), Tronti wrote, "We too have worked with a concept that puts capitalist development first, and workers second. This is a mistake. And now we have to put the problem on its head, reverse the polarity, and start again from the beginning: and the beginning is the class struggle of the working class" (1979: 1). Words far removed from Adorno's, yet here is the question, the interweaving of autonomist and critical theory. Tronti (and the other theorists-practitioners of *operaismo*) turned orthodox Marxism on its head and put working-class struggle (and not capital) at the centre of their analysis. Adorno (and the other members of the Frankfurt School) turned orthodox Marxism on its head and put non-identity at the centre of their analysis. Adorno probably did not meet Tronti and quite possibly would not have wanted to, but we can make them meet.

"Dialectics is the consistent sense of non-identity." Dialectics means thinking the world from that which does not fit, from those who do not fit, those who are negated and suppressed, those whose insubordination and rebelliousness break the bounds of identity, from *us* who exist in-and-against-and-beyond capital. This is surely the same as the autonomist project formulated by Tronti: less explicitly political, but it goes much deeper, because the attack on identity goes to the core of life itself, touches directly who we are and how we think. The autonomist project of *operaismo* was ambiguous precisely because it did not go far enough, because it did not question the identitarian concept of the working class as an identifiable group. It turns the capital–labour relation on its head, but to be consistent, it should have turned the whole world on its head; putting non-identity at the centre of the way we breathe and how we think. It is this limitation that leads, then, to the later unfortunate and stultifying union of some autonomist thinkers with poststructuralism, a tradition that denies the centrality of the subject and hence of working-class struggle.

The development of the autonomist project (the drive towards social self-determination) requires critical theory (just as, indeed, the development of critical theory requires the autonomist project, and not the social-democratic ruminations of Habermas, for example). Why? Because the autonomist project puts working-class struggle (or anti-capitalist struggle) at the centre of our understanding of the world, as driving force and not as reaction, and because the project of critical theory also puts working-class struggle (as non-identity) at the centre of our understanding of the world, as driving force, not as reaction. Am I, then, saying that we can replace "working-class struggle" for "non-identity" in Adorno: "dialectics is the consistent sense of working-class struggle"? Yes, but obviously only if we understand class struggle as the movement of non-identity (a tautology, since non-identity can only be understood as movement). Thus: "We too have worked with a concept that puts identity first, and non-identity second. This is a mistake. And now we have to put the problem on its head, reverse the polarity, and start again from the beginning: and the beginning is the movement of non-identity." Is this not doing violence to both Adorno and Tronti? Of course, but is it a creative violence, does it take us forward in the struggle against capitalism, against the identity of a system built on death?

Non-identity is creativity, identity is the negation of creativity: everything *is*. In capitalism, non-identity exists "under the aspect of identity" (1990: 5), creativity exists in the form of non-creativity, doing exists in the form of alienated labour. The strength of the subject exists as the "fallacy of constitutive subjectivity": "to use the strength of the subject to break through the fallacy of constituted subjectivity – this is what the author felt to be his task ever since he became to trust his own mental impulses" (1990: xx). Dialectics turns the strength of the subject against the fallacy of constituted subjectivity: the "subject [is] the subject's foe" (1990: 10). Dialectics is the consistent sense of that which lies hidden: the non-identity that exists under the aspect of identity, the creativity that exists as the fetishised rule of things, the strength of the subject that is concealed by the "fallacy of constitutive subjectivity." "Our thinking heeds a potential that waits in the object ... the resistance of thought to mere things in being, the commanding freedom of the subject, intends in the object, even that of which the object was deprived by objectification" (1990: 19). Dialectics seek to bring to light the power of human creativity that lies in all that negates that power, to understand the world and not just the capital–labour relation (understood in traditional identitarian terms) from the perspective of human creativity. That is why dialectics has to be at the core of the autonomist project and why the autonomist project has to be at the core of critical theory. Without that connection they both dry up, become academic playthings, and Adorno becomes an intellectual adornment, part of the culture industry which he hated.

"Thought as such, before all particular contents, is an act of negation, of resistance to that which is forced upon it" (1990: 19). Life too.

REFERENCES

Adorno, T. W. (1990) *Negative Dialectics*. London, Routledge.
Tronti, M. (1979) "Lenin in England," in Red Notes, *Working Class Autonomy and the Crisis*. London, Red Notes.

3

PIED PIPERS AND POLYMATHS: ADORNO'S CRITIQUE OF PRAXISISM

Adrian Wilding

For many readers the philosophy of Theodor Adorno has become synonymous with esoteric intellectualism, cultural elitism, the isolation of the theorist from the social struggles of his day. The English philosopher Bryan Magee voiced this widespread feeling towards Adorno's thought back in 1978 in a television interview with another member of the Frankfurt School, Herbert Marcuse. He put it to Marcuse that Adorno's writings were "turgid," even "unreadable," and that they erected a barrier between the author and any political agent who might possibly realise their aspirations (Magee 1978: 72). Marcuse's response was surprising in its magnanimity, given what we know of the tensions between him and Adorno. He repeated a claim he had already made, that Adorno was "without doubt a genius," that he knew of no one "so equally well at home in philosophy, sociology, psychology, music." Whenever Adorno spoke, Marcuse continued, the words could be printed verbatim, so fully-fledged were his formulations. And the difficulty of the ideas Adorno expressed was testament not to a wilful obscurantism but to the opacity and contradictoriness of the social system he attempted to comprehend. Marcuse's spirited defence was echoed some years later in remarks by the leading light of the second-generation Frankfurt School, Jürgen Habermas. According to Habermas,

Adorno was a genius; I say that without a hint of ambiguity ... [He] had an immediacy of awareness, a spontaneity of thought, and a power of formulation which I have never encountered before or since. One could not observe the process of development of Adorno's thoughts: they issued from him complete – he was a virtuoso in that respect ... As long as one was with him, one was caught up in the movement of thought. Adorno did not have the common touch; it was impossible for him, in an altogether painful way, to be commonplace. (Habermas 1992: 220)

What Habermas puts down to personality, Marcuse – interestingly – politicises. Adorno's difficult style is said to be grounded in its very subject matter, the *verkehrte* world of late capitalism. In such a topsy-turvy world of systematic illusion it might be that divining the truth about the social whole requires a language and a thought process unafraid of contradiction and complexity. In a time when abstract labour and exchange value come to permeate not only social relations but even language and thought, the language of critique included, it might be a necessary cause to resist "premature popularisation of the terribly complex problems we face" (Magee 1978: 72).

One reason why Adorno is viewed as a philosopher at one step removed from the *sensus communis* is surely the curious and slightly farcical detail of his final months. Adorno's language alienated him not just from Anglo-American philosophers whose objections Magee voiced, but equally from the student radicals of the late 1960s who mocked his political aloofness and ridiculed him in ways which probably contributed to his fatal heart attack. The now infamous scene in which two female students attacked him with flowers and slogans – "Adorno as an institution is dead!" – reflected a widespread feeling that even this theorist of repression shared in society's repressive tendencies (Jäger 2004: 198–207). Such judgements must have been all the more galling for Adorno, who meanwhile was watching the meteoric fortunes of his one-time colleague Marcuse participating in the student protests in just those ways which Adorno resisted.

With the publication of Adorno's *opus postumum*, specifically his lectures from the mid to late 1960s, it may be possible finally to determine the truth of this picture of a remote and politically impotent intellectual. But it may also be possible to test the truth of Marcuse's assertion that what Adorno said could stand on its own, verbatim, unedited, because the lectures Adorno gave in the final decade of his life at the University of Frankfurt were improvised and largely spontaneous. These lectures are all the more remarkable for this and confirm the picture of a man whose extemporising could be committed straight to paper and to press. Not only their spontaneity but the sheer variety of lecture topics covered, the sustained erudition on themes across the humanities and social sciences, do indeed support Marcuse's portrait of an intellect totally at home in whichever topic he spoke on.

But while one can admire the polymath erudition of these lectures, one can fall into the trap of confirming a cult of genius which Adorno's own intellect sought critically to engage. To this extent it may be more illuminating to read these lectures in their historical context rather than as the disembodied thoughts of a "free-floating intellectual," which it seems Adorno's student critics took him to be, but which he had already exposed as fundamentally rooted in that same capitalist division of labour which divided hand and mind, intellect and action, and was itself to be overcome (Adorno 1983: 42).

A useful way to read these lectures, therefore, might be not simply as philosophy or theory but also as an expression of the politically momentous times in which they were delivered. To read Adorno in a way which is consistent with his own avowed "materialism" – not a crude materialism which reduces philosophy and ideas to history or to class interests, but in such a way as would do justice to his own notion of the philosophical moment of the whole, where thought is able to articulate a crisis-ridden historical conjuncture, and yet through this come to something "essential"; to read Adorno, in other words, just as we will see Adorno read Kant's philosophy, not just as philosophy but "as a kind of coded text from which the historical situation of spirit could be read, with the vague expectation that in doing so one could acquire something of truth itself" (Adorno 2001: 251, fn. 7).

"THIS IS THE AUSCHWITZ GENERATION"

This requires some background to the events of the late 1960s in which Adorno's lectures were delivered and some knowledge of the trajectory which led him back to Frankfurt after the war and to the position he would attain as one of the leading men of German letters. Some of this background is familiar to readers on the left today: the works which had generated Adorno's fame by the time of the Frankfurt School's exile in America from Nazi Germany are now widely read, even if they are too often taken in isolation from the particular experiences which inspired them. The intellectual touchstones of Adorno's collaboration with Max Horkheimer for instance, *Dialectic of Enlightenment* – Schopenhauer, Nietzsche and de Sade – were testament to just how far the experience of Fascism had dislodged faith in the humanist traditions of the German Enlightenment. In the immediate postwar era, not only were Horkheimer and Adorno's political assumptions rethought (though their 1920s prediction of Fascism was confirmed with chilling accuracy), both had started to believe in a deep complicity between the philosophy of the Enlightenment with its championing of the rational mastery of external and internal nature, and the kinds of worldviews characterising totalitarianism. Instead of the leading figures of German Idealism and the Enlightenment, Horkheimer and Adorno turned to the Enlightenment's harshest critics. Though not wholly abandoning the Enlightenment project, they had certainly lost faith in its cosmopolitan and pacific ideal. If in the 1760s Voltaire could confidently argue that torture and similar human atrocities would soon be things of the past, to Horkheimer and Adorno, writing in exile as news reached them of the Holocaust, this judgement seemed increasingly Panglossian. For Adorno, only the "dark writers of the bourgeoisie" could now lay claim to have recognised the world's course, the reversal of an ostensibly self-perfecting humanity into barbarism.

The period between the publication of *Dialectic of Enlightenment* (1947) and Adorno's own *magnum opus*, *Negative Dialectic* (1966) is perhaps less well known in its influence on the direction of critical theory. It was an era in which the trends foreseen by

Horkheimer and Adorno could not have been further from the dominant consciousness of the German society to which they returned from exile. Germany's recent past was strenuously being played down in favour of ideological unity, economic reconstruction and political re-education, the schooling of democratic values into the new generation. Sure enough, Germany was witnessing the beginnings of its *Wirtschaftswunder*, that remarkable growth in productivity and consumption that would eventually give it dominant economic status in Europe. But, for a writer like Adorno, there was something worryingly unchanged in German society: the political re-education which the Allies sought to instil in the young was leaving their parents' generation largely untouched.

On the political left there was a growing recognition that the Fascist chapter of German history was not over. The continuities in political personnel, state structure and corporate power between postwar Germany and the twelve years of Fascism were now there for many to see. To a growing number of people 1950s Germany seemed not a new democracy but a "restoration society" (Thomas 2003: 13). For Adorno particularly, the structural preconditions for Fascism's recrudescence had in no way been thoroughly excised. In an essay from 1959 he argues that "the past will have been worked through only when the causes of what happened then have been eliminated. Only because the causes continue to exist does the captivating spell of the past remain to this day unbroken" (Adorno 1998: 103). What Horkheimer and Adorno had already posited in the 1930s as a continuum rather than a strict opposition between liberal democracy and Fascism was now recognised as the dark secret of the postwar settlement.

By the mid 1960s the residual Fascism which these authors found deep within the mass consumption society was becoming clear to the student generation too; that many former Nazis retained their jobs in the universities brought the issue particularly close to home. A Chancellor-led state, unresponsive to opposition by parliamentary means, paralleled an undemocratic, hierarchical university structure; both were perceived by students as run by the same "authoritarian personalities" already diagnosed by the Frankfurt School. For the younger generation a rising standard of living was having the paradoxical effect of fuelling disaffection with the consumer-led economic boom which had ostensibly vindicated the direction of postwar development. German youth found themselves politicised not just by a rejection of their parents' wartime complicities, but by the emergence of new cultures of personal expression and experimentation which made use of the very free time afforded by economic growth. When fuelled by the wider international protests against the Vietnam War this made for an explosive mix. Not that one should overlook the provocative actions of a right-wing German popular press, which informed its readership that students were a fifth column dangerously close to the heart of German society. During the 1960s the media empire of Axel Springer was feeding off the increasing number of extra-parliamentary confrontations, telling its readers that the students were a Soviet-backed insurrection. The vilified would respond in kind: in 1968 the Berlin Film School was occupied by its students, who set about making an *agitprop* work, *Manufacturing a Molotov Cocktail*, a film which ends with an inviting still of the glass-fronted Springer newspaper building (Elsaesser 1989:156).

Many students needed no such provocation. On June 2, 1967, during protests against the visit to Berlin of the fascist Shah of Iran, a young man named Benno Ohnesorg was shot in the back by a plain clothes police officer from the "political crimes" squad (Thomas 2003: 112). When the police tried to cover up what had happened, tens of thousands of students in both Berlin and Frankfurt took to the streets. Later the same day a young woman named Gudrun Ensslin, grand-daughter of the grand-daughter of a certain G. W. F. Hegel, spoke to a meeting of radical students: "This fascist state means to kill us all .... Violence is the only way to answer violence. This is the Auschwitz generation and there's no arguing with them" (Aust 1987: 44). Soon after, Ensslin, along with her boyfriend Andreas Baader, would plant incendiary bombs in a large Frankfurt department store, describing the act as "sharing with the rich capitalists something of the reality of the Vietnam War."

Such actions raised the stakes in the struggle considerably. Sure enough, the West German state was not standing idly by. A grand coalition was busy hurrying through the *Notstandgesetze* (Emergency Laws), allowing them free rein "in time of emergency" to censor the press, ban strikes, increase surveillance on dissidents and call in the army to break up demonstrations. An oppressively enforced consensus politics was authorising a suspension of the very guarantees which the *Bundesrepublik*'s constitution had meant to enshrine. It seemed that a dialectical reversal of Enlightenment had been joined by a dialectical reversal of democracy.

"THE FALSE PERSONA OF A GURU"

When unfavourable comparisons are made with the radical figureheads of the German student movement it is forgotten that Adorno himself made several keynote speeches showing sympathy for their aims to rid the universities of politically tainted personnel, and resisting the emergency legislation (Wiggershaus 1995: 627–8). But the student revolts also saw Adorno come under increasing pressure to go further and give intellectual leadership to their cause. Radicals in the student movement levelled against Adorno the same charge Marx and Engels had made against "The German Ideology" – that his philosophy was lost in the mists of speculation. Adorno, many felt, had privileged theory over practice and abandoned the revolutionary project at just the moment when a new revolution seemed possible. Not oblivious to the clamour around him, Adorno explicitly addressed the issue in his Frankfurt University lectures.

> I have found again and again that when carrying out theoretical analyses – and theoretical analyses are essentially critical in nature – I have been met by the question: "Yes, but what shall we do?" and this question has been conveyed with a certain undertone of impatience, an undertone which proclaims: "All right, what is the point of all this theory? It goes on far too long, we do not know how we should behave in the real world, and the fact is we have to act right away!" (Adorno 2001: 3)

Adorno finds himself having to respond explicitly to the increasingly tense situation and the political pressures placed upon him. He tells his students that the call for direct political action is problematic, because it is a desire for immediacy amidst the most mediated, amidst the complex and opaque capitalist society in which both student and teacher find themselves: "there is nowadays a great danger," he says, "of what might be termed an illicit shortcut to practical action" (Adorno 2001: 3). Such shortcuts, he tells them, rest ironically on the reverse of that which philosophy is accused, a subordination of theory to practice (and an attenuation of the original meaning of both terms), and in this subordination Adorno sees an unholy alliance of radical politics with the most instrumental attitudes of the ruling ideology, a *symptom* of alienation rather than the solution to it.

Adorno's turn in these lectures to a careful and remarkably sympathetic exposition of the philosophy of Kant can be read as his own way, within the restrictions of an academic syllabus in a philosophy department, of examining such illicit shortcuts to practical action. Kant's moral philosophy, Adorno reminds us, always maintained an interest in action and "practical reason" as moral thinking was revealingly called. Kant in turn drew on the resources of ancient philosophy, in particular Greek philosophy's foregrounding of praxis and "practical wisdom" (Aristotle's *Phronesis*) in its examination of "the good life." But by Kant's time practical reason had already lost many of the nuances which the concept of praxis evoked for the Greeks. The heyday of the Enlightenment coincided with an emergent division of labour which was busy parcelling up experience into separate spheres such that philosophies like Kant's could respond only with their own specialised critiques. By the mid twentieth century, Adorno argues, this attenuation of praxis had only worsened, becoming mere "practicality," guided by a wholly instrumental and anti-theoretical idea of action. For Adorno the rhetoric of "practicality" is symptomatic rather than illuminating of a state of unfreedom:

> The more uncertain practical action has become, the less we actually know what we should do, and the less we find the good life guaranteed

to us – if it was ever guaranteed to anyone – then the greater our haste in snatching at it. This impatience can very easily become linked with a certain resentment towards thinking in general, with a tendency to denounce theory as such.[1]

Ironically, the denigration of theory and the intellectual by those outside the academy sits alongside its opposite within the academy: a submissive *over-valuation* of the intellectual, who becomes something of a superego or even "father-figure," able to bring decisiveness to a moment of political uncertainty. This too, Adorno suggests, is to be resisted: "precisely because I am aware that very many of you have great confidence in me, I would be extremely reluctant to abuse that confidence by presuming to slip into – even if it were only through my lecturing style – the false persona of a guru, a sage" (Adorno 2001: 2). The over-valuation of the intellectual is, Adorno argues, a kind of transference, symptomatic of a powerlessness instilled in the individual from an early age and is reproduced in the hierarchical structure of society in much the same way as the Frankfurt School's *Studies on Authority and the Family* from the 1930s had shown individuals' susceptibility to authoritarian leaders being nurtured in the most intimate structures of the family. The students' high regard for their teacher could easily switch into masochistic abasement before charismatic power. A teacher's responsibility at a moment of crisis was to avoid such temptations. The art of imparting practical wisdom becomes for Adorno a tightrope walk, using the authority of the speaker to empower the addressee in non-pathological ways.

The desire for decisive leadership in a moment of political crisis is caught up in a whole series of societal mediations, not the least being the existing structure of hierarchy and authority. Not that Adorno is simply denying immediacy in favour of mediation; this itself would be undialectical. But the philosophical point had some political reasoning behind it: Adorno seems to anticipate how easily direct actions on the part of the students would be used to legitimise repressive countermeasures by the state, turning latent into manifest power, and limiting the possibilities for future struggle. And yet he acknowledges that in even drawing attention to this possibility he will be accused of reaction.

> However, I do not think that because we ruthlessly define the blocked state and disproportionate power relationships of the present situation, we should therefore be branded with quietism or resignation. For anyone who shrinks back from analysing the existing structure for the sake of a thesis to be demonstrated or a goal to be achieved thereby betrays both truth and theory; and that is quite certainly not what has ever been meant by the unity of theory and practice. (Adorno 2002: 28)

Recognition of the mediation of the immediate does not render the immediate *aufgehoben*; on the contrary, it is equally true that there is no mediation without a moment of immediacy (Adorno 1993: 91).[2] It is not that spontaneous actions are to be condemned. It is just that the student movement had not had, in Adorno's eyes, "that slightest experience," as Hegel calls it, which would have revealed the dialectical nature of its political activity.

Adorno's formulations are not without their problems. His notion of "the blocked state" (2001: 3), a condition as much intellectual as social in which every attempt to change society radically seems closed off, would appear to hypostasise in the form of a structural constraint something which is surely more contradictory and fluid. In his lectures on Kant's *Critique of Pure Reason* Adorno seems to respond to this criticism, condemning a similar conception of the "blocked state" which led Kant to see individual freedom as "noumenal," incapable of being experienced. This notion, Adorno tells us, may merely register a limit in the bourgeois society of Kant's time. It would be the duty of a critical theory of society to refuse the boundary-setting of Kantian philosophy and to think of a freedom actualised and actualisable.

"A CODED TEXT OF THE HISTORICAL SITUATION"

Not only does Adorno use these lectures to warn his students of the complex relation of theory to practice, he also makes thematic the very practical situation in which his students find themselves, their social position as future labour power in an education system mediated by economic imperatives. It is as part of the university's preparation of its students for a life of "socially useful work" (as Adorno quotes Marx's ironic phrase) under the sign of increasingly "anonymous and opaque economic processes" that they have come to his lectures in the first place (Adorno 2002: 3, 24). Like Weber in his 1918 essay on "Science as a Vocation," Adorno begins his 1968 lecture series *Introduction to Sociology* by warning of the perils of studying the very subject the students have embarked on. Where Weber had warned of the "Americanisation" of the academy – there a student treats the lecturer as selling knowledge "just as the greengrocer sells cabbage" (Weber 1991: 149) – Adorno half a century later tells his students that they will find their academic work no less subject to the capitalisation of the life of the mind. He also warns that the kind of insights upon society which their subject will give them could make it very difficult for them to adapt to that same society and to find in it their station and its duties. "Today this fact – that the better one understands society, the more difficult it is to make oneself useful within it – has probably become a regular part of the consciousness of the intellectually progressive sector of students, and at any rate, I expect, of those in this hall today" (Adorno 2002: 3).

These words come from April 1968, almost at the height of the protests, and show Adorno was well aware of how radicalised his students had become. But he was also cognisant of how that radicalism could be abused by those who presumed to speak on the students' behalf. A rift was clearly emerging between the Frankfurt School and the student leadership. Demands for critical theory to lead the way in political intervention, to "describe a concrete utopia" as the student figurehead Rudi Dutschke asked of the School (Wiggershaus 1995: 622), were for Adorno anathema to the very dialectical nature of the social object critical theory analyses. It was bad theory which indicted theory as such for having no clear praxis.

Not that one could thereby explain or excuse all of Adorno's actions during the height of student unrest: his calling the police to evict striking students from the Frankfurt University building has become infamous – and rightly so – but probably only because it is so easily contrasted with Marcuse's enthusiastic part in the sit-ins at American campuses. The contrast may reflect merely the directness and perspicuity of Marcuse's version of critical theory rather than something inherently conservative in Adorno's. Indeed, Adorno seems to have felt the call for him to lead his students out of the lecture theatres and onto the streets as just the sort of Pied Piper role – what Weber called "charismatic authority" – of which a genuinely critical intellectual should be deeply suspicious.

One reason why Adorno might have been reluctant to endorse such activity may have been – surprisingly – the influence of one of his students, Jürgen Habermas. Habermas had already conducted research at Frankfurt into the political consciousness of the generation coming into their majority during the postwar reconstruction. *Students and Politics* (1957) was the result of extensive polling which sought to determine how students were coping with the *Bundesrepublik*'s attempt to instil democratic values. Habermas's study drew on the techniques of the First Generation Frankfurt School's research on authority, which in the early 1930s had found the germs of authoritarianism in various strata of German society. Habermas found similarly entrenched ambivalence towards democratic ideas in the postwar period. What he learned in his *Students and Politics* research would be ammunition for his belief in the late 1960s that the student revolts might well be doomed to failure.

Habermas went further than Adorno in criticising the student revolts, and in more striking language. When Rudi Dutschke (responding to the death of Benno Ohnesorg which had made incendiaries of Ensslin and Baader) voiced the relatively tame demand for "continuous action against all forms of authority," Habermas called Dutschke's "a voluntarist ideology which in 1848 one would have called utopian socialism," but which in 1967 amounted to "left fascism" (Ryan 2003: 16). These words were a red rag to the bulls of the student movement and Habermas would not be forgiven for them. He was unrepentant, though. Reflecting in 1969 on the previous year's actions, he argued that the student protests had been a "phantom revolution," which like the rebellious act of the sons against their father in Freud's *Moses and Monotheism*, had succeeded only in re-inscribing patriarchal state power. Identification on the part of the protesters with revolutionary struggles in the Third World was, according to Habermas, an illusory compensation for the derailing of the revolutionary project in the First World and underlined the symptomatic nature of the revolt. What had happened in Germany, he argued, had left the existing order intact, only further legitimising the state of emergency. There was something to this: the German chief of police certainly welcomed the blank cheque he was given to root out and incarcerate "terrorists," now firmly linked in the public mind with student activists, the result of a skilfully orchestrated press campaign. The deaths in Stammheim prison a few years later of Ensslin and Baader would give some idea of the ferocity of the state's backlash. Ironically, the Frankfurt School would be held partly responsible for the ideology of groups like Baader-Meinhof, though mostly on the evidence of a prominent member of the Christian Democratic Union with a particular distaste for critical theory, a certain Josef Ratzinger (Ryan 2003:16).

Such posthumous smears on the Frankfurt School's First Generation were the ideological aspect of the state's victory in the struggle. They are all the more reason to look carefully beneath the surface of a history of 1960s Germany that has been "written by the victors." But this also requires going beyond the apparent silence in Adorno's lectures on what was happening *extra muros*, and realising that the political events are, despite appearances, reflected in them at a deep level, through Adorno's choice of academic subject matter, concepts and language. We need to hear, as it were, the "noises off," occasionally registered by the *Lectures*' editor, for instance in the cheers which attend Adorno's more committed statements. We also need to realise what was at stake in an intellectual turning the academic syllabus towards topics he would have known were of theoretical and practical import to the political actions occurring outside. Even in the seemingly abstruse topic of lectures on Kant's *First* and *Second*

Critiques Adorno can be seen to lay before his students new ways of conceiving the relation of theory to social actuality. The practical resources contained within the tradition of German philosophy were themselves threatened by a crude but popular Marxism, which had ostensibly "solved" the problems of philosophy. It may be possible too that Adorno was trying to impart something of the inspiration of his first encounter with Kant's *Critique of Pure Reason*, as a 17-year-old schoolboy. Adorno suspected that there was more than met the eye in this forbidding tome: "I experienced the work from the beginning not as mere epistemology, not as an analysis of the conditions of scientifically valid judgments, but as a kind of coded text from which the historical situation of spirit could be read" (Adorno 2001: 251, fn. 7). He found in Kant's *First Critique* the expression of an early bourgeois world, emergent modernity, in which the scientific Enlightenment, flushed with the ideal of progress, has nevertheless put restrictions on reason and knowledge and turned its face towards the practical:

We might say that the achievement of the *Critique of Pure Reason* is that a whole series of these great metaphysical, fundamental concepts vanished from the horizon of what could be rationally decided .... It is a critique of the ability of reason to pose such [metaphysical] questions, to do them justice. We may say perhaps that the enormous impact of the *Critique of Pure Reason* has its source in the circumstance that it was in effect the first work to give expression to the element of bourgeois resignation, to that refusal to make any significant statement on the crucial questions, and instead to set up house in the finite world. (Adorno 2001: 6)

Kant's philosophy turned away from metaphysical speculation, put a "no entry" sign around the Absolute (that "block" again) and, whilst turning its gaze heavenward (as Kant's *Second Critique* famously ends), actually resigned itself to the mundane practical sphere: "We might almost say, then, that what has been codified in the *Critique of Pure Reason* is a theodicy of bourgeois life which is conscious of its own practical activity while despairing of the fulfilment of its utopia" (Adorno 2001: 6). It is just that resignation, that despair of realising its utopia, that Adorno warns against, clearly aware that the same charge has been levelled at his own work. Statements such as this, where Adorno seems to defend that metaphysical impulse which Kant castigated for "straying into intelligible realms," suggest in their own coded form an allegiance to a utopian image unrealisable within the framework of bourgeois life. Not the concrete, well-planned utopia demanded by the student leaders, but an ideal definable only negatively, by its negative relation to everything bourgeois.

This theme is dealt with in more depth in one set of Adorno's lectures, those he gave during 1964–5 on Hegel, Kant and the philosophy of history. Entitled *Zur Lehre von der Geschichte und von der Freiheit* [Towards a Theory of History and Freedom], they show Adorno clarifying his relation to the philosophies of Hegel and Kant, and the attitude of both towards notions of historical progress. Early lectures from this semester see Adorno dealing with the recurring theme of "mediation and immediacy," but also developing his own philosophy of history negatively, out of a critique of Hegel's own treatment of these topics. A later lecture is devoted to a close reading of Walter Benjamin's theses "On the Concept of History," a powerful critique of those progressive theories born of the Enlightenment. It is instructive that Benjamin's argument for a discontinuous history of revolutionary "leaps" and his championing of "a real state of emergency" over its repressive state-imposed analogue is explored by Adorno at this time of great political upheaval.

The most intriguing of the *History and Freedom* lectures deals with a term drawn from Hegel's *Phenomenology of Spirit*, the notion of the *Weltlauf* [Course of the World]. By this term Hegel meant the perception of a malign and perverse character to historical events. In the moral philosophies of his day Hegel saw a tendency to set the virtue of the individual against "the way of the world" understood as "universally perverted." According to Hegel, virtuous moral individuals protested loudly but vainly against the supposed madness of this *Weltlauf* and in doing so failed to recognise their own part in the very world they denounced.

Something in this notion of the *Weltlauf* appeals to Adorno, who increasingly adopts it as shorthand for the malign and seemingly irrational tendency of his own late-capitalist world. True, he will castigate Hegel for having hypostatised the "way of the world" as something inevitable and against which the individual is impotent – thus the charge in these lectures that Hegel's is an "appeasing" philosophy. I have argued elsewhere that in key parts of the *History and Freedom* lectures Adorno misrepresents this part of Hegel's philosophy and in ways which are revealing of weaknesses in Adorno's own politics (Wilding 2007). But here the focus must lie with Adorno's specific use of this concept. The key lies in the notion that a society could be "generally perverted," set on a wholly irrational course. For Adorno, the *Weltlauf* stigmatises the protesting individual as irrational and so legitimises its own irrationality.

> The irrationality of society is *devolved*: it appears to be not society that is mad, but the individual. However, the irrational individual in turn aligns himself with the irrational world, through a kind of perverse identification with general perversion.
>
> This sets up a catastrophic vicious circle in which human beings have an objective interest in changing the world and in which this change is quite impossible without their participation. However, these mechanisms of identification have stamped themselves on people's characters to such a degree that they are quite incapable of the spontaneity and the conscious actions that would be required to bring about the necessary changes. This is because, by identifying with the course of the world, they do so in an unhappy, neurotically damaged way, which effectively leads them to reinforce the world as it is. And that, I would say, is the truth about the situation of human beings in history. (Adorno 2006: 76)

It would be easy to read this as Adorno's epitaph for the student movement. But it must be taken with a pinch of salt – there is something deliberately hyperbolical about the formulation, as its author must have realised: how could the protesting individual (Hegel's "virtuous moraliser") articulate this vicious circle if his delusion were as complete as is suggested, if the subject's reactionary identification with the *Weltlauf* is total? And if the world's course is wholly irrational, then what individual could with reason articulate this fact and expect to be heard? Adorno seems to realise that his formulation is untenable, and pulls back from it in a letter to Horkheimer.

It is only the other side of the same coin that, with the current course of the world [*Weltlauf*], situations may arise today or tomorrow which, while they are very likely to be catastrophic, at the same time restore the possibility of praxis which is today obstructed. As long as the world remains antagonistic and itself perpetuates contradictions, the possibility of changing it will be a legacy. (Wiggershaus 1986: 628)

Here the world course appears unpredictable, not the unstoppable movement it is imputed to have in Hegel and which it tended to become for the Adorno of the lectures on *History and Freedom*; it can favour repression, yet it can open up revolutionary counter-tendencies. This formulation is undoubtedly more dialectical and more plausible. It lines up with the many examples given above where Adorno, rather than being the epitome of a resigned philosopher, points to ways out of political resignation, indeed indicts resignation for its wrong-headedness. In fact, resignation is just what Adorno finds pervading the social sciences, in the discipline of sociology for instance, a subject which he feels has abandoned a critical theory of society for specialised, fragmented knowledge: "one no longer dares to conceive of the whole since one must despair of changing it."[3] Critical theory, by contrast, understands that conceiving the social whole means overcoming the divisions within and between the disciplines, that grasping the whole is immanently related to the conceivability of changing it.

"AS IF IN HIS IVORY TOWER"

In a sense the very polymath quality of these lectures, the sheer scope of Adorno's attempt to make sense of the social whole and to pass on these insights to his students, is as important a legacy as their various reflections on the mediation of theory and practice. This polymathy can be seen to take one Enlightenment tradition – the encyclopaedic approach of the *philosophes*, of

Goethe, Schiller and even Weber's "Faustian universality of man" (Weber 2001: 123) – and set it against the compartmentalised thinking of that other great Enlightener, Kant, the limitations of whose philosophy are shown to be those of bourgeois society itself. In Adorno's hands polymathy consciously breaks down the intellectual division of labour, attempts to halt the relentless drive towards academic specialisation and seeks to apprehend an alienated whole.

Though this will hardly reassure those for whom such philosophical traditions are of dubious relevance to political practice. Any re-examination or rehabilitation of Adorno within a left-wing context will always have to negotiate a prejudice that the Frankfurt School in general and Adorno in particular embody: the historical pessimism of intellectuals separated from the revolutionary movements of their time. The *doxa* on Adorno is that his philosophy was devoid of a politics and was proved hopelessly impotent in the face of real political praxis; worse, that he helped quench the fires of revolutionary enthusiasm. The Adorno of these *Lectures*, critics will argue, is the perfect illustration of how hidebound academics can be, unable to engage with the political activism of students or the class struggles being waged beyond the university walls.

The above should have rendered such a charge more difficult to sustain. It is not borne out by a careful reading of these texts which do reveal the influence of the times in which they are written, and address them in a philosophical language which does justice to their complexity and their mediatedness. Politics does not somehow become less mediated in a period of intensified struggle. This is the illusion of a certain kind of spontaneity, and one reason why it can have disastrous political results. Adorno does not pass a negative judgement on the possibilities of spontaneous action, but only on "thought bowing irrationally to the primacy of practice" (Adorno 1973:143–4), a practice which in its anti-theoreticism is left at "the prey of power," whether that of charismatic leaders or revolutionary parties.

Among Marxists the contrast between Marcuse's and Adorno's reactions to the events of the late 1960s will no doubt continue to be the lasting memory of the postwar Frankfurt School, even if the way it is presented today is still couched in stark terms which have changed little in the century and a half since Charles Augustin Sainte-Beuve praised Victor Hugo over Alfred de Vigny:

> Hugo, strong partisan ... fought in armour,
> And held high his banner in the middle of the tumult;
> He still holds it; and Vigny, more discreet,
> As if in his ivory tower, retired before noon.
>
> (Sainte-Beuve 1938: 98)

It is to Sainte-Beuve that we are indebted for the term "ivory tower" with all its unfortunate connotations of the separation of the academy from politics and society, philosophical thought from political practice. But we cannot imagine – especially today – that the academy is somehow immune to the influence of the "outside world," to what goes on *extra muros*. It is subject to the same imperatives and exhibits the same struggles, as Adorno already recognised, over the reduction of life and mind to labour, struggles that pervade ever more corners of society. These *Lectures* allow us to begin to dismantle the caricature of Adorno as a thinker removed from Sainte-Beuve's "tumult," to dismantle, too, the legacy of anti-theoreticism which still derides the polymath as a "jack of all trades and master of none." To resist the desire for an intellectual figurehead, a Pied Piper, whilst defending the critical role – neither crudely committed to every cause nor free-floating – of the polymathic intellectual in a specialised, instrumentalised world: in these final lectures Adorno forces his way beyond these false alternatives.

In 2003 an Adorno centenary conference took place in the infamous lecture theatre VI of Frankfurt University, where in 1969 a bare-breasted student had announced "Adorno as an institution is dead." What brought the delegates together was a recognition that Adorno's thought, whether institutionalised or not, is very much alive. The gradual publication and translation of these lectures from the 1960s demonstrate an afterlife of thought that is more vibrant than that of many other twentieth-century philosophers, whose surface radicalism has often failed to stand the test of time.

That the non-institution which is Adorno is very much living is, I suggest, testament to its radical and prophetic core.

NOTES

1. Compare the essay "Marginalia to Theory and Praxis," where Adorno says that in a situation where experience has become "blocked," praxis is likewise "damaged" and therefore "longed for, distorted and desperately overvalued" (1998: 260).
2. Compare Hegel (1988: 99): "Only slight experience is needed to see that where there is immediate knowledge there is also mediated knowledge, and vice versa. Immediate knowledge, like mediated knowledge, is by itself completely one-sided."
3. Adorno, "On the Logic of the Social Sciences," in Adorno et al. (1976: 121).

REFERENCES

Adorno, T. W. (1973) *Negative Dialectic*. London, Routledge.

Adorno, T. W. (1976) "On the Logic of the Social Sciences," in T. W. Adorno et al., *The Positivist Dispute in German Sociology*. London, Heinemann.

Adorno, T. W. (1983) "The Sociology of Knowledge and its Consciousness," in *Prisms*. Cambridge, MA, MIT Press.

Adorno, T. W. (1993) *Hegel: Three Studies*. London, MIT Press.

Adorno, T. W. (1998) "The Meaning of Working through the Past," in *Critical Models: Interventions and Catchwords*. New York, Columbia University Press.

Adorno, T. W. (2001) *Kant's Critique of Pure Reason*. Cambridge, Polity, 2001.

Adorno, T. W. (2001) *Problems of Moral Philosophy*. Cambridge, Polity.

Adorno, T. W. (2002) *Introduction to Sociology*. Cambridge, Polity.

Adorno, T. W. (2006) *History and Freedom*. Cambridge, Polity.

Aust, S. (1987) *The Baader-Meinhof Group: The Inside Story of a Phenomenon*, London, Bodley Head.

Elsaesser, T. (1989) *New German Cinema: a History*. London, Macmillan.

Habermas, J. (1992) "Critical Theory and the Frankfurt School", in P. Dews (ed.), *Autonomy and Solidarity: Interviews*. London, Verso.

Hegel, G. W. F. (1988) *Lectures on the Philosophy of Religion*, ed. P. Hodgson, London, University of California Press.

Jäger, L. (2004) *Adorno: a Political Biography*. London, Yale University Press.

Magee, B. (1978) "Herbert Marcuse and the Frankfurt School," in *Men of Ideas*. London, BBC.

Ryan, A. (2003) "The Power of Positive Thinking," in *New York Review of Books*, vol. 50, no. 1 (16 January).

Sainte-Beuve, C. A. (1838) *Pensées d'Août*. Brussels, Laurent.

Thomas, N. (2003) *Protest Movements in 1960s West Germany*. Oxford, Berg.

Weber, M. (1991) "Science as a Vocation," in H. H. Gerth and C. Wright Mills (eds.), *From Max Weber*. London, Routledge.

Weber, M. (2001) *The Protestant Ethic and the Spirit of Capitalism*. London, Routledge.

Wiggershaus, R. (1986) *Der Frankfurter Schule*. München, Carl Hanser Verlag.

Wiggershaus, R. (1995) *The Frankfurt School: Its History, Theories and Political Significance*. Cambridge, Polity.

Wilding, A. (2007) "The World's Course and its Discontents," *Studies in Social and Political Thought*, no. 14 (September).

Wilding, A. (2008) "Max Weber and 'the Faustian Universality of Man'," *Journal of Classical Sociology*, vol. 8, no. 1 (Spring).

II

Negative Dialectics versus Neo-Structuralism

4

ANTAGONISM AND DIFFERENCE: NEGATIVE DIALECTICS AND POST-STRUCTURALISM IN VIEW OF THE CRITIQUE OF MODERN CAPITALISM

Alberto R. Bonnet *

I

The present notes were inspired by a discussion held at the permanent seminar on *Subjectivity and Critical Theory*, which is run at the Institute of Social Sciences and Humanities of the Autonomous University of Puebla (*Instituto de Ciencias Sociales y Humanidades de la Universidad Autónoma de Puebla*) and has allowed me, on many occasions, to harvest the best of ideas. At the instigation of Sergio Tischler, one of its participants, the seminar's group took on the arduous task of reading and discussing Theodor Adorno's *Negative Dialectics*. It was, more specifically, an intervention by John Holloway in that discussion that inspired this chapter.[1] In short, Holloway justified the proposal to read and discuss *Negative Dialectics* with a political argument: Adorno helps us go deeper in our critique of modern capitalism. I agreed with this and I still do, no matter how strange and paradoxical it might seem considering the "abstract" character of *Negative Dialectics* or the "conservatism" of Adorno's political positions while he was writing it. And the argument seemed to me to be timelier than ever, arriving at a moment when the recent commemoration of the centenary of his birth, in September 2003, had ratified that, indeed, Adorno was well and truly dead in many academic circles.

41

So the purpose of these notes is to reaffirm the importance of negative dialectics to the critique of contemporary capitalism.

Negative dialectics, as a modality of thought that consistently takes on board the antagonistic character of capitalist society, is, we shall argue, a revolutionary critique of the same capitalist society. However, to argue this today does not entail a vindication of the critical character of negative dialectics as opposed to the apologetic character of positive dialectics inherited from idealism, on which Adorno predominantly insisted in his *Negative Dialectics*, but rather a defence of the relevance itself of concepts that have been somewhat underestimated in the revolutionary critique of capitalist society, such as *antagonism* and *dialectic negativity*. We will justify this shift in our emphasis later. For now, we will say in anticipation that we believe the problem today does not lie so much in the fact that anti-capitalist political practices are conceived in terms of a reactionary positive dialectics – such as the one already dead and codified in the Soviet DIAMAT – but in that they are conceived in terms of a philosophy which is quintessentially alien, or even opposed, to any dialectics, in particular poststructuralist philosophy.

II

In fact, *Negative Dialectics* is a "largely abstract" document, as Adorno warns in the Preface. However, we must not forget that it was Adorno himself who questioned all the contemptuous uses of this adjective, usually accompanied by a vindication of the "concrete things" which equally condemns irrationality in political theory and practice. There is nothing more reified and, therefore, more remote from a critique of capitalist society than a way of thinking which worships "things themselves!" Therefore, *Negative Dialectics* is not an "abstract" document in that derogatory sense, for it approaches a modality of thought whose characteristics – its dialectic and negative character, but also its own "abstract" character – derive from highly "concrete" determinations of its object.

It is enough to have a quick look at the first movements of *Negative Dialectics* in order to confirm this. Dialectics emerges from the observation of the difference between the object and its concept, Adorno argues (1990: 4), a difference which becomes contradiction *vis-à-vis* the inherently identifying nature of thought. Thus, dialectic thinking is an *index falsi* of reality. However, neither that difference between the object and its concept nor the conversion of this difference into a contradiction can be attributed to dialectics – which would then be implicitly reduced to a method – but to reality itself. "Concept and reality display the same contradictory nature," Adorno argues.

> The principle of dominion, which antagonistically rends human society, is the same principle which, spiritualized, causes the difference between the concept and its subject matter; and that difference assumes the logical form of contradiction because, measured by the principle of dominion, whatever does not bow to its unity will not appear as something different from and indifferent to the principle, but as a violation of logic. (1990: 48)

So, identification and the absence of identity, which this identification converts into contradiction, are both dimensions of antagonistic society itself. Identification refers us in the last instance to the conversion of a plurality of qualitatively diverse concrete labours into quantities of a single, undifferentiated, abstract labour through the process of exchange. Lack of identity sends us in turn, definitively, to the exploitation underlying this exchange of equivalents. However, as dimensions that are inherent in antagonistic society, they cannot be overcome in thought if they are not reconciled in reality. Let us quote Adorno *in extenso*:

> If mankind is to get rid of the coercion to which the form of identification really subjects it, it must attain identity with its concept at the same time. In this, all relevant categories play a part. The barter principle, the reduction of human labour to the abstract universal concept of average working hours, is fundamentally akin to the principle of identification. Barter is the social model of the principle, and without the principle there would be no barter; it is through barter that non-identical individuals and performances become commensurable and identical. The spread of the principle imposes on the

whole world an obligation to become identical, to become total. But if we denied the principle abstractly – if we proclaimed, to the greater glory of the irreducibly qualitative, that parity should no longer be the ideal rule – we would be creating excuses for recidivism into ancient injustice. From olden times, the main characteristic of the exchange of equivalents has been that unequal things would be exchanged in its name, that the surplus value of labour would be appropriated. If comparability as a category of measure were simply annulled, the rationality which is inherent in the barter principle – as ideology, of course, but also as a promise – would give way to direct appropriation, to force, and nowadays to the naked privilege of monopolies and cliques. When we criticize the barter principle as the identifying principle of thought, we want to realize the ideal of free and just barter. To date, this ideal is only a pretext. Its realization alone would transcend barter. Once critical theory has shown it up for what it is – an exchange of things that are equal and yet unequal – our critique of the inequality within equality aims at equality too, for all our scepticism of the rancour involved in the bourgeois egalitarian ideal that tolerates no qualitative difference. If no man had part of his labour withheld from him any more, rational identity would be a fact, and society would have transcended the identifying mode of thinking. (1990: 146–7)

The identity resulting from this reduction of the plurality of specific labours to the unity of abstract labour is, at the same time, illusory insofar as exploitation underlies it, and objective in that it springs from the production and exchange of commodities. It is precisely as this socially necessary appearance, that is, as ideology, that this identity makes its mark on philosophical systems. On this Adorno writes: "However fraudulently the promotion of unity to a philosophy may have exalted it at the expense of plurality, its supremacy, though not the *summum bonum* a victorious philosophical tradition since the Eleatics took it for, is an *ens realissimum*. It really has a touch of the transcendence which the philosophers praise in the idea of unity" (1990: 314). The Hegelian system – where positive dialectics culminates in a reconciliation of the social totality in the Absolute Spirit – is its major exponent, that is, the system in which that identity reaches simultaneously its truest and falsest expression. Thus Adorno can say:

if Hegel's philosophy fails in terms of the highest criterion, its own, it thereby also proves itself true. The nonidentity of the antagonistic, a nonidentity it runs up against and laboriously pulls together, is the nonidentity of a whole that is not the true but the untrue, the absolute opposite of justice. But in reality this very nonidentity has the form of identity, an all-inclusiveness that is not governed by any third, reconciling element. This kind of deluded identity is the essence of ideology, of socially necessary illusion. Only through the process whereby the contradiction becomes absolute, and not through the contradiction becoming alleviated in the absolute, could it disintegrate and perhaps find its way to that reconciliation which must have misled Hegel because its real possibility was still concealed from him. (1993b: 31)

For its part, negative dialectics aspires to display a fidelity to this antagonistic character of capitalist society: it is a dialectic modality of thought because society is antagonistic; negative because this antagonism cannot be overcome through thought; and certainly utopian, because it continues to hope for a reconciled reality.

However, the abstract character of negative dialectics also points towards a determination of society, because its abstraction is not a subjective abstraction which belongs to the realm of thought, but an abstraction which is rooted in its object: society. Therefore, in relation to Kant's transcendental subject, Adorno writes:

As the extreme borderline case of ideology, the transcendental subject comes close to truth. The transcendental generality is no mere narcissist self-exaltation of the I, not the *hubris* of an autonomy of the I. Its reality lies in the domination that prevails and perpetuates itself by means of the principle of equivalence. The process of abstraction – which philosophy transfigures, and which it ascribes to the knowing subject alone – is taking place in the factual barter society. (1990: 178)[2]

In this sense the Hegelian system, in its idealism, also approaches reality.

He who attributes a conceptual character to social reality should not fear the objection of idealism. I am not referring so much to the conceptual constitution of the cognising subject, as to the one that prevails in the thing itself: in the doctrine of the conceptual mediation of everything that

is, Hegel also pointed towards something decisive from the standpoint
of reality. Exchange is the law which guides humanity's fatal destiny. But
that law is not pure immediacy, but rather something conceptual: the act
of exchange entails the reduction of the exchanged commodities to their
equivalent, something abstract, in no way, as it is usually said, material.
(Adorno 2001b: 30)

Therefore, there is no more abstraction in negative dialectics than
that inherent in the very society which motivates it.

III

Negative Dialectics was published in Frankfurt in 1966.
Difference and Repetition, by Gilles Deleuze, in Paris, in 1968.
At the end of the 1960s, the French and German Mays challenged
the "identifying" character of postwar advanced capitalism:
mass production and mass consumption of undifferentiated
commodities, commodification of art and culture, repetitive
activities in factories and schools, imposition of homogeneity in
hospitals and jails. Both texts, which probably aspired to the same
vindication of difference in the face of a crudely "identifying"
way of thought and reality, were not alien to this conjuncture.
As Deleuze writes in his Preface, the vindication of difference was
"manifestly in the air" (1995a: xvii).

However, while Deleuze called for the rejection of dialectics
in order to think of "a concept of difference without negation,"
Adorno called for the construction of a negative dialectics
conceived as a "consequent conscience of difference." Naturally,
it is not that Adorno was oblivious to the terrible consequences
that the reduction of difference to negation brought upon thought,
but rather he considered them to be the price one inevitably had
to pay for an operation that reality itself imposed on thought.
"Contradiction is nonidentity under the rule of a law that affects
the nonidentical as well" he recognized in the first pages of his
Negative Dialectics, only to warn that

This law is not a cognitive law, however. It is real. Unquestionably, one who
submits to the dialectical discipline has to pay dearly in the qualitative

variety of experience. Still, in the administered world the impoverishment of experience by dialectics, which outrages healthy opinion, proves
appropriate to the abstract monotony of that world. Its agony is the world's
agony raised to a concept. Cognition must bow to it, unless concretion
is once more to be debased into the ideology it starts becoming in fact.
(1990: 6)

In contrast, it was dialectics rather than reality that Deleuze was
held responsible for "substituting the labour of the negative for
the play of difference and the differential," and *Difference and
Repetition* closes with the declaration that

> history progresses not by negation and the negation of negation, but by
> deciding problems and affirming differences. It is no less bloody and cruel
> as a result. Only the shadows of history live by negation: the good enter
> into it with all the power of a posited differential or a difference affirmed.
> ... That is why real revolutions have the atmosphere of *fêtes*. Contradiction
> is not the weapon of the proletariat but, rather, the manner in which the
> bourgeoisie defends and preserves itself. (1995a: 268)[3]

Subordination of difference to negation, dialectic discipline,
adaptation of thought to the painful poverty of the world; the
affirmation of difference beyond negation, a game of differences
and celebration. The clash between the arguments is so direct
that it resonates in two languages; to be more precise, in the
contrast between Adorno's words of hurt and Deleuze's words
of rebellion. And let us remember that, while Deleuze joined
the rebellious Parisian students, Adorno evicted students from
Frankfurt University. Nevertheless, going against what these
languages and political positions might suggest, we shall insist
on the critical character of Adorno's negative dialectics, just as
we shall assert the ambiguous character of Deleuze's philosophy
of difference. Naturally, we do not claim that one should simply
get rid of these specific languages or political positions without a
second thought, as if they were mere accessories. Adorno was fully
conscious of the connection between philosophical language and
thought, and it was not by chance, for example, that he named
his fragments "melancholic science," in opposition to Nietzsche's

"gay science" (2006a: 15). His highly painful rejection of the new left of the end of the 1960s could also accompany arguments, true or false, but in no case alien to the whole of his thought (see 1993a). All we argue for is that the immediate reactions that this language and these political positions might motivate should not substitute the analysis of the arguments at stake.

So let us set out the arguments. Adorno and Deleuze both recognise that this reduction of difference to negation, an operation which is inherent in any dialectics, involves violence against difference. "Contradiction is nonidentity under the aspect of identity; the dialectical primacy of the principle of contradiction makes the thought of unity the measure of heterogeneity" (Adorno 1990: 5). "On what condition is difference traced or projected on to a flat space? Precisely when it has been forced into a previously established identity, when it has been placed on the slope of the identical which makes it reflect or desire identity, and necessarily takes it where identity wants to go – namely, into the negative" (Deleuze 1995a: 51). The two begin to diverge when Adorno decisively rejects any effort to emancipate difference from negativity in the sphere of thought as long as this emancipation has not occurred in the sphere of reality, and Deleuze tries, no less forcefully, to do precisely that. The object and its concept cannot be reconciled in the sphere of thought – as Hegelian dialectics set out to do – but neither can this difference between the two be emancipated in the sphere of thought from its reduction to negativity, as the Deleuzian philosophy of difference claims. This tension aspires to harbour in thought the antagonistic character of the thought reality, the antagonism which is inherent in capitalist social relations and is constitutive of Adornian negative dialectics. "On its own, by conceptual dispositions, it [consciousness] cannot eliminate the objective contradiction and its emanations. It can comprehend it; everything else is idle protestation. ... Dialectics need not fear the charge of being obsessed with the fixed idea of objective conflict in a thing already pacified; no single thing is at peace in the unpacified whole. The aporetical concepts of philosophy are marks of what is objectively, not just cogitatively, unresolved" (1990: 152–3). However, in this precise tension also lies the critical character of negative dialectics. For if this tension is constitutive of Adornian negative dialectics, as we have said, its resolution in the sphere of thought – whatever the direction of this resolution, i.e. whether it is towards the unity of a system which is identical to itself or towards a multiplicity of differences – is constitutive of the Adornian notion of ideology.

IV

The specific ideology that concerns us, if we are talking about a non-antagonistic coexistence of differences in multiplicity, is liberalism. Indeed, liberalism is a ghost that persistently haunts Deleuze's pages, leaving its mark in his repeated precautions against the figure of the beautiful soul – a final Hegelian vengeance! The Deleuzian warning already mentioned, that although history does not progress by negation it is no less bloody and cruel as a result, is a precaution against this beautiful soul. However, there are more explicit warnings.

> There are certainly many dangers in invoking pure differences which have become independent of the negative and liberated from the identical. The greatest danger is that of lapsing into the representations of a beautiful soul: there are only reconcilable and federative differences, far removed from bloody struggles. The beautiful soul says: we are different, but not opposed ... Nevertheless, we believe that when these problems attain their proper degree of *positivity*, and when difference becomes the object of a corresponding affirmation, they release a power of aggression and selection which destroys the beautiful soul. (1995a: xviii)

Deleuze tries to eliminate the marks of this beautiful soul by evoking the figures of Marx and Nietzsche.

So, in his analysis of existing problems, more specifically of the multiplicity in the Idea, he warns that "the philosophy of difference must be wary of turning into the discourse of beautiful souls: differences, nothing but differences, in a peaceful coexistence in the Idea of social places and functions ... but the name of Marx is sufficient to save it from this danger" (Deleuze 1995a: 259). And that should be enough but it *is not*, for the figure evoked by

Deleuze is not the Marx who criticises the antagonistic nature of capitalist social relations, but a quasi-Durkheim dedicated to the sociology of the division of labour. "Those commentators on Marx who insist upon the fundamental difference between Marx and Hegel rightly point out that in *Capital* the category of differentiation (the differentiation at the heart of a social multiplicity: the division of labour) is substituted for the Hegelian concepts of opposition, contradiction and alienation"(1995a: 207).[4] And in his approach to difference, Deleuze argues that

> in its essence, difference is the object of affirmation of affirmation itself. In its essence, affirmation is itself difference. At this point, does the philosophy of difference not risk appearing as a new version of the beautiful soul? The beautiful soul is in effect the one who sees differences everywhere and appeals to them only as respectable, reconcilable or federative differences, while history continues to be made through bloody contradictions. (1995a: 52)

However, this time it is Nietzsche that Deleuze calls upon to clear the marks of the beautiful soul. "There are two ways – he claims – to appeal to 'necessary destructions': that of the poet, who speaks in the name of a creative power, capable of overturning all orders and representations in order to affirm Difference in the state of permanent revolution which characterizes eternal return; and that of the politician, who is above all concerned to deny that which 'differs', so as to preserve or prolong an established historical order, or to establish a historical order which already calls forth in the world the forms of its representation" (1995a: 52). This return to Nietzsche seems more promising in the sense that, unlike Marx, there is no doubt that Nietzsche rejected dialectics. And it is precisely in this anti-dialectic sense that he is evoked by Deleuze and the other French poststructuralists.[5] As for Hegelian dialectics, Deleuze had already written that "the man of resentment needs to conceive a not-I, after opposing himself to this not-I, in order to finally assert himself as him. A strange sociologism, that of the slave: he needs two negations in order to achieve an appearance of assertion. We already presage under what form the syllogism of the slave has had so much success in philosophy: *dialectics*" (1986: 171). And he had denounced it in terms of an "ideology of resentment," a "speculation of the plebs" and other similar aristocratic expressions.

But let us return to our figure of the beautiful soul. "To the speculative element of negation, opposition or contradiction, Nietzsche opposes the practical element of *difference*: object of assertion and pleasure," Deleuze writes (1986: 18).[6] This affirmation of difference, with its potential for aggression and selection, is precisely what would dissolve this pluralism of differences into a peaceful coexistence which is common in the beautiful soul. But this recurring to Nietzsche is not enough either. The capitalist market and democracy are the quintessential names which denote the habitat of this coexistence of differences within liberal ideology. And anyway, the aggressiveness and selectivity which are liberated by this affirmation of difference are in no way alien to this habitat: there is a certain Darwinism amongst the constitutive elements of the concept itself of the capitalist market. Naturally, this assertion of difference can acquire various degrees of brutality – just as the strategies of competition can go from the bloodiest inter-imperialist wars, justified by calling upon racial difference, to the most subtle differentiations in the product – but in no case does it seem incompatible with the market. Even the expression *faire la différence*, which Deleuze chooses and uses regularly in *Difference and Repetition*, cannot be distinguished from its use in referring to competition amongst workers in the privileged segments of the labour market: one must *make the difference* in relation to others if one wants to impose oneself in the selection of personnel. Of course, in Deleuze's philosophy of difference, it is not the staff management but the eternal Nietzschean return that makes the selection. So, he writes: "Nietzsche reproaches all those selection procedures based upon opposition or conflict with working to the advantage of the average forms and operating to the benefit of the 'large number.' Eternal return alone effects the true selection, because it eliminates the average forms and uncovers 'the superior form of everything that is" (1995a: 54–5). However, when this assertion of difference adopts the guise of a revolution, or this eternal return adopts the guise of a permanent revolution, political ambiguity floods Deleuze's pages.

V

Certainly, liberalism is not a ghost that exclusively haunts Deleuze's work. The warnings against liberalism appear again when Deleuze's concept of the multiplicity of differences, which continues to be of a somewhat philosophical nature, tries to adopt a more explicit political edge – with some help from Spinoza – in Negri's or Virno's concept of multitude.[7] "The notion of multitude seems to share something with liberal thought because it values individuality but, at the same time, it distances itself from it radically because this individuality is the final product of a process of individuation which stems from the universal, the generis, the pre-individual. The seeming nearness is overturned and becomes the maximum distance" (Virno 2004: 76). Virno's notion of multitude would thus separate itself from liberalism in that the concept of the individual associated with this notion of multitude would occur *a posteriori* in relation to a process of individuation, while the liberal concept of the individual would occur *a priori*. "The liberal idea of the individual and the idea of the singularity of the multitude are like twins who, however, oppose one another," Virno clarifies in an article. "They are very similar, but they have two profoundly different meanings. Because the liberal thinks the individual is a primary element and the comprehension of how the individual acts in relation to others and the state comes later. From the standpoint of the multitude, the individual, singularity is the result of a process."[8] And, indeed, this distinction between *a priori* and *a posteriori* concepts of the individual allows us to separate the notion of the individual from the natural law liberalism of the seventeenth and eighteenth centuries, which built its concepts of state and market on the basis of philosophical anthropologies. However, it is doubtful that the same would apply to John Stuart Mill's liberalism and it would certainly not apply in the case of the liberalism of Richard Rorty. Furthermore, the facts, social relations themselves – mediated by the production and exchange of commodities – are a decisive component of the pre-individual sphere from which this individuation parts, as Virno himself seems to admit, and there is no reason to assume that this concept of the individual, which recognises such an individuation on the basis of the market, is incompatible with liberalism. In other words, there is nothing that prevents the political science of capital from assuming this notion of the individual reduced to a combination of the commodity brands he/she consumes, promoted by its own marketing, as it has certainly done so many times with so many other market concepts.

Very like Virno, in *Empire* Negri and Hardt assert: "the multitude is a multiplicity, a plane of singularities, an open set of relations, which is not homogeneous or identical to itself, and bears an indistinct, inclusive relation to those outside of it" (2000: 103). However, faced with the need to distinguish their notion of multitude from the liberal tradition, they do not take up the relation between multitude and individual but between multitude and class. "Multitude is a class concept," Negri and Hardt state (2004: 103). However, they argue, the economic conceptions of class have the inconvenience of imposing a false option between unity (Marxism, the capitalist and working classes) and plurality (liberalism, racial, ethnic, gender and sex differences, etc.). "The mandate to choose between unity and multiplicity treats class as if it were merely an empirical concept and fails to take into consideration the extent to which class itself is defined politically"(Negri and Hardt 2004: 104). This argument is not without certain ambiguities, but we accept its conclusion: "An investigation of economic class, then, like an investigation of race, should not begin with a mere catalogue of empirical differences but rather with the lines of collective resistance to power" (Negri and Hardt 2004: 104). And this conclusion decisively exorcises the ghost of liberalism. Indeed, if the concept of multitude is defined in terms of collective resistance against power, it becomes incompatible with the coexistence of differences which liberalism embraces. However, this rigorously dialectic definition presents the drawback of being no less rigorously incompatible with the aforementioned definition and with any other definition based on a substitution of negation with difference, or antagonism with multiplicity. Negri and Hardt pay the price for expurgating the concept of multitude from the ghost of liberalism; in short, they sacrifice Nietzsche to Hegel.

And let us warn that one cannot escape this quagmire by invoking a supposed priority and externality of resistance in relation to power. In this sense, Deleuze draws from Foucault (especially 1990 and 2001) that "the final word on power is that *resistance comes first*, to the extent that power relations operate completely within the diagram, while resistances necessarily operate in a direct relation with the outside from which the diagrams emerge. This means that a social field offers more resistance than strategies, and the thought of the outside is a thought of resistance" (Deleuze 1988: 89, 90). Later, when this resistance has been assimilated to desire or life, we shall return to this point. Let us simply mention here that this solution does nothing but shift the problem: it is now presented as a tension between resistance defined in relation to power and resistance which is prior or external to power.[9] And the solution remains dialectic: both resistance and power are reciprocally constituted in antagonism and any priority or externality is a mere illusion.

Let us pick up the thread of our argument. In short, we suspect that the difficulties faced by Deleuze and Negri or Virno in exorcising the ghost of liberalism from concepts such as multiplicity or multitude lie finally in that these concepts were intentionally conceived in the absence of dialectics, or in that its objects were deprived of their innate antagonistic character, which in the end comes down to the same thing. This is the key difference between concepts such as society as antagonistic totality or class as the result of class struggle, on the one hand, and multiplicity of differences or multitude of singularities, on the other. And thus, almost imperceptibly, we return to Adorno and his negative dialectics. For, as we have mentioned, negative dialectics can be defined, precisely, as the mode of thinking which fits this antagonistic character of capitalist society, even though it aims at overcoming it. "In fact, dialectics is neither a pure method nor a reality in the naïve sense of the word," Adorno writes:

It is not a method, for the unreconciled matter – lacking precisely the identity surrogated by the thought – is contradictory and resists any attempt at unanimous interpretation. It is the matter, not the organizing drive of thought, that brings us to dialectics. Nor is dialectics a simple reality, for contradictoriness is a category of reflection, the cogitative confrontation of concept and thing. To proceed dialectically means to think in contradictions, for the sake of the contradiction once experienced in the thing, and against that contradiction. A contradiction in reality, it is a contradiction against reality. But such dialectics is no longer reconcilable with Hegel. Its motion does not tend to the identity in the difference between each object and its concept; instead, it is suspicious of all identity. (1990: 144–5)

More than this. The legitimacy of negative dialectics itself as a way of thinking does not outlive the historical existence of this antagonistic society: "Dialectical reason's own essence has come to be and will pass, like antagonistic society" (1990: 141).[10]

VI

For now, let us leave definitions aside and explore some of the implications of the confrontation between Adorno's negative dialectics and Deleuze's philosophy of difference. Adorno's negative dialectics inherits the Hegelian mandate of thinking without starting from principles – in the sense of αϱχή – keeping in mind the mediated character of all immediacy. Let us recall, for example, the Adornian critique of the Heideggerian conversion of *Sein* into a transcendental principle. "He pursues dialectics to the point of saying that neither the subject nor the object are immediate and ultimate; but he deserts dialectics in reaching for something immediate and primary beyond subject and object. Thinking becomes archaistic as soon as whichever scattered entity is more than entity will be transfigured into a metaphysical αϱχή" (1990: 106, see also 2006). Despite its immanentist intensions and rigorous critique of transcendental philosophic traditions, the Deleuzian philosophy of difference ends up postulating a similar principle.[11] The assertion of difference itself, associated with the Nietzschean *will to power*, already seemed implicitly elevated to a transcendental principle in these texts, and appears once again and even more evidently in later works under the names of *desire* and *life*. Let us focus a little more on this issue.

It is well known that, in their critique of psychoanalysis, Deleuze and Guattari stress the productive nature of desire, dissociating it not only from the absence of real objects but also from the production of mere phantom realities. Desire, thus, is productive in a strict sense – and social production is but desiring production under certain conditions. The problem with psychoanalysis is that it would oedipalise this desiring production, that is, it would reduce the multiplicity of partial objects to parental representatives. "So the entire process of desiring-production is trampled underfoot and reduced to parental images, laid out step by step in accordance with supposed pre-oedipal stages, totalized in Oedipus, and the logic of partial objects is thereby reduced to nothing" (Deleuze and Guattari 1998: 45–6). So schizo-analysis intends to "schizophrenize the domain of the unconscious" in order to "rediscover everywhere the force of desiring-production" (1998: 53), "undo the expressive Oedipal unconscious, always artificial, repressive and repressed, mediated by the family, in order to attain the immediate productive unconscious" (1998: 98)[12] In this sense, the key argument of Deleuze and Guattari is that the nature of the repressed cannot be deduced on the basis of its repression, that is, the oedipal nature of desire cannot be deduced from its oedipalisation by the family. "But it [repression] in fact implies an original double operation: the repressive social formation delegates its power to an agent of psychic repression, and correlatively the repressed desire is as though masked by the faked displaced image to which the repression gives rise" (1998: 119). So what is left is to specify the nature of desire, of that third element independent of both its repression and the image that this repression imposes of it, regardless of either.

Let us recall the role that Deleuze and Guattari attribute to Freudian psychoanalysis in the rupture between the classic episteme of representation and the modern episteme of production, which Foucault (1994) pointed out.

Just as Ricardo founds political or social economy by discovering quantitative labour as the principle of every representable value, Freud founds desiring-economy by discovering the quantitative libido as the principle of every representation of the objects and aims of desire. Freud discovers the subjective nature or abstract essence of desire, just as Ricardo discovers the subjective nature or abstract essence of labour, beyond all representations that would bind it to objects, to aims, or even to particular sources. Freud is thus the first to disengage desire itself (*le désir tout court*), as Ricardo disengages labour itself (*le travail tout court*), and thereby the sphere of production that effectively eclipses representation. (Deleuze and Guattari 1998: 299–300)

Indeed, political economy can be considered to have made a significant move forward when it referred the value of commodities to this concept of labour devoid of any specificity as commercial, manufacturing, agrarian, etc., labour, which, in some way, opens the way for the Marxian concept of abstract labour. However, it is not correct but blind when he assumes that this concept bears no relation to any analytical or historical determination – those determinations that are in the mutual mediation between the abstraction of labour and the salarisation and monetisation of social relations in the Marxian concept of abstract labour.[13] For value does not refer to indeterminate labour, but to labour abstracted from its specific determination as diverse concrete labours. More important still, while this abstract labour exists objectively, as an objective abstraction which results from the production of commodities for exchange, that indeterminate labour barely exists as an idea which is more or less devoid of content, as a subjective abstraction resulting from the enclosing in parenthesis of all determinations of thought which differentiate the diverse historical labours. *Labour itself,* conceived in this way, could only aspire to being a residual concept, almost devoid of content. Now, could the concept of *desire itself,* which Deleuze and Guattari tirelessly pursue, aspire to a different destiny? It certainly cannot be argued against Marx that he determined this concept of *labour itself* as abstract, commodity-producing labour. Could it be objected to Freud that he insisted on considering this *desire itself* as a desire linked to specific oedipal objects and purposes? Marx cannot be accused of being a "commodifier" for reducing labour to this abstract, commodity-producing labour. Could we accuse Freud of being an "oedipaliser" for having reduced desire to oedipal objects and purposes?

But let us take another step forward. This Marxian determination of *labour itself* as abstract labour is not only an analytical determination, but also an historical one. We know the historical character of oedipal desire, in its explicit Freudian conception, is more controversial. However, in its inevitable reference to the triangle of a determined family structure, this desire is implicitly more historical than any assumed *desire itself*. And yet another step. Because of the mutual mediation, already mentioned, between the abstraction of labour and the salarisation and monetisation of social relations, antagonism is inherent in the Marxian concept of abstract labour. The generalised conversion of different and specific acts of labour into a single abstract labour cannot be separated from the conversion of the worker into a salaried worker, separated from the means of production, exploited by capital. However, antagonism also lies in the Freudian concept of oedipal desire, which cannot be separated from paternal law, as the exercise of social repression delegated in the family. In both cases, determination is negation. And, in both cases, this negation amounts to the inscription of antagonism.

Of course, Deleuze and Guattari do not claim it was Freud who invented Oedipus, but that the dominant psychoanalytic practice, which is both psychologistic and adaptationist, tends to reinforce its mechanisms: "We are not saying that Oedipus and castration do not amount to anything. We are oedipalized, we are castrated; psychoanalysis didn't invent these operations, to which it merely lends the new resources and methods of its genius" (1998: 67). "Psychoanalysis does not invent Oedipus; it merely provides the alter a last territoriality, the couch, and a last Law, the analyst as despot and money collector" (1998: 269). This critique of predominant psychoanalytical practice is largely justified. However, the problems appear when Deleuze and Guattari assess Freudian theory in its totality – as well as its

Lacanian new reading – on the basis of this bad praxis. For the critical cutting edge of a theory capable of stripping naked the marks of repression in subjectivity cannot be eradicated by the conservatism of therapeutic praxis, which actually validates this repression, not even when this praxis is faithfully inspired in this theory.[14] However, this cutting edge can be blunted if, in the name of an unspecified desire, repression is shifted from the key position that this theory grants it in the genesis of subjectivity, even when this shift is aimed at supporting a more progressive praxis. For Freud's insistence on the connection between desire and repression is, even beyond his own intentions, a denunciation of repressive society. Freud's grandeur thus lies in that he "refuses to pretend a systematic harmony exists where things are torn in themselves," in that "he reveals the antagonistic character of social reality insofar as it touches his theory and his practice, inside a pre-inscribed division of labour," Adorno asserts (1979: 117).

Bridging differences between Deleuze and Guattari, on the one hand, and Fromm and Horney, on the other, the Adornian critique of psychoanalytic revisionism naturally takes a relevant path in this context. Indeed, Adorno flatly rejected any rushed attempt to sociologise psychoanalysis: "in tenaciously focusing on the atomistic existence of the individual, Freud has managed to see the essence of socialization, beyond the usual casual glimpse at social circumstances." "The more psychoanalysis is sociologized, the more blunt it becomes as an instrument to achieve a knowledge of conflicts of a social origin" (1979: 105, 107). Adorno also defended the importance that psychoanalysis attributes to childhood traumatic experiences occurring within the family – *par excellence*, the oedipal castration in the genesis of neurosis – because "what exactly led Freud to concede a special importance to certain singular aspects of childhood is – although he never formulated it – the concept of injury. A totality of character, such as the one that revisionists take for granted, is an ideal which could only be achieved in a non-traumatic society" (1979: 104).[15] To assert that this character, invoked by the revisionists, was indeed something more than a "system of scars," according to Adorno, amounted to an apology for the society in which this character was formed. "In the actual constitution of existence, the relations between humans are not a result of free will or instinct, but rather of social and economic laws, which have their way above them; and if in such situation psychology becomes human or suitable for society, operating as if society were determined by men and their most intimate I, it grants a human gleam to an inhuman reality" (1979: 113–14). Does Deleuze and Guattari's unceasing quest for a desire itself, lacking oedipal determination, not bring them to the verge of a similar apologetics?

VII

However, Adorno had also responded *avant la lettre* to the late Deleuzian vitalism – and, not by chance, in his critique of Bergsonian vitalism, which in its turn is one of the decisive inspirations of the former. "The matters of true philosophical interest at this point in history are those in which Hegel, agreeing with tradition, expressed his disinterest. They are nonconceptuality, individuality and particularity – things which ever since Plato used to be dismissed as transitory and insignificant, and which Hegel labeled 'lazy Existenz'," Adorno recognises, in words to which Deleuze would perhaps have subscribed. However, a bit further on he adds that, in confrontation with this tradition,

> Bergson, in a *tour de force*, created another type of cognition for the sake of nonconceptuality. The dialectical salt was washed away in an undifferentiated tide of life; solidified reality was disposed of as subaltern, not comprehended along with its subalternity. The hater of the rigid general concept established a cult of irrational immediacy, of sovereign freedom in the midst of un-freedom. He drafted his two cognitive modes in as dualistic an opposition as that of the Cartesian and Kantian doctrines he fought had ever been; the causal-mechanical mode, as pragmatistic knowledge, was no more affected by the intuitive one than the bourgeois establishment was by the relaxed unselfconsciousness of those who owe their privileges to that establishment. (1990: 8)

This "cult of irrational immediacy, of sovereign freedom in the midst of unfreedom" adequately defines in advance late Deleuzian thought. Adorno's critique of this cult equally concerns Bergson and Deleuze:

> Every cognition including Bergson's own needs the rationality he scorns, and needs it precisely at the moment of concretion. Absolutized duration, pure becoming, the pure act – these would recoil into the same timelessness which Bergson criticises in metaphysics since Plato and Aristotle. He did not mind that the thing he groped for, if it is not to remain a mirage, is visible solely with the equipment of cognition, by reflection upon its own means, and that it grows arbitrary in a procedure unrelated, from the start, to that of cognition. (1990: 9)

"The illusion of taking direct hold of the Many would be a mimetic regression, as much a recoil into mythology, into the horror of the diffuse, as the thinking of the One, the imitation of blind nature by repressing it, ends at the opposite pole in mythical dominion. The self-reflection of enlightenment is not its revocation; it is corrupted into revocation only for the sake of today's status quo" (1990: 158).[16] This rejection of any effort to leave behind the characteristic violence exercised by the concept on the object through a supposed immediate access to this object is constitutive of negative dialectics. At this point Adorno positions himself closer to Hegel than to Bergson, because "he knew that any critique of a reifying, divisive, alienating consciousness that merely sets up a different source of knowledge from the outside as a contrast to it is impotent" (1993b: 72–3).

But let us continue. Adorno does not stop at a philosophical critique of Bergsonian vitalism, he continues to make an historical critique of its key concept, life. In the pages of *Negative Dialectics* dedicated to reflecting on freedom/necessity in terms of the imposition of the law of value on formally free individuals, he recovers the concept of life:

> While life keeps reproducing itself under the prevailing conditions of unfreedom, its concept, by its own meaning, presupposes the possibility of things not yet included, of things yet to be experienced – and this possibility has been so far reduced that the word "life" sounds by now like an empty consolation. ... The anarchy in the production of goods is a

manifestation of the social primitivity that vibrates in the word "life", in the use of a biological category for a thing that is social in essence. If the social process of production and reproduction were transparent for the subjects, if the subjects determined that process, they would no longer be passively buffeted by the ominous storms of life. (1990: 262-3)

Thus, the irrationality of the concept of life responds to the irrationality of its object, that is, the reproduction of social life as reproduction of capital, and if this object were to stay behind it would drag its concept along with it. Of course, this has not happened so far, the reproduction of social life continues to unfold as the reproduction of capital, but perhaps the meaning of this concept of life has been modified in the meanwhile by the changes in capitalist reproduction itself. Let us merely go over certain suggestive images. The *storms of life* mentioned by Adorno refer to the homonymous piece for piano by Franz Schubert: this romantic creation brought to life at the end of the eighteenth century definitely left its mark on the concept of life of the vitalism at the end of the nineteenth century. But Deleuzian images are less passionate. The comatose life of the villain in Dickens's *Our Mutual Friend*, who survives his execution and enjoys the empathy of those who had condemned him but now look after him. This tale is well chosen. Deleuze concludes that "between his life and death, there is one moment which is but a moment of *one* life playing with death" (1995b: 2). Deleuze's concept of *one life* is intended as a synonym for absolute immanence and, therefore, must be a singular – though not individualised or personalised – conscious or subjective life. Certainly, this completely indeterminate concept of life is yet one more of the phantasmagorias that Adorno denounces. However, before continuing, let us note the contrast between that stormy life and this comatose one, between that animal and this vegetative life, a contrast which is symptomatic, if we paraphrase Adorno, of how little life there is left in life: a life reduced to bare self-preservation (1990: 262), or, more precisely, self-preservation that has lost its prefix. In its immanence in itself, in its non-belonging to a subject and its non-remission to an object, in its consequent indifference to distinctions such as activity and passivity or potential and act, this vegetative life is a blind perseverance: a "complete power and beatitude" as that which insists in the moribund (Deleuze 1995b: 2), a "mere contemplation without knowledge" such as that which leads a rat to adopt a habit (Deleuze and Guattari 1991: 215). And that other concept of desire has no more luck, for it is also conceived as immanent in itself, that is, as an enjoyment of oneself.[17] Deleuze thus insists that desire is not related to lack or law, nature or spontaneity, or even to pleasure and sexuality: it requires an "ascesis" that, just as in courteous love or masochism, allows "desire [to] fill itself up" (Deleuze and Parnet 2002: 100). Life and desire are thus both reduced to a "vacuous and needy residue" – just as the one resulting, according to Adorno, from the reductive procedures of Husserl or Heidegger.

VIII

But let us return to our theme of the critique of capitalism, although we have not strayed as far as it might seem: these Deleuzian notions of life and desire do not only operate as his philosophical principles in a broader sense, but also aspire to be principles of his political insights. Deleuze declares, in solidarity with the later Foucault, that "life becomes resistance to power when power takes life as its object" (1988: 92), that is, when power becomes biopower.[18] However, this concept of life is as philosophically indeterminate as it is politically neutral. The vegetative life of Dickens's character can hardly aspire to maintain any politics, but if it were so, the attribution of any defined political sign to such a politics would be random. The Adornian critique in the sense of the political availability of the philosophies based on the concept of existence (1990) equally applies to a philosophy founded on the concept of life. Heideggerian existentialism was able to adapt to Nazism just as Sartrean existentialism was to Communism – although his moderate readers have no reason to be alarmed for, in the facts, Deleuzian vitalism accommodates itself to much less extreme political orientations.[19]

However, desire has no better luck than life as a basis for critical political thinking. Shortly after the French May and inspired by it, Deleuze and Guattari had proclaimed that "desire is revolutionary in its essence" (1998: 116). A revolutionary schizo-desire, then, was confronted quite schematically with the neurotic-paranoid ongoing repression. The irruption of the unconscious desire of the group, rather than conscious class interest, sparked the revolution (1998: 253f). "Capitalist society," they conjectured, "can endure many manifestations of interest, but not one manifestation of desire" (1998: 379). In this context, the goal of schizoanalysis is to "de-oedipalize the unconscious in order to reach the real problems" (1998: 81), in order to "reach the immediate productive unconscious" (1998: 102). However, to assume that a supposed desire itself is revolutionary is as arbitrary as it would be to assume the opposite, that is, that the same desire is reactionary. Rather, the characterisation of revolutionary or reactionary could be attributed, in the best of cases, to desires in the plural and not the singular, to desires determined according to their purposes and goals and not to indeterminate desire. And let us add that capitalist society can endure a few manifestations of desire: it even promotes them through marketing when consumption is its goal and commodity its object. So this invocation of a supposed desire itself is no more revolutionary than the hedonistic invocation of a pleasure itself. In the 1940s, that is long before May 1968 and the ultimate conversion of this May into a profitable commodity, Adorno was already warning: "the admonitions to be happy, voiced in concert by the scientifically epicurean sanatorium-director and the highly-strung propaganda chiefs of the entertainment industry, have about them the fury of the father berating his children for not rushing joyously downstairs when he comes home irritable from his office" (2006a: 62–3). (And what if the father's mandate were: enjoy!? – but let us leave aside this complication). Consequently, Adorno refused to allow psychoanalysis to assume the task of restoring to humans their capacity for pleasure:

> As people have altogether too few inhibitions and not too many, without being a whit the healthier for it, a cathartic method with a standard

other than successful adaptation and economic success would have to aim at bringing people to a consciousness of unhappiness both general and – inseparable from it – personal, and at depriving them of the illusory gratifications by which the abominable order keeps a second hold on life inside them, as if it did not already have them firmly enough in its power from outside. (2006a: 62)[20]

Naturally, Deleuze and Guattari's appeal to desire is intended to be more radical than this admonition to be happy, that is, to feel a pleasure which is decreed and manipulated by the system, and which Adorno criticises. But as soon as this indeterminate desire begins to acquire a certain determination, ambiguities start to appear: Deleuze and Guattari themselves insistently point out the relationship between capitalist social production and desiring schizophrenic production, both operating as flux decoders. However, they argue, the difference is that the former is forced to become inhibited, recurring to family and the state as recoding instances, while the latter can develop without inhibitions. This kind of paraphrase – a quite mechanistic reading – of certain Marxian assertions referring to the relation between the forces of production and relations of production will be forgotten later, certainly, along with the concept of revolution itself. The revolt of the French May, in a retrospective reading, resulted from molecular lines of escape, decoding flows which escaped the binary coding machines of the state. So, on the one hand, we have a molar dominion of representations (classes and their organisations, such as political parties and trade unions, resulting from this codification) and, on the other, a molecular dominion of desires (the masses or decoding flows). So, decoding movements, such as that May, begin as escapes: "these are not contradictions," Deleuze and Guattari state, "but escapes" (1987: 242). The concept of escape is thus rendered the substitute of the concept of contradiction, or, in more political terms, the concept of exodus replaces that of antagonism.[21]

But what would a politics of escape consist of? Deleuze tries to specify the concept of escape by warning that "to flee is not to renounce action: nothing is more active than a flight"; "the great and only error lies in thinking that a line of flight consists in fleeing from life; the flight into the imaginary, or into art. On the contrary, to flee is to produce the real, to create life" (Deleuze and Parnet 2002: 36, 49). The concept of escape thus refers to the concepts of life and desire immanent to themselves in such a way that a politics of escape is defined as biopolitics, as a creation of life itself. So, then, does following a line of escape consist, in short, of following the advice of a self-help manual one has written oneself? Let us see. This biopolitics would overlap with a new era of political struggle inaugurated by May '68, of transversal and immediate struggles (not centralised or mediated) for a subjectivity without identity (non-creators of identity). Deleuze, with Foucault, wrote in this sense that "the struggle for a modern subjectivity passes through a resistance to the two present forms of subjection, the one consisting of individualizing ourselves on the basis of constraints of power, the other of attracting each individual to a known and recognized identity, fixed once and for all. The struggle for subjectivity presents itself, therefore, as the right to difference, variation and metamorphosis" (Deleuze 1988: 105–6). And although those good old days of May are over, Deleuze asserts that "there is no blossoming of desire wherever it happens – in an unremarkable family or a local school – which does not call established structures into question" (Deleuze and Parnet 2002: 78–9). So let us forget the barricades of the rebel students and sit at the family table of the anorexic; that is, let us examine one of the few illustrations that the later Deleuze offers of the biopolitical escape he has in mind: anorexic desire as micropolitics:

> The anorexic void has nothing to do with a lack, it is on the contrary a way of escaping the organic constraint of lack and hunger at the mechanical mealtime. ... Anorexia is a political system, a micro-politics: to escape from the norms of consumption in order not to be an object of consumption oneself. It is a feminine protest, of a woman who wants to have a functioning of the body and not simply organic and social functions which make her dependent. (2002: 110)

In its most extreme expression, this micropolitics of anorexia faces, as Deleuze recognises, the risk that the militant involved might die of starvation. And he is right. But he forgets that, right from the start, it faces another danger, maybe less dramatic for the anorexic, but devastating for the philosopher's argument: the danger that the behaviour of the real-life anorexic – and not this persona which lives together with other no less strange Deleuzian schizophrenics and masochists – has been dictated by the anorexic ideal of the female body imposed by fashion shows and magazines. To follow a line of escape, in this case, is not even to follow the advice of a self-help book written by oneself, but by others.

Faced with this biopolitics or, even better – to use the Foucauldian concept – faced with the ethics of taking care of oneself, it is enough to put forward the sharp Adornian aphorism that a "wrong life cannot be lived rightly" (2006a: 39). However, if the cutting edge of this aphorism were not enough, let us recall some insights on subjective identity from *Negative Dialectics*. "Within a reality modelled after the principle of identity", Adorno writes on the Kantian subject,

> there exists no positive freedom. Where men under the universal spell seem inwardly relieved of the identity principle, and thus of the comprehensible determinants, they are not more than determined, for the time being; they are less than determined. As schizophrenia, subjective freedom is a destructive force which incorporates men only so much more in the spell of nature. (1990: 241)

And, more importantly, its inverse evaluation of the pair neurosis–schizophrenia:

> This truth content of neuroses is that the I has its unfreedom demonstrated to it, within itself, by something alien to it – by the feeling that "this isn't me at all!" Neuroses are true insofar as they demonstrate the ego's unfreedom precisely where its rule over its inner nature fails ... yet nothing that fails to invade the zone of depersonalization and its dialectics can be intellectually relevant any longer. Schizophrenia is the truth about the subject, from the viewpoint of the philosophy of history. (1990: 222. 281)

IX

Let us sum up and specify our arguments. What can Adorno's negative dialectics – and not Deleuze's philosophy of difference – contribute to the critique of modern capitalism? Before continuing, we should stress that both share the same utopian dimension and even use almost the same words to describe this utopia. "To rescue difference from its maledictory state seems, therefore, to be the Project of the philosophy of difference," Deleuze writes (1995b: 29). And, in the same sense, Adorno writes: "[Dialectics] would come to an end in reconcilement. Reconcilement would release the nonidentical, would rid it of coercion, including spiritualized coercion; it would open the road to the multiplicity of different things and strip dialectics of its power over them" (1990: 6). "Accompanying irreconcilable thoughts is the hope for reconcilement" (1990: 19). "Utopia would be above identity and above contradiction; it would be a togetherness of diversity" (1990: 150). "The reconciled condition would not be the philosophical imperialism of annexing the alien. Instead, its happiness would lie in the fact that the alien, in the proximity it is granted, remains what is distant and different, beyond the heterogeneous and beyond that which is one's own" (1990: 191). Rather, the difference between the two lies in that, in negative dialectics, fidelity to this utopia demands a rejection of all efforts to emancipate difference from negativity in the sphere of the concept (of dialectics), insofar as this emancipation has not happened in the sphere of the object (of society).[22] Fidelity to utopia is a synonym of critique in negative dialectics. Indeed, all our previous arguments are no more than variations of this one argument.

Nevertheless, this difference, however suggestive, tells us nothing conclusive about its possible contributions to the critique of modern capitalism. Is a philosophy such as the Deleuzian one centred in a concept of difference which intends to escape negativity truly apologetic? Is a dialectics such as Adorno's, which remains anchored in a negativity that points towards the antagonistic character of social relations, truly critical? Let us see. The immediate answer to the first question can only be no. Deleuze's philosophy of difference, as we have said, has a strong utopian dimension. One could object that all ideologies, especially the liberalism mentioned in connection with various Deleuzian arguments, have a utopian dimension. But even this objection is not enough to change our initial response, for the Deleuzian philosophy of difference cannot simply be assimilated to liberalism or to any other ideology which is openly apologetic of capitalist society. On the other hand, the Deleuzian philosophy of difference obviously recovers many motifs from the tradition of anarchist thinking: life as resistance, the state as a despotic machine, externality of resistance in relation to power, the rejection of dialectics itself and, naturally, its repeated and explicit invocations of the multiplicity of differences as crowned anarchy and other similar expressions. The Deleuzian philosophy of difference can then be assumed – and is thus assumed by many of its followers – to be anarchist or, even better, post-anarchist. Nevertheless, even with that not everything has been said. We must leave aside internal criticism for a moment and reflect on the relation between this post-anarchist philosophy of difference and the dominant ideology in modern capitalism.

Perhaps the most unequivocal reply to this question lies in the provocative questions that Slavoj Žižek asks in relation to the scene, drawn by Jean-Jacques Lecercle, of a yuppie reading Deleuze and Guattari's *What is Philosophy?* in the subway:

And if there were no puzzlement, but rather enthusiasm, as the yuppie reads about the communication of affective intensities below the level of meaning ("Yes, that's how I design my publicity!") or when he reads slogans such as exploding the limits of the subjectivity which exists within itself and directly connect man and machine ("This reminds me of my son's favourite game, the superhero that transforms into a car!') or on the need of permanently reinventing oneself, opening up to the multitude of desires which push us to the limit ("Isn't that the goal of the new virtual sex videogame I'm developing? It's no longer about reproducing sexual bodily contact, but about exploding the limits of the established reality and imagine new intense and unprecedented ways of sexual pleasure!"). Indeed, there are certain features that justify our calling Deleuze the ideologist of late capitalism. (Žižek 2004: 11–12)

Perhaps this answer is too categorical and provocative, but we believe it has a core of truth. If an ideological mutation had taken place in such a way that the dominant ideology no longer rested on universalistic values such as those associated with the concepts of totality and system, universal history, subject and object identical to one another and dualistically distinguished, etc., if the fragmentary and multiple nature of differences, the dissolution of dualism and the identities of subject and object as well as the event were key values of the dominant ideology in modern capitalism, then the critical character of a philosophy such as Deleuze's could not be approached a-critically. A philosophy that vindicates difference in an immediate way, i.e. a difference which avoids negativity, would be condemned in such a context, in the best of cases, to a radicalised version of the discourse on the harmonious cohabitation of differences within the horizon delimited by the capitalist market and democracy, characteristic of the liberalism dominant in this context. And maybe in this radical gesture it would bring a utopian dimension into play; but, at the same time, it would be betraying its own utopia of an emancipation of difference.

Terry Eagleton mentions just such an ideological mutation:

There was a time, back in the days of classical liberal capitalism, when it was still thought possible and necessary to justify your actions as a good bourgeois by an appeal to certain rational arguments with universal foundations. ... As the capitalist system evolves, however – as it colonizes new peoples, imports new ethnic groups into its labour markets, spurs on the division of labour, finds itself constrained to extend its freedoms to new constituencies – it begins inevitably to undermine its own universalist rationality. For it is hard not to recognize that there are now a whole range of competing cultures, idioms and ways of doing things, which the hybridizing, transgressive, promiscuous nature of capitalism has itself helped to bring into being. ... The system is accordingly confronted with a choice: either to continue insisting on the universal nature of its rationality, in the teeth of the mounting evidence, or to throw in the towel and go relativist, gloomily or genially accepting that it can muster no ultimate foundations to legitimate its activities. The uptight conservatives take the former road, while the laid-back liberal pragmatists take the latter. ... In its post-imperial phase, and in a supposedly multicultural society, the system can no longer plausibly claim that its values are superior to those of others, simply – key postmodern term – different. (1996: 39–40)

However, speaking of the system as antinomy, in *Negative Dialectics* Adorno had already philosophically anticipated this ideological dialectics originating in the tension between the universalization of capitalist social relations and the subordination of differences. "Kant had already held," Adorno writes, "that the emancipated *ratio*, the *progressus ad infinitum*, is halted solely by recognizing nonidentities in form, at least. The antinomy of totality and infinity – for the restless *ad infinitum* explodes the self-contained system, for all its being owed to infinity alone – is of the essence of idealism. It imitates a central antinomy of bourgeois society. To preserve itself, to remain the same, to 'be', that society too must constantly expand, progress, advance its frontiers, not respect any limit, not remain the same" (1990: 26). The historical tendency towards the universalisation of capitalist social relations (Adorno has in mind the Marxian assertions on the global nature of capital) translates into the systematic tendency of idealism. The subsuming of labour in capital is ideally reproduced as subsuming difference in the identity of the system. There is no need to say that this is the philosophical imperialism which would reach its peak in Hegel's system. "The Hegelian system in itself was not a true becoming; implicitly, each single definition in it was already preconceived. Such safeguards condemn it to untruth" (Adorno 1990: 27). However, at the same time, it is this very difference that holds up the system: if it were to dissolve in its self-sufficiency, in totality without infinity, in static without dynamics, in an undifferentiated identity with itself, the system would dissolve – perhaps in a multiplicity of differences? To the very success of that tendency of subsuming the difference inherent in idealist systems – and to that of its other side, the tendency of subsuming labour in capital – Adorno rightly ascribes the crisis of the idealist systems in the seventeenth and eighteenth centuries, from the end of the nineteenth century: "the process in which the systems decomposed, due to their own insufficiency, stands in counterpoint to a social process. In the form of the barter principle, the bourgeois *ratio* really approximated to the systems whatever it would make commensurable with itself, would identify with itself – and it did so with increasing, if potentially homicidal, success. Less and less was left outside" (Adorno 1990: 23).

But let us return to the end of the twentieth century: does the Deleuzian philosophy of difference – as well as postmodern philosophy in total – not represent a subsequent moment of this crisis of idealist philosophical systems? To be more precise, does it not point towards a new encounter between the remains of this universalistic reason, of which these philosophical systems had constituted the maximum expression, and the proliferation of differences unleashed by the French May – but also of the later assimilation of these differences, not through this universalistic reason in crisis but a new imminent relativist reason, within the boundaries of capitalist market and democracy? If that were the case, the Deleuzian philosophy of difference could offer very little to the critique of the dominant ideology in modern capitalism. And the Adornian negative dialectics could offer more insofar as, in its insistence on the antagonistic character of capitalist social relations, it is incompatible with any illusion surrounding a true emancipation of difference in relation to negativity within these limits of the capitalist market and democracy. As we said at the beginning, Adorno's *Negative Dialectics* is worth reading. But let it be made clear that we are not talking of any reading of *Negative Dialectics*. We are not talking of reading it as an immediate vindication of difference, thus adding it more or less imperceptibly to the spectrum of postmodern philosophical thought. Because this reading – apart from violating its content – would sever its critical character towards an ideology which turned this very same vindication of difference – always within the boundaries of the capitalist market and democracy – into one of its decisive values. So let us leave this reading to literary criticism – or the micropolitical militancy – of American universities. We are talking of a reading of *Negative Dialectics* as a dialectics of class struggle.

* Translated by Anna-Maeve Holloway

NOTES

1. This intervention by Holloway, as well as one of my own, has been published in the electronic review *Topos y Tropos* 4, Córdoba, www. toposytropos.com.ar, 2005.
2. Although in consonance with Adorno, it was Sohn-Rethel (1978) who highlighted better than anyone this externality of the cognitive structures of the transcendental subject, deriving them from the inherent abstraction in commodity exchange.
3. In the same sense, Foucault, in his reception of Deleuze's *Difference and Repetition*, wrote: "to tell the truth, dialectics does not liberate that which is different; on the contrary, it guarantees it will always remain trapped. The dialectical sovereignty of that which is the same consists in letting it be, but under the law of the negative, as the moment of not being ... In order to liberate difference we need a thinking without contradiction, without dialectics, without negation: a thinking that says 'yes' to difference, an affirmative thought that uses disjunction as a tool; a thinking of the multiple – of the dispersed and nomadic multiplicity which does not limit nor regroup any of the coactions of that which is the same" (Foucault 1999: 32–3).
4. Deleuze naturally points towards the Althusserian reading of Marx (Althusser and Balibar 1985). There is no way of overestimating the influence of the Althusser of *Ecole* of the 1970s – an influence not always recognised by his disciples – in the formation of French poststructuralism. And that definitely includes many of his worst vices. Nevertheless, Althusser should not be blamed for the crude reduction of Marx to Durkheim that Deleuze performs.
5. Negri and Hardt argue that, rather than in the Marxist recuperation of dialectics in the 1920s, it is in the Nietzschean poststructuralist recuperation of the 1960s that the critique of European modernity reaches its peak. "For the real clarification of this scene, we are most indebted to the series of French philosophers who reread Nietzsche several decades later, in the 1960s [a reference to Deleuze, Foucault and Derrida]. Their rereading involved a reorientation of the standpoint of the critique, which came about when they

began to recognize the end of the functioning of the dialectic and when this recognition was confirmed in the new practical, political experiences that centered on the production of subjectivity. This was a production of subjectivity as power, as the constitution of an autonomy that could not be reduced to any abstract or transcendent synthesis. Not the dialectic but refusal, resistance, violence, and the positive affirmation of being now marked the relationship between the location of the crisis in reality and the adequate response" (Negri and Hardt 2000: 378). That can be confronted with the very different role that Adorno and Horkheimer attribute to Nietzsche, in his quality of the "black writer of the bourgeoisie," in *Dialectic of Enlightenment* (2002).

6. Let us mention in passing that here we can distinguish the Nietzschean origin of the Bacchanalian language of Deleuze. "Nietzsche's 'yes' is opposed to the dialectical 'no'; affirmation to dialectical negation; difference to dialectical contradiction; joy, enjoyment, to dialectical labour; lightness, dance, to dialectical responsibilities ... It is an exhausted force which does not have the strength to affirm its difference, a force which no longer acts but rather reacts to the forces which dominate it – only such a force brings to the foreground the negative element in its relation to the other. Such a force denies all that it is not and makes this negation its own essence and the principle of its existence" (Deleuze 2006: 9).

7. The concept of multitude used by Negri or Virno has a Spinozan origin (particularly Negri 1993), but the content attributed to him would be inconceivable without the mediation of the Deleuzian philosophy of difference.

8. "Crear una nueva esfera pública, sin Estado" [Creating a public sphere, without a state], article on Virno by H. Pavón, published in *Clarín*, 27 December 2004.

9. It is no coincidence that Deleuze points, at this moment of his argument on Foucault, towards the "inversion" of M. Tronti. "We too have worked with a concept that puts capitalist development first, and workers second. This is a mistake. And now we have to turn the problem on its head, reverse the polarity, and start again from the beginning: and the beginning is the class struggle of the working class" (1979: 1). The confrontation between Adorno and Tronti proposed by Holloway in his intervention (see note 1 above) is, in this sense, highly pertinent: the priority and externality of potential in relation to power in Negri's new autonomism finds its precedent in this autonomist inversion of Tronti, that is, in this assertion of the priority and externality of labour in relation to capital. And

both operations are included in the same dialectical critique, which in Adorno's negative dialectics acquires its higher expression.

10. Also in this sense, the Adornian negative dialectics differs from the Deleuzian philosophy of difference in that, as an heir of structuralist formalism in that respect, it dreams of "systems subject to eternal return," in mechanics, natural science, biology, psychology, literature, etc. (Deleuze 1995a: 126), with a "system of multiple, non-localizable connections between differential elements" such as scientific atomism, the biological organism, society (1995a: 183), etc.

11. His own anti-Aristotelian thesis on the univocality of being, formulated in *Repetition and Difference*, is a good synthesis of that immanentist intention. "Being is said in a single and same sense, but that it is said, in a single and same sense, of everything of which it is said, but that of which it is said differs: it is said of difference itself" (1995a: 36). This thesis of the univocality of being can be found, according to Deleuze (1992), as for the relation between substance and mode, in Spinoza.

12. There is no need to add that this "schizophrenization of the unconscious" is the psychoanalytical correlate of that task of liberating difference from its reduction to negativity that Deleuze had announced in *Repetition and Difference*. "The phenomena of the unconscious – he already said back then – cannot be understood in the overly simple form of opposition or conflict" (1995a: 106).

13. Marx ascribes to Smith, despite his ambiguities, this concept of labour itself: "It was an immense step forwards for Adam Smith to throw out every limiting specification of wealth-creating activity – not only manufacturing, or commercial, or agricultural labour, but one as well as the others" (Marx 1993: 104). But he immediately points out that that concept, which approaches the simplest social relation which exists in all societies, can only be conceived as the result of the development of capitalist society. Both concept and its object are historical products, very specific abstractions. "This example of labour shows strikingly how even the most abstract categories, despite their validity – precisely because of their abstractness – for all epochs, are nevertheless, in the specific character of this abstraction, themselves likewise a product of historic relations, and possess their full validity only for and within these relations" (Marx 1993: 105).

14. It is in this assertion of the critical character of Freudian psychoanalysis, as well as in the rejection of the revisionist interpretation that we will mention further on, without ignoring other differences, that Marcuse (1974: I–IV) coincides with Adorno.

15. There is no need to add that, in the Adornian critique of revisionism, there is an adherence to a Freudian orthodoxy in play. Adorno recognized the conservative streak of a Freudian reasoning that "materialistically pursued conscious behaviour into the basis of its unconscious grounding in the drives, yet simultaneously accords with the bourgeois contempt for the drives, which is itself the product of precisely those rationalizations, which he demolishes" (2005, aphorism 37). Rather, it is a dialectic strategy of assimilation of psychoanalysis that aims at overcoming this conservatism parting from the radicalization of the critical dimensions which are inherent in psychoanalysis itself – a strategy which is justly similar to the one adopted by Adorno before the assertive Hegelian dialectics. This is the meaning, worth generalising, in the aphorism that "nothing is true in psychoanalysis except its exaggerations" (2005: aphorism 28).

16. This Adornian reflection overlaps, naturally, with the dialectics of enlightenment in its entirety. Adorno and Horkheimer's slogan that "enlightenment must take conscience of itself, if it does not wish for men to be totally betrayed" amounts to the rejection of any regressive effort in relation to illustrated reason, such as the Bergsonian in his case – and the Deleuzian in ours?

17. In relation to the link between life and desire in Deleuze, Agamben (1998) explains that life is "the field of variable immanence of desire" and that, therefore, life designates the immanence of desire to itself.

18. Naturally, there are important affinities between the Deleuzian and Foucauldian philosophies in general, and in particular, in their last works they share the same preoccupation for life. But we do not believe it is as clear as saying that in the late works of Foucault we can find the vitalism Deleuze attributes to him: in Foucault, life continues to appear predominantly as an object of power rather than as the origin of a resistance against the same.

19. The correlate of this political availability is a certain decisionism which, in postwar French existentialism, led to the effort to "desperately oppose to the omnipotence of society an isolated, presumably ontological concept of subjective spontaneity" (Adorno 1993: 41).

20. Once more, in relation to the supposed Adornian argument that "people have altogether too few inhibitions and not too many, without being a whit the healthier for it", we should remember the Marcusian reflections on repressive "desublimation" and "tolerance" (Marcuse 1991: III; 1969). In reflections such as this, Adorno and Marcuse discern the profound mutation in dominant ideology that we will refer to below.

21. We talk of a more political language simply because it is the one employed by Negri and Hardt in their political writings (2000; 2004) – although this exodus ends up adopting forms as politically ambiguous as the migratory fluxes.

22. We should clarify that that does not mean there are no glimpses of freedom, that is, truly human relations where that which is different does not give rise to identifying violence, before society as a whole is emancipated. The Adornian aphorism "you will be loved only where you can show your weakness without provoking force" (2006) wants to define love as one of those relations.

REFERENCES

Adorno, T. W. (1976) *Terminología filosófica I*, Madrid, Taurus.

Adorno, T. W. (1979) "La revisión del psicoanálisis," in M. Horkheimer and T. W. Adorno, *Sociológica*, Madrid, Taurus.

Adorno, T. W. (1986) *Sobre la metacrítica de la teoría del conocimiento*, Barcelona, Planeta-Agostini.

Adorno, T. W. (1990) *Negative Dialectics*, London, Routledge.

Adorno, T. W. (1993a) "Notas marginales sobre teoría y praxis," in *Consignas*, Buenos Aires, Amorrortu.

Adorno, T. W. (1993b) *Hegel: Three Studies*, Cambridge, MA, MIT Press.

Adorno, T. W. (2001a) "Sociedad," in *Epistemología y ciencias sociales*, Madrid, Cátedra.

Adorno, T. W. (2001b) "Sociología e investigación empírica," in *Epistemología y ciencias sociales*, Madrid, Cátedra.

Adorno, T. W. (2005) *Mínima Moralia. Reflections on a Damaged Life* www.marxists.org/reference/archive/adorno/1951/mm/ch01.htm (accessed 23 May 2008). (Also available as Adorno, T. W. (2005) *Mínima Moralia. Reflections on a Damaged Life*, trans. E. F. N. Jephcott. London, Verso.)

Adorno, T. W. (2006) *The Jargon of Authenticity*, London, Routledge.

Adorno, T. W. and Horkheimer, M. (2002) *Dialectic of Enlightenment*, Stanford, CA, Stanford University Press.

Agamben, G. (1998) "L'immanence absolue," in E. Alliez (ed.), *Gilles Deleuze, une vie philosophique*, Paris, Synthélabo.

Althusser, L. and Balibar, E. (1998) *Reading Capital*, London, Verso.

Deleuze, G. (1986) *Nietzsche y la filosofía*, Barcelona, Anagrama.

Deleuze, G. (1988) *Foucault*, London, Athlone.

Deleuze, G. (1992) *Expressionism in Philosophy: Spinoza*, New York, Zone Books.

Deleuze, G. (1995a): *Difference and Repetition*, New York, Columbia University Press.

Deleuze, G. (1995b) "L'immanence: une vie ...," in *Philosophie* 47, Paris.

Deleuze, G. and Guattari, F. (1987) *A Thousand Plateaus*, Minneapolis, MN, Minnesota University Press.

Deleuze, G. and Guattari, F. (1991) *¿Qué es la filosofía?* Barcelona, Anagrama.

Deleuze, G. and Guattari, F. (1998) *Anti-Oedipus. Capitalism and Schizophrenia*, Minneapolis, MN, Minnesota University Press.

Deleuze, G. and Parnet, C. (2002): *Dialogues*, New York, Columbia University Press.

Eagleton, T. (1996) *The Illusions of Postmodernism*, London, Wiley Blackwell.

Foucault, M. (1990) *The History of Sexuality. Vol. 1: An Introduction.* New York, Vintage Books.

Foucault, M. (1994) *The Order of Things, An Archaeology of Human Sciences*, London, Vintage.

Foucault, M. (1999) "Theatrum Philosophicum," in M. Foucault, and G. Deleuze, *Theatrum Philosophicum seguido de Repetición y diferencia*, Barcelona, Anagrama.

Foucault, M. (2001) "El sujeto y el poder," Postcript in H. L. Dreyfus and P. Rabinow (eds.), *Michel Foucault: más allá del estructuralismo y la hermenéutica*, Buenos Aires, Nueva Visión.

Marcuse, H. (1969) "Represive tolerance," in AAVV: *A Critique of Pure Tolerance.* London, Jonathan Cape.

Marcuse, H. (1974) *Eros and Civilization*, London, Beacon Press.

Marcuse, H. (1991) *One Dimensional Man*, London, Beacon Press.

Marx, K. (1993) *Grundrisse: Foundations of the Critique of Political Economy*, London, Penguin Classics.

Negri, A. (2000) *The Savage Anomaly: The Power of Spinoza's Metaphysics and Politics*, Minneapolis, MN, Minnesota University Press.

Negri, A. and Hardt, M. (2000) *Empire*, London, Harvard University Press.

Negri, A. and Hardt, M. (2004) *Multitude*, New York, Penguin Press.

Sohn-Rethel, A. (1978) *Intellectual and Manual Labour*, London, Macmillan.

Tronti, M. (1979) "Lenin in England," in *Working Class Autonomy and the Crisis,* London, Red Notes.

Virno, P. (2004) *A Grammar of the Multitude.* New York, Semiotext(e) Foreign Agent Series.

Žižek, S. (2004) *La revolución blanda*, Buenos Aires, Parusía.

5

ADORNO AND POST-VANGUARDISM

Darij Zadnikar

It should already be obvious, but I want to remark: I shit on all the revolutionary vanguards of this planet. (Subcommandante Insurgente Marcos)

THE VIEW FROM SOUTHEAST EUROPE

From my perspective, coming from post-socialist Slovenia which was a part of the failed Yugoslav experiment, a consideration of Western Marxism,[1] the Frankfurt School and particularly Adorno may be different in some way. Here we are living in an environment which, while openly renouncing the whole Marxist tradition, nevertheless at the ideological level of so-called common sense accepts the authoritarian idea of the state, parties and representative democracy, which are conditioned by the legacy of bureaucratic Marxism. In this respect it is similar to other East European countries, yet there is a difference, for in the former Yugoslavia there was a strong academic reception of Western Marxism and, even more, a significant contribution to it by the Praxis group (Gajo Petrović, Milan Kangrga, Mihajlo Marković, etc.), which was important in the debates beyond the Yugoslav frontiers. In the other East European countries, which were under the dominance of Soviet Union and Stalinist ideology, the tradition of Western Marxism was ignored and even prohibited as bourgeois and reactionary intellectualism. Even so, the rich and influential presence of anti-Stalinist Marxism could not prevent the breakdown and failure of the Yugoslav experiment. Even more: some of the most famous philosophers, as is the case with

Mihajlo Marković, contributed to the expansion of the most aggressive nationalism and supported Slobodan Milošević[2] and other nationalistic leaders. In the late 1970s and 1980s a lot of young intellectuals abandoned Western Marxism in favour of postmodernism. Slavoj Žižek, the most famous Slovenian philosopher, is one of them. His philosophical development from the Frankfurt School to Lacanian psychoanalysis and postmodern eclecticism[3] is significant, even paradigmatic for the intellectual climate of this country.

In my opinion we have to think afresh the relation of the emancipatory and liberation theories towards and within the emancipatory and liberation movements. My contribution to the debate on the role of Adorno's thought for contemporary alternative-globalisation movements expresses our historic sensitivity within these movements and concentrates on the rupture between theory and practice in the form of vanguardism and elitism.

THE MULTITUDES AGAINST VANGUARDISM

If we want to understand the actual and future condition of the new social movements that emerged after the Seattle protests, then we have to grasp the structural changes and particularities of contemporary capitalism. The insurgency in southeast Mexico in January 1994 has pointed to neo-liberal globalisation as the core problem that threatens the existence of indigenous people at the local level. Neo-liberal globalisation overrides the division between local and metropolitan not only in the organisation of economic life, but also at the level of resistance. There is no longer a privileged actor and script of emancipation, as was imagined there was in the era of the industrial capitalism. Therefore, we can witness all the heterogeneity and multiplicity of contemporary resistance. In general all such resistance arises from the specific conditions, but with a more or less clear awareness of neo-liberalism as the common enemy. This distinguishes it from the politics of identity and lifestyle of the 1980s, and also from the humanitarianism of the NGOs. The plurality of emancipatory narratives creates the multidimensional experiences and practices of resistance. The boundaries between political activism, artistic expression, lifestyle, fighting, surviving, enjoying, etc. are dissolving. Even the difference between the political and intimacy is lost in this climate of militancy. The movement for global justice consists largely of these heterogeneous elements, of multitudes[4] which are dynamic and fast moving, anarchic, even chaotic. It resembles the so-called Brown's chaotic movement of microscopic particles in a heated liquid, which until Einstein did not have a full explanation. As the social sciences are more self-deluding than natural science, they tend to interpret the new realities through old schemata or to play down their importance or even to ignore them. This is mirrored itself also in mainstream politics, culture, educational rituals, media and at other ideological levels. Because of the plurality, heterogeneity and chaotic nature of these movements, they have greater difficulties in the processes of self-reflection than the ruling ideologists have in producing their dogmatic falsifications (that is, producing the phantasm of "anti-globalism"). But even in this chaotic and fast-moving environment of resistance, new, non-institutional forms of consensus-building are emerging. The multitudes do not strive to gain hegemony in movements, they do not try to impose their ideas and priorities, but more to express them in a creative way that can impact and infiltrate the other subjects. This lack of a classic, discursive aim at consent is not in all cases the strong side of these movements, but it is, on the other hand, the principal means of rapid communication amongst the neuron-shaped webs. This structure of resisting multitudes makes it impossible to build a metanarrative of resistance, as in the industrial era. The multitudes generally express themselves, their means of fight and survival, denying the possibility of privileged metanarratives and their representatives.

Despite the new shape of global resistance, it has from the outset been accompanied by some old-fashioned organisational forms, such as parties, trade unions, etc. Some of them contributed a lot to the movement materially as well as in the sense of shared experiences. After the protests in Genoa in summer 2001, the movement was widely recognised as a political force, despite corporate propaganda. In the following months some of the biggest trade unions accepted the ideas of the global movement. These parts of the movement had an important role in providing material and infrastructural support for some bigger events (social forums, etc.). Amongst the multitudes these old-fashioned organisations were often derided. The classic socialist workers' parties were described as the Salvation Army or Jehovah's Witnesses.[5] There are three main reasons for refuting and being cautious of such organisations: they are hierarchic and autocratic, they have a linear conception of history and they introduce vanguardism into the movement.

Although the Marxist revolutionary movements understood the state in the context of broader social transition, the reality was a total fetishisation of state power. They understood their "historic" task in terms of taking state power (by elections or revolution, social democrats and communists alike) as an instrument for social change. So they had to build militaristic and bureaucratic parties.

> The induction into the conquest of power inevitably becomes an induction into power itself. The initiates learn the language, logic and calculations of power; they learn to wield the categories of a social science, which has been entirely shaped by its obsession with power. ... Manipulation and manoeuvring for power become a way of life. (Holloway 2002: 15–16)

The result was a profound impoverishment of emancipatory goals and methods and their subordination to state-oriented ends. The disciplinary society was built on the model of the factory. The hierarchical organisation of political life has been conceived as the proper rational basis of society itself, as though society were just an extended factory. Politics became engineering and bureaucratic administration. With such a mentality the members of old-fashioned trade unions and parties cannot adapt themselves to the dynamic and chaotic ways of contemporary social movements. They miss the meetings with appointed delegates, agendas, minutes, speakers, etc. They want order and clear instructions. All the plurality of resistant multitudes and their ways of expressing rebellion is seen as a childish charade. They are solemn. They act like church dignitaries. They know. They are respectable and this shows in their ties and clothes. They do not have dreadlocks, piercings or tattoos.

This organisational closeness to clergy shows a deep connection with Judeo-Christian conceptions of society and history. For them history is an explicable drama with a cathartic dénouement. History is seen as a linear progression towards this dénouement. It is measured by the criteria of industrial advance. It is more a Protestant than a Catholic version of Christianity. It is always possible to recognise the "ethics" of work in the criteria of historic progress. Work that produces surplus value, of course. There is not much scope outside these criteria. I want to stress here that a linear notion of history reduces itself to a unique criterion of progress. Such a history consists of reduced narration. It is an impoverishment that is constructed with the exclusion of plural narratives, or at least with their hierarchisation. The end of history, its dénouement or Day of Judgement, is of course the revolution, which establishes the heavenly kingdom on earth, Communism or anarchy. The question is: how to identify this *file rouge* of history and not miss the historic point of revolutionary dénouement. The revolutionary clergy, the party intellectuals and bureaucracy have to decipher this historical point. Following their Christian predecessors, there are some revolutionaries who patiently wait for it and others who are hatching a plot in their kitchens of history. As the narratives of contemporary global movement, the multitudes are plural, dispersed, non-centric, chaotic, anarchic, non-hierarchic, etc., and history loses its one-dimensional characteristic. It loses its emphatic explicability, it becomes the stage for various scripts rather than a single truth. It does not mean we have to subject ourselves to any kind of fancy, postmodern scepticism, but it does mean we have a broader task than the revolutionary bureaucrats would like to admit. From the standpoint of grassroots multitudes and the multiplicity of their resistances, the revolution is real, it is happening right now. So the multitudes are working out their plural and divergent tasks without waiting for the proper historic time or realising an emphatic programme. The notion of revolution and of the revolutionary working class from the industrial era followed the example of the French Revolution, when the revolutionary bourgeoisie overthrew the aristocracy, so that capitalism took the place of feudalism in the "historic line." The party revolutionaries overlooked the fact that the world of bourgeois life had already overwhelmed feudalism. The alternative now existed at the level of everyday experience. In the case of the industrial party revolution, the working class has been idealised, though it did not build much in the way of positive alternatives at the level of everyday life. And this is precisely the point of Marxist understanding of the revolutionary proletariat: it is its total social negativity, which is realised through the commodification of labour. The proletariat is the excess of alienation, the point from which you have to step out from the realm of work. The proletariat is the point of self-destruction of capitalism, it is not an idealised actor of history. It is the end of humanity. It is the standpoint from which freedom is seen only beyond work. The nomadic and contingent characteristics of the multitudes regarding the systemic imperatives of neo-liberalism are opening up the cracks in the history, the pockets of resistance, the exodus from Empire, the revolution. It is productive and inventive through its negativity. The plurality of possible different worlds is actual, but not in the sense of a gigantic historical swap. The multitudes are inconsistent and contradictory, therefore the system wants to normalise them. We have to understand them in Georges Bataille's term *heterogeneity*. They have to build the practices of transgression. The actual notion of revolution, which goes through and beyond the world of capital, is comparable with composting in organic gardening. The multitudes have to decompose the system by means of a plurality of rebellious life practices into something that is suitable and worth living.

I can understand the position of some British comrades (for example, Callinicos 2003) from the viewpoint of the rich tradition of the British labour movement. But what they offer us is the nationalisation of industry, which could only strengthen the state and integrate the workers into the capitalist mode of production. Still more: such a nationalised economy can function only within nationalistic and protectionist frameworks. It is no coincidence that this so often idealised working class is the social basis for right extremism. The idealisation of the working class, so foreign to the Marxian concept of the proletariat as social negativity, is consequent on the contemplative view of history as linear progress. This view needs, intellectually and from above, to identify the social actors of history, the subjects of history. History no longer emerges from the rebellious negativity of social groups, but these have to fulfil the task of history as heroes. The problem is that either they do not see this historic task, or do not care about its long-term goals: the revolution is missing its revolutionary subject. As we know, it has been substituted by "revolutionary" parties, their bureaucracies and militants and leaders. They have to bring the subject to its senses, by fair means or foul. The clerical vision of history is the birthplace of vanguardism. This vanguardism is blind to all social movements which cannot be manipulated and which express their rebellious visions by themselves. Vanguardism is the absolute realisation of representative politics. As we have said, it is manipulative and totalitarian. The dictatorship of the proletariat is in fact the dictatorship of the party vanguard, which seized state power to fulfil the task of history. As they separate themselves from the heterogeneity of negative life (creativity) they cannot see emancipated society outside the visions of factory management. The "ruling" working class becomes that which it can only be inside the factory boundaries: executors of orders. The more this class is exploited and repressed, the more its social image is idealised. They become the superheroes of work (living in poor conditions). It is similar to the idealisation of women (virgin mother) in patriarchal societies. The multitudes are useless for vanguardists. They do not accept the supreme historic task. They do not accept the representatives. They are difficult to read. They are not serious. They are networking and swarming instead of organising themselves. They are useless and therefore invisible. This vanguardism constitutes an obstacle for a lot of parties, groups and trade unionists, irrespective of their socialist, anarchist or other origins. The objectives of their struggle are defined from nineteenth- and early twentieth-century books, so they are often missing the point of today's fight. The anarchistic standpoint towards the state is as a rule defined by old-fashioned images of state power, which have little to do with the reality of the society of control that is emerging in post-industrial societies. The socialists are dreaming of a state with full employment. The communists are discussing the differences between Leninism, Maoism, Trotskyism and other "-isms".

It seems that on the field of contemporary struggles it is only the project that counts. In fact, the project is a projection of individual, collective and "natural" life. At the boundaries and cross-sections of the multitudes the new world could be born. Of course, it does not mean that it will, because the multitudes do not have history on their side. In this narrow sense of "history" they are a-historic. Somehow they have accelerated to the point of absence of time. It is more or less the result of new communicative technologies, which changed not only the flow of information but also the cognitive styles and perceptive sensitivity. The outcomes of fights are therefore unpredictable. Let us take two examples: Genoa 2001 and Madrid 2004. The battle of Genoa strengthened the movement despite the hostile media coverage and violence of the Italian forces. The mobilisations after Genoa were even more numerous, irrespective of the decoy of the so-called Black Bloc, which started in Genoa and ended in Thessaloniki 2003. The global peace movement of February 2003 did not stop the aggression against Iraq. But the Spaniards did not react to the terrorist bombing in March 2004 with primitive patriotism and anti-Islamism. The activists, who organised themselves against the war a year earlier were able to mobilise the masses within a few hours: "Your war, our deaths!" In the elections the socialists did not win on the basis of their own manifesto, as they were forced by the multitudes to change their policy and immediately withdraw the Spanish army from Iraq, followed by some other contingents. When the corporate media sarcastically asked what the efficiency of peace protests in winter 2003 was, nobody could predict the reaction and impact of the Spanish multitudes. They managed to instrumentalise the political parties, which usually instrumentalised so-called public opinion. In this sense the impact of the multitudes is equal to the decomposition of public opinion, which consists of passive voyeurism of corporate media and political parties.

The people we are learning from to recover dignity are the indigenous peoples, from oppressed women we learn how to gain courage, from the Argentinian *piqueteros* to rebuild urban society, from the Slovenian "erased" or the *sans-papiers* in Europe how to survive, from the migrants how to transform their adopted countries and not just assimilate, from punks how to squat for living and amusement, from Brazilian peasants how to occupy large estates, etc. There are numerous questions: What to eat? What to breathe? How to buy? There is no single doctrine which can give us all the answers. There is no unique method to win the fight. There is no guarantee of success. The localisation of struggles could be successful, when it takes into consideration how the globalised neo-liberal system is functioning at their local level. At this moment the process of extending the society of control, which follows the disciplinary society, could be overcome by the tactics of acceleration and speed, divergence and rhizomatic connectability, by surpassing and autonomy, by hiding in the web and emerging from the shadows, by interruptions of flows, deceptions and piracy, nomadism and techno-fanaticism, to shirk work and go on protests, be playful and creative. And shit on all vanguards!

DID ADORNO DIE?

We can easily refute the importance of Adorno's thought for the contemporary multiplicity of social struggles by referring to his scepticism towards the student movement of 1968 or maybe even by quoting his denial of mass culture. At that time the student protestors interrupted his lecture and he died not long after. But we can sarcastically add that the student movement died not long after Adorno. Even though there are some comparisons between 1968 and the global movement, the duration, utopias and political representation of the student movement are not of great importance for now, as it failed utterly at the political level, failing to overcome the over-ideologisation of their goals. But the splinters of 1968 survived at the (counter-) cultural level and are constitutional for the movements after Seattle 1999. We have here an interesting analogy with Adorno and the Frankfurt School in general. The "historic role" of the working class failed to prevent the rise of fascism[6] and the revolutionary subject disappeared. The project of Western Marxism, as derived from Karl Korsch's *Philosophy and Marxism*, was no longer possible. In this respect refuge in the academic sanctuary and a shift to *Kulturkritik* seem reasonable. In this fragmented sense Adorno's thought could be as important for the (self-) reflection of the movements. Even more: Adorno's entire work is some kind of systematic fragmentation and vice versa (see Adorno 1973). Self-reflection from the singularities of resistance which make up the global movement is possible as a work of *micrology*, which is an important concept for Adorno's notion of negative dialectics.

Enlightenment leaves as good as nothing left of metaphysical truth-content, *presque rien* after a modern musical term. What shrinks back becomes ever smaller, just as Goethe portrayed in the parable of the little box of the New Melusine, which names an extremity; ever more inconspicuous; this is the reason that, in the critique of cognition as much as in the philosophy of history, metaphysics migrates into micrology. This latter is the place of metaphysics as the refuge from what is total. (Adorno 1994: 399)

The micrological thought prevents dialectical reconciliation in the totality. In negative dialectics, the reconciliation is "mediation on the no-longer-hostile multiplicity":

Dialectics develops the difference of the particular from the generality, which is dictated by the generality. While it is inescapable to the subject, as the break between subject and object drilled into the consciousness, furrowing everything which it thinks, even that which is objective, it would have an end in reconciliation. This would release the non-identical, relieving it even of its intellectualized compulsion, opening up for the first time the multiplicity of the divergent, over which dialectics would have no more power. Reconciliation would be the meditation on the no-longer-hostile multiplicity, something which is subjective anathema to reason. (Adorno 1994: 18)

Such a concept of negative dialectics deviates considerably from the fashionable general rejection of dialectical thought by Derrida, Deleuze (1994) and others, and especially amongst the notable thinkers who are close to the new movements, for example Antonio Negri, who explicitly declares himself to be "Deleuzian." This brings us back to the problem of vanguardism, which is emerging from within the movements as a kind of new activist *post-vanguardism*. It can be detected in Negri and Hardt's passage on the militant in *Empire* (2001). My thesis is that post-vanguardist activists are uncoerced, where Adorno and others from the Institute for Social Research were forced to go by the threat of fascism.

There is no need for the reduction of the idea of dialectics to Hegel's logic. A vast post-Hegelian reconceptualisation of dialectics has been carried out and Adorno's negative dialectics is just one of the best known. What we have to bear in mind is the original meaning of the word *dialegein* and the need to expose the communicative dimension of dialectics over its logical meaning. Micrology derives from speech and interaction before diving in-and-against metaphysics. In the absence of the dialogical/dialectical component, there is only the residue of shattered and unconnected monologues. We can enjoy their wittiness, but there is no need to take a stand, where we can, as in the supermarket of ideas, just change them, like old clothes or TV channels. It is not the reconciliation of and in differences – it is simply ignoring them. In this respect we can critically point to professional activists and the activists by mission, the new age missionaries, who are like medieval Franciscan monks wandering through the networks of resistances. Yesterday they were on the streets of Genoa, today they are preparing Food-not-Bombs in the No Border Camp, tomorrow visiting a new squat in Croatia and they are already contemplating where to participate for Euro Mayday. These activists-by-mission can contribute experience at the local level, but also leave the scene instantaneously if the situation becomes complicated or boring. Such a postmodernist activism cannot replace the need for communication between the communities in resistance, which is the only way of building global solidarity against neo-liberalism. The "Franciscan" activist assumes an intellectual standpoint – the gaze from above – describing and proscribing, interpreting and naming, applying theories in order to "understand" and "direct" the situation. It is not the way of micrology, it is rather a functionalism of social scientists.

The idea of non-Hegelian dialectics is based on deriving the logic of a thing and not on applying a logical-theoretical concept to it. It means that revolutionary thought has to be strongly interwoven with local struggles, aiming for more global perspectives through patient dialogue of the singularities, acquiring consent more by way of slow sedimentation[7] than by argumentative contests. The theories, which the movements need for self-reflection, have to be modest and remote from the emphatic ideologies of the past, but also from contemporary intellectual eclectic "applicationism."

Such a post-vanguardism of the activists reminds us of the more theoretical than political *bíoi* (Aristotle) of Adorno and other members of Frankfurt School – theoretical not in the sense of non-involvement, which in the case of contemporary activism is out of the question, but in the sense of a sublimity, which makes possible the gaze and micro-logical interpretation. There is some resemblance concerning the (non-)accessibility to academic sanctuaries. But Western Marxism was left alone in the revolutionary vacuum of Fascism, so that the turn to *Kulturkritik* and academic Marxism is reasonable. Reasonable also is that Adorno (unlike Marcuse) did not recognise the revolutionary potential of '68 and did not get involved in any social movement. We can decipher the "reasons" of sublime academic Marxists like Mihajlo Marković, who gave the Serbian nation and their leader the historic task of genocide. Floating intellectuals were easily transformed from "revolutionaries" into nationalists. It would be perhaps be better for them to stick with their academic sublimity of non-involvement as Adorno did. Sublimity of vacuum and academic excellence are better than shifting from the theoretical gaze-from-above (intellectual vanguardism) to bureaucratic interventionism (party vanguardism and state terror).

The theory and theorists of the new global and multitude-based movements in this respect have to reconsider their role.

MODESTY OF THOUGHT

What I am proposing is a notion of *dialectics as micro-logical dialegein*. It is not just approaching things but also reconstructing and restructuring them: it is in-spiralling and out-spiralling, listening and acting. This metaphor refers to the Zapatistas' idea of the *Caracol*. The Zapatistas are reconstructing and recuperating their communities on the basis of *encuentrismo*[8] and the *Caracoles* are the spaces of these processes.

> They say here that the most ancient say that other, earlier ones said that the most first of these lands held the figure of the shell in high esteem. They say that they say that they said that the conch represents entering into the heart, that is what the very first ones with knowledge said. And they say that they say they said that the conch also represents leaving the heart in order to walk the world, which is how the first ones called life. And more, they say that they say that they said that they called the collective with the shell, so that the word would go from one to the other and agreement would be reached. And they also say that they said that the conch was help so that the ear could hear even the most distant word. That is what they say that they say that they said. I don't know. I'm walking hand in hand with you, and I'm showing you what my ears see and my eyes hear. And I see and hear a shell, the "pu'y'", as they say in their language here. (Subcomandante Insurgente Marcos, 2003)

The new social praxis has to refashion its own theory, and the theory of the movements cannot come from the universities and institutes[9] (or from the party and trade union offices). Even more: such a theory needs a new activist epistemology which transcends the division between subject and object. Its objectivity has to be gained by and through the constituting of rebellious subjectivity. Is this not the sense of Marx's *11th Thesis on Feuerbach*?

But is it just my wishful thinking or does it have any real basis beyond the magic of the Mayan language? It seems that the Zapatistas are quite successful in reshaping their (and our) world, so their magic could become a usable epistemology. The problem is that it is not completely translatable because the conditions of our and other struggles are different.

An example of non-vanguardism is the *Colectivo Situaciones*[10] and its relation with/in *MTD Solano*, which is one of the most radical groups of Argentinian *piqueteros*. It is radical in the sense of a creative inventing of non-hierarchic sociability through opposition to neo-liberal capitalism, *encuentrismo*, reshaping of everyday life and reflective imagination. *Colectivo Situaciones* is a group of militant researchers who have in their projects destroyed the hierarchy of narratives and are constructing something which we could paraphrase in the Zapatista way as interpreting by listening. The interpretation, of course, is not self-sufficient, it seems that militant research is providing the conceptual possibilities and terms for actions and reflections of the *piqueteros*. The theory is constantly digested in the praxis, and the praxis in turn gains from theory its reflexive possibilities.

> *Situaciones* tries to be a literary project 'within' the struggle, a phenomenology (genealogy) and not an 'objective' description. Because only in this manner can thought be affirmative and assume a function of creation, and stop being merely a reproduction of the already existent. And because only with this fidelity with immanence is the act of thinking a real and dynamic contribution, which is the absolute opposite of a programme or outline that frames and saturates all action. (quoted in Khorasanee 2005)

The friends from the collective have been telling me how in the meetings of mostly unemployed workers and residents of the suburban neighbourhoods quite theoretical theorems were used in the discussions to cast light on the issues of everyday practices. In this way we can hardly perceive any of the vanguardism or the striving of the party intellectuals to lead the people like a herd, tending to reshape their narratives into the goals of history. Let us hope we can learn from them and build the micro-logical multiplicity of *dialegein* to recuperate our own world and life.

In conclusion we can say that the Hegelian form of dialectics in its most primitive and degraded way embodied itself as designing history from above through vanguardism and even dictatorship, but that refuting such a vanguardism by a Deleuzian abolition of dialectical thought seems to restore an activist post-vanguardism. Adorno's concept of the negative dialectic, which respects and preserves the differences, could survive and communicate to us (who are involved in global movements) in a fruitful way, in spite of his political withdrawal from the struggles of '68.

NOTES

1. With the thought of G. Lukács and K. Korsch as a departure point.
2. Mihajlo Marković, a philosopher of great significance in the Praxis circle, was a co-author of the Memorandum of the Serbian Academy of Sciences and Arts, which formed the ideological basis of Milošević's policy of Great Serbia.
3. His philosophy is a brilliant rhetoric, which is beyond the mere theoretical sybaritism quite controversial. Even though he was one of the key ideologists of the ruling Liberal Democrat Party and supported the annexation of Slovenia to the NATO Pact, outside of Slovenian borders he is considered as a leftist thinker.
4. I do not believe that at this moment the debate over the term *multitude* in Negri's or Virno's sense and its relation to the notion of *class* is of great importance to the new movements. Just like they need to place stress on their heterogeneity through the first term, they need the (non-sociological) concept of class to position themselves with regard to the relations of capital.
5. But they are not to be underestimated, as we saw at the London European Social Forum, where the authoritarian and even violent organisation of the event by the SWP ruined it.
6. Leftist parties did not support the students in 1968, nor did they significantly recognise the importance of the movements after Seattle.
7. We have seen such a method in the rebellious indigenous communities in Mexican Chiapas.
8. In Spanish *encuentro* means meeting or encounter.
9. It can visit them or play at hide-and-seek for a while. But nowadays in European universities, where the so-called Bologna process is

taking place, changing the universities from academic sanctuaries into production for the labour market, the survival of our thought is almost impossible.
10. www.situaciones.org.

REFERENCES

Adorno, T. W. (1973–74) *Philosophische Terminologie, Zur Einleitung*, 2 vols, Frankfurt, Suhrkamp.
Adorno, T. W. (1994) *Negative Dialektik*, Frankfurt, Suhrkamp.
Deleuze, G. (1994) *Difference and Repetition*, New York, Colombia University Press.
Holloway, J. (2002) *Change the World Without Taking Power*, London, Pluto Press.
Negri, A. and Hardt, M. (2001) *Empire*, London, Harvard University Press.
Subcomandante Insurgente Marcos, *Chiapas: The Thirteenth Stele, Part One: A Conch*, www.dostje.org/Aguas/Besedila/23jul03.htm

6

NEGATIVE AND POSITIVE AUTONOMISM. OR WHY ADORNO? PART 2[1]

John Holloway

I

To ask why Adorno, we start this time the other way round, not with Adorno but with the *operaista* or autonomist inversion of orthodox Marxism (see Tronti 1979). Where orthodox Marxism, and indeed nearly all left discourse, starts from capital or domination, the *operaistas* insisted on starting from below, from the struggle of the working class, or, more broadly, anti-capitalist struggle. This is an inversion of fundamental importance, simply because to begin from domination means to enclose oneself within the categories of domination, so that the only possible way of breaking from domination is through the intervention of an external force, such as a vanguard party. The inversion is therefore of crucial importance in liberating Marxism from the dead weight of the vanguard party tradition.

Nevertheless, there are two ways of interpreting the autonomist inversion, a positive and a negative one. This distinction has important political and theoretical implications and it is in this context that the tradition of negative or critical theory (Adorno, Bloch, Marcuse, Benjamin, Horkheimer, and so on) acquires crucial political relevance.

II POSITIVE AUTONOMISM

In this interpretation, the autonomist inversion goes only halfway, for it is not accompanied by a conceptual revolution.[2]

The working class is seen as the starting point, but it is understood as a positive subject. The working class replaces capital as the driving force of capitalism. It struggles against capital on the basis of a certain class composition; capital responds, trying to decompose the working class, which leads to a recomposition of the working class and a new wave of struggle, a new decomposition, and so on in a constant movement of composition–decomposition–recomposition. Capitalism develops under the impulse of the struggles of the working class, and the working class recomposes itself with each wave of struggle.

It seems that this movement dissolves everything, and to some extent this is the case. However, since there is in this approach no questioning of the positivity of the categories, attention is focused almost exclusively on the composition of the working class, and this becomes easily confused with a sociological analysis. This reproduces within the autonomist inversion an identitarian concept of the working class not dissimilar to that which characterises orthodox Marxism. Thus:

- The flow of composition–decomposition–recomposition is replaced in practice by a static concept of composition, that is, by the attempt to identify the present class composition, to classify, to construct paradigms. Thus, the movement of composition is seen in terms of a series of jumps from one paradigm to another: from mass worker to social worker to multitude, with corresponding steps in the development of capitalism, from factory to social factory, to integrated world capitalism (IWC), to Empire – all petrifications and exaggerations of real tendencies. This paradigmatic approach is accompanied by an explicit rejection of dialectics as a method.
- There is a slippage in this paradigmatic thought from the emphasis on the force of struggle to a characterisation of the

present phase of capitalism. That is, the original inversion of *operaismo* becomes forgotten or, at most, there is a token obeisance to the initial autonomist impulse, followed in practice by a focus on the analysis of domination.

- Since the conceptualisation of the subject is positive, the polar antagonism that gives meaning to class as class gets lost. Contradiction is dissolved in a multiplicity of differences and the struggle against capital becomes diluted into a struggle for genuine democracy.

- Since the centrality of the struggle against capital is lost, the struggle can easily reappear in the form of a struggle between different expressions of capitalism: between European capitalism and American capitalism, between progressive capitalism and reactionary capitalism.[3]

III NEGATIVE AUTONOMISM

This approach starts from a much more radical interpretation of the initial inversion. The starting point is not just the working class in place of capital, but also negativity in place of positivity.

The point of departure is the struggle of the working class and the point of departure is *no*, the scream. That is, the point of departure is the working class as negation, not as a positive but as a negative subject.

The working class exists as negation of capital, that is, as crisis. The emphasis, then, is not on the restructuring of capital (as tends to be the case in positive autonomism), but on crisis. Crisis is not so much an empirical statement as a theoretical option. Crisis is the centre of thought because what interests us is not the stability of capitalism but its instability, its fragility. Marxism is not a theory of the reproduction of capitalism, but of its crisis.

The working class is the negation and crisis of capitalism and therefore the negation and crisis of itself. To negate capital is to negate that which creates capital, that is, abstract or alienated labour. To negate abstract labour is to struggle for the emancipation of that which is negated every day by abstract labour, that is to struggle for the emancipation of useful or creative doing, the doing that pushes towards its own emancipation. Class struggle is not just the struggle of labour against capital, but, at a much profounder level, the struggle of doing against (abstract or alienated) labour and therefore against capital. And that means the struggle against the whole edifice of classification that is constructed on the basis of abstract labour, and that means a struggle against the working class itself as a class and as (abstractly) working.

The subject of anti-capitalist struggle is, therefore, an anti-identitarian subject. We can call the subject the working class, but only if we understand by that an anti-working anti-class, that is, the movement against being classified and against being subjected to alienated labour. Or we can call the subject simply *we*, but understanding *we* not as an identity but as an anti-identity, a negation, an open question. Or perhaps we can call ourselves the anti-identity, the subject without name.

As anti-identity we do not seek to define, but move against-and-beyond all definition. Or, more precisely, we define but go beyond the definition in the same breath. We are indigenous, but more than that. We are women, but more than that, gays, but more than that. If the negation of the definition is not included in the definition itself, definition becomes reactionary. We conceptualise because we cannot think without concepts, but we negate the concept in the same breath because every concept is inadequate, every concept becomes an obstacle to movement and therefore the class struggle. Every concept contains, but does not contain, and we are the force of that which does not allow itself to be contained; we overflow. Our struggle is the struggle of non-identity in-against-and-beyond identity.

The movement of anti-identity opens. It is not simply negative, but a movement that opens towards a different doing, a movement of negation and creation, a movement of creating cracks in the texture of domination, spaces or moments of alternative creation: cracks that expand and multiply.

Anti-identity attacks identity and opens it, seeking its own movement which identity contains and does not contain. It attacks the categories of political economy to discover the antagonism between abstract labour and useful or creative doing, which the categories contain and yet do not contain. It attacks all the categories of bourgeois thought in an *ad hominem* critique, a critique that constantly seeks human doing and its contradictory existence as the source of all movement. It attacks nouns to liberate the verbs that those nouns hold imprisoned, frozen and yet not frozen. It attacks clocks that contain and yet do not contain the creative rhythms of doing, and shoots at them to show that the only revolution is revolution here and now,[4] that the idea of a future revolution is non-sense. It attacks the state to find that which it contains and yet cannot contain: the struggle for self-determination. The movement of anti-identity is the movement of the revolution without name.[5]

IV TWO AUTONOMISMS, THEN

One autonomism is positive, it classifies, seeks to put everything in its place, slides into sociology, flirts with progressive governments. The other is a delirium, a vertiginous critique, a corrosive movement of non-identity, with no paradigms, nothing firm to hold on to, an asking not a telling. The one still trapped in the identities of abstract labour, the other pushing against and beyond all identities, part of the budding and flowering of useful-creative doing. The distinction matters politically.

V WHY ADORNO, THEN?

That's why.

NOTES

1. An earlier version of this chapter was presented in a colloquium on La Autonomía Posible, at the Universidad Autónoma de la Ciudad de México, on 25 October 2006.
2. In this section I am thinking primarily of what is sometimes called *post-operaismo*, represented by such authors as Negri, Hardt, Virno: see especially Hardt and Negri (2000, 2004), Negri and Cocco (2006) or Virno (2004). The theoretical positivism is, however, present in

the earlier autonomist literature: for a more detailed criticism, see Holloway (2005).

3. See, for example, the support expressed by Negri for the governments of Argentina, Brazil, Bolivia and Venezuela.

4. See Thesis XV of Benjamin (1969).

5. The expression is taken from Vaneigem (1993).

REFERENCES

Benjamin, W. (1969) "Theses on the Philosophy of History," in *Illuminations*. New York, Schocken Books, pp. 153–64.

Hardt, M. and Negri, A. (2000) *Empire*, Cambridge MA, Harvard University Press.

Hardt, M. and Negri, A. (2004) *Multitude,* New York, Penguin Books.

Holloway, J. (2005) *Change the World without Taking Power*. New, revised edition, London, Pluto.

Negri, A. and Cocco, G. (2006) *GlobAL: Biopotere e Lotte in America Latina*, Rome, Manifestolibri.

Tronti, M. (1979), "Lenin in England," in Red Notes, *Working Class Autonomy and the Crisis*, London, Red Notes.

Vaneigem, R. (1993) *The Revolution of Everyday Life*, London, Left Bank Books and Rebel Press.

Virno, P. (2004) *A Grammar of the Multitude*, New York, Semiotext(e).

III

Emancipation and the Critique of Totality

7

ADORNO: THE CONCEPTUAL PRISON OF THE SUBJECT, POLITICAL FETISHISM AND CLASS STRUGGLE

Sergio Tischler *

I

If the theoretical starting point for the critique of capitalism is class struggle, as it is in our case, does Adorno have anything important to say?

We believe that Adorno's critique of positivism, Hegelian dialectics and all identitarian thought are a fundamental starting point for a non-identitarian approach to class struggle. In this sense, the Adornian idea of the negative subject, conceived as a struggle that does not culminate in a new synthesis or a positive totality of a different sign, is a central aspect in this theoretical process.

According to Adorno, the core concept in the dialectic of the negation of the negation, subordinated as it is to synthesis or identity, forms part of a constellation of power which prolongs the abstract material and symbolic form of domination. In this sense, the negative, non-identitarian subject is a critique of the synthetic form of production of the categories of social change, mainly the notion of the revolutionary subject as a figure of totality and synthesis. That is why, in Adorno, the category of particularity becomes a main critical category. Following his line of argument, particularity expresses the *surplus* of the existing confronted with what is dominant, or the system, a *surplus* or *excess* created by social antagonism.

If perceived in this way, particularity is understood in its dialectical (negative) function as *crisis of totality*; social change renders particularity its principal category, as opposed to positive dialectics – which reaches its peak with Hegel – where totality and synthesis play the leading roles. In other words, according to Adorno, the overcoming of capitalism (the system) demands the critique of the conceptual horizon of the bourgeois form of science and philosophy. The destructuring of the identitarian form of the concept, a constitutive part of bourgeois subjectivity, is central in Adorno's critique of theoretical fetishism. While it is true that he considers Marx to be the great critic of that form, there are inadequate theoretical developments in the latter's work which have been paid for and continue to be paid for at the price of a "bad practice," and it is because of them that the bourgeois form of thought has not yet been radically overcome in Marxist and revolutionary thought.

Adorno's criticism of the absolute character of the identifying function of the concept is a horizon which opens up possibilities for thinking about how even a revolutionary concept like class struggle can be imprisoned by a mystifying conceptual form. In this sense, Adorno allows for a distinction between negativity, the No, and the specific figures of political organisation, a fundamental distinction for an open-minded reflection on the dialectics between organisation and struggle, and not a reduction of the No to an organisational synthesis. Likewise, we believe Adorno represents a very important theoretical opening that allows for a non-identitarian reading of Marx. As we shall see, at the centre of such a reading lies the theoretical approach of the *crisis of the value form*, which implies a conceptual unfolding that departs from use value and living labour as fundamental critical categories.

II

One of the main focuses of attention in *Negative Dialectics* is the critique of the Hegelian version of Lukácsian Marxism.[1] For Lukács (1969), the revolutionary concept of class struggle is closely linked to that of totality. From this standpoint, the proletariat is a revolutionary class because it is the embodiment of a new totality whose goal is to overcome the totality of capital. This movement of transformation would be mediated by *class consciousness*. For that reason, the philosophical subject of class consciousness, linked to the issue of totality, is rendered in Lukács the main subject of historical materialism.

Unlike Hegel, to whom totality is a matter of the real movement of the world apprehended by the philosopher, Lukács matches that category with the figure of the party and the proletariat. Thus, the subject is no longer the bourgeois form reified in the figure of the Absolute Spirit, but the proletariat. It is not, however, the proletariat outright as the object of capitalist exploitation, but the proletariat redefined as a subject due to its transformation by class consciousness. If, in Hegel, the subject/object unity is produced in a subjective synthesis, a synthesis brought about by the subject in the form of the Absolute Spirit (objective idealism), in Lukács this unity occurs with the overcoming of the bourgeois form through the intervention of the proletariat; which, by virtue of its objective characteristics, would have the possibility of producing a real unity from the tearing apart of the world, a true identity between subject and object.

One could claim that Lukács set out somehow to surpass Hegel, while retaining and preserving the method of the latter: The true synthesis is not the Absolute Spirit, but the proletariat transformed into the ruling class. In that sense, in Lukács the issue of totality and the subject is resolved on the basis of the central character of class consciousness and the proletariat in the historical process.[2]

Possibly due to this Hegelian heritage, two – sometimes contradictory – ways of approaching totality can be perceived in the writings of Lukács: on the one hand, as a critical category and, on the other, as a positive one. First, as a critical category, Lukács apprehends totality as a unifying knowledge of a reality which is torn apart and contradictory. This knowledge, as we have said, is not a matter of isolated individuals. Its core is in the (theoretical) consciousness of the social subject (the proletariat) which opposes capital. So totality is not a cognitive category, unattached to revolutionary practice. To put it in other words: totality is struggle, class struggle.[3]

On the other hand, when referring to the proletariat as the subject that can think of totality because it is a kind of alternative totality itself, Lukács tends to give a positive twist to this category. As we have seen, when he talks of the proletariat as *the subject*, he does not refer to the whole of the proletariat (the empirical proletariat), but to a part which has assumed class consciousness, that is, the revolutionary proletariat. However, he supports the thesis that the whole proletariat has the objective possibility of becoming a revolutionary proletariat. Revolutionary consciousness is a "possible" consciousness for the whole proletariat. Nevertheless, it is only a fraction of the proletariat which in practice acquires class consciousness, and that process demands a fundamental mediation: the class party. Thus, the elaboration of the concept of the subject slowly shifts from the proletariat in total to one illuminated fraction of it, a vanguard. This vanguard would be a kind of synthesis of the proletariat. The subject, then, is understood in terms of a new synthesis: revolutionary organisation.

This line of argument presents one main problem. Synthesis, when conceived in that way, forms part of an abstraction: the political form which separates and autonomises itself to produce a new figure of hierarchic organisation. That is why, here, synthesis does not overcome the subject/object division, but extends it as the unity of power and rule; an issue which is akin to the Hegelian sphere of the concept, in its turn directed towards the production of a homogeneous subject whose theoretical core is a normative or abstract totality (Jay 1984a: 115).

However, what matters here is that Lukács's conceptualisation elaborately expresses a *mode of conceptual organisation* on the basis of which class struggle is thought. Here, the main character is synthesis: the class, the party, the state, all are figures of synthesis. That means that the theory of the primacy of the political over the social, according to which the latter is defined in terms of subordination to the former, forms part of this mode of conceptual organisation; which, on the other hand, is constitutive of the conceptualisation of the dialectics between the class and the party in Lenin's *What is to be Done?* and in the (Leninist) way of conceiving class struggle in a vanguard way.

At this point, Adorno's critique of the Hegelian concept of totality is essential because it is aimed at the mode of conceptual organisation which makes it possible to think of social change in a vanguard way.

III

In the Preface to *Negative Dialectics*, Adorno formulates his theoretical programme as an effort to liberate dialectics from the primacy of the identity principle. "As early as Plato, dialectics meant to achieve something positive by means of negation; the thought figure of a 'negation of negation' later became the succinct term." This text seeks to "free dialectics from such affirmative traits without reducing its determinacy" (Adorno 1990: xix).

Negative dialectics presupposes totality; however, far from placing it at the centre of knowledge and of the elaboration of a revolutionary theory of the subject, as in Lukács, it turns what is negated in totality into an epistemological starting point. Departing from this principle, it will no longer be possible to think of radical social change in terms of an alternative totality which is fully identified with the subject.[4]

As we said, one of the points of focus of negative dialectics is the critique of the Lukácsian theory of the subject, based in the final analysis on Hegelian totality. This critique aims, among other things, at dismantling the forms of power and domination which enclose and conceal the concept as an expression of the identity principle. That is why Adorno renders contradiction the fundamental principle of dialectics, in clear opposition to the centrality of the category of totality in positive dialectics.

However, the Adornian critique of the epistemic centrality of totality does not amount to the conceptual annihilation of the latter. It means thinking of totality in negative terms; that is, starting from its crisis. In other words, the negation of the negation does not move towards synthesis, towards a new totality represented by an abstract and homogeneous subject. What is new emerges from the crisis of totality and its main figures are particularity and constellation.

> The categories of a critique of systems are at the same time the categories in which the particular is understood. What has once legitimately transcended particularity in the system has its place outside the system. The interpretive eye which sees more in a phenomenon than it is – and solely because of what it is – secularizes metaphysics. Only a philosophy in fragment form would give their proper place to the monads, those illusory idealistic drafts. They would be conceptions, in the particular, of the totality that is inconceivable as such. (Adorno 1990: 28)

For Adorno, particularity is the quintessential critical category. It is the system's excess, and that excess can be understood as the crisis of totality organised as a system.[5] Thus, the centre of the question of the subject in Adorno is radically shifted towards particularity, leaving positive totality as that which must be overcome.[6] That is, the overcoming of totality does not imply *another* totality, which is not the same but symmetrical in its logical structure, but the unfolding of the excess negated in totality.[7]

According to Lukács, capitalist totality is overcome by another totality, the proletariat. There is a shift from a bad or perverse totality to another one, where the unity of subject/object is achieved; thus, the social world is liberated from exploitation, domination and estranged forms of existence. Following this line of thought, the logical structure remains unaltered: totality is conceived in terms of identity. The subject/object identity cannot be produced in capitalism because of class antagonism, but Communism is its realisation. The goal is full totality, full identity. The subject is conceived as totality and through figures of totality: class, party, state. Thus, the liberation from class antagonism would, at the same time, be the production of an identitarian synthesis formed in the new figures of totality.

On the contrary, Adorno claims that to think of radical social change in terms of figures of totality is part of a process of perversion and fetishisation of the idea of revolutionary change.

To imagine it in that way leads to identifying totality with the system; that is, renouncing totality as a category destined to dissolve with emancipation.

Thus the category of totality is critical only if thought of as contradictory, that is, starting from its overflowing or excess. So one could claim that particularity, conceived as the crisis of totality, is the theoretical effort to think of the overflowing in non-identitarian, anti-system terms. Its utopia is the abolition of society as a reification that subsumes the individual. That is why, for Adorno, a philosophy of the future would not be tied to totality and dialectics (Jay 1984a: 267).

The Adornian critique of totality renders visible what is negated in synthesis. And this is where Adorno introduces the centrality of pain as a figure which is negated *in* and *by* the concept.

But what is pain? Pain is a who: the oppressed and negated by the system. Pain is an *us* (see Holloway, chapter 2 above) because, for Adorno, "Its [dialectics'] agony is the world's agony raised to a concept" (1990: 6).

In other words, Adorno's starting point is the subject negated by the objective reality turned into system, that is, in a "negative objectivity ... not the positive subject" (1990: 20). That "negative objectivity," that is, the objectivity which negates the "positive subject," dictates the guidelines of the universal as rule and repression. That is why negative dialectics "unfolds the difference between the particular and the universal, dictated by the universal" (1990: 6). A difference that is contradiction and antagonism, for dialectics is the "subject–object dichotomy ... brought to mind" (1990: 6). Its goal is reconciliation through the emancipation of the non-identical, that is, of the repressed and subordinated in totality, which "would open the road to the multiplicity of different things and strip dialectics of its power over them" (1990: 6).

In other words, in negative dialectics the concept is at the service of non-identity; that is, of the excess of reality which overflows the unity achieved at the expense of the mutilation that homogeneity implies. As an anti-identitarian category, particularity is the scream of rebellion raised to a concept against the system.

According to Adorno, the failure of positive dialectics to think of particularity[8] without subordinating it to totality had a perverse historical effect in revolutionary practices. This was also expressed in the impossibility of truly thinking of individuality as a cultural figure. On this, it is interesting to note how Bakhtin (1984), in his well-known essay on Dostoyevsky, establishes his theory of the polyphonic novel, rightly pointing out the impossibility of imagining the cultural figure of individuality on the basis of Hegelian-type dialectics.

IV

We must point out that the Adornian critique of positive dialectics in particular, and of identitarian thought in general, is at the same time an unveiling of the bourgeois constellation that this concept conceals.[9] On the one hand, as we have mentioned, it is a critique of homogeneity; on the other, it implies the unveiling of a subjectivity impregnated by *class fear*. On that, Adorno writes:

> The *ratio* which in accordance with bourgeois class interests has smashed the feudal order and scholastic ontology, the form of the intellectual reflection of that order – this same *ratio* no sooner faced the ruins, its own handiwork, than it would be struck by fear of chaos. It trembled before the menace that continued underneath its own domain, waxing stronger in proportion to its own power. This fear shaped the beginnings of a mode of conduct constitutive for bourgeois existence as a whole: of the neutralization, by confirming the existent order, of every emancipating step. (Adorno 1990: 21)

Fear is part of the theoretical process which leads to the autonomisation of the concept and the idea of the system as "autonomous objectivity" (1990: 21). In other words, the "reification ... of the concept" (1990: 12) is a form of paralysis produced by the antagonistic nature of bourgeois society. That is, identitarian thought has the function of closing antagonism through the fetishism of the concept. In other words, Adorno argues that it is impossible to think of the world radically with identitarian thought, especially with Hegelian dialectics: Hegelianism is part of a bourgeois constellation, of a subjectivity of that sign.

One could argue, following Adorno, that the extension of Hegel into a philosophy of the state (dialectical materialism and historical materialism) is part of a specific power constellation where human emancipation has not been produced. The unfolding of identitarian thought is part of a social relation based on hierarchy and relations of domination. In Benjamin's words, the "temporal core"[10] referred to by the concept is an historical situation where the project of emancipation failed.[11] Thus, conceptual production derived in ideology, in a subjectivity of power.

> The loathing which materialist dialectics felt for any crude *Weltanschauung* made it prefer an alliance with science, and yet, in its decline to a means of political rule, dialectics itself turned into such a *Weltanschauung*. ... A materialism come to political power is no less old on such practices than the world it once wanted to change; it keeps fettering the human consciousness instead of comprehending it and changing it on its part. On the threadbare pretext of a dictatorship (now half a century old) of the proletariat (long bureaucratically administered), governmental terror machines entrench themselves as permanent institutions. (Adorno 1990: 200, 204)

As part of this historical process, theory had been turned into the servant of practice, and gnoseology transformed into a "reflection theory."[12] In other words, for Adorno, practice is not plain and clear but contradictory; it requires theory as a moment of self-criticism. That implies the existence of a subject of change which has not been reified or suspended in the movement of transformation of the world. On the contrary, one could say that the state form, the party form, the totality linked to the figures of synthesis, are for Adorno the expression of power constellations that confront the emancipation of humanity and the free deployment of the individual.

V

To conceive particularity as a crisis of totality leads us to the critique that Benjamin advanced in relation to the Marxism of his time, which would play a decisive role in the Adornian elaboration of particularity and constellation. That is why we will allow for a small parenthesis on this issue. According to Benjamin:

> Thinking involves not only the flow of words, but their arrest as well. Where thinking suddenly stops in a configuration pregnant with tensions, it gives that configuration a shock, by which it crystallizes into a monad. A historical materialist approaches a historical subject only where he encounters it as a monad. In this structure he recognizes the sign of Messianic cessation of happening, or, put differently, a revolutionary chance in the fight for the oppressed past. He takes cognizance of it in order to blast a specific era out of the homogeneous course of history – blasting a specific life out of the era or a specific work out of the lifework. As a result of this method the lifework is preserved in this work and at the same time cancelled; in the lifework, the era; and in the era, the entire course of history. (Benjamin 1968: 262–3)

From this perspective, to think is to break with the concept of a temporality of rule penetrated by abstraction and homogeneity. This possibility is an attribute, according to Benjamin, of the revolutionary subject, which is class *in* struggle. Thus, the concept is the blow which stirs up that which is negated in the homogeneous and empty totality of time as a *continuum* of domination. That is why, according to Benjamin, it is necessary to free Marxism from the idea of progress, a representation linked to such a type of temporality (homogeneous and empty). In this sense, Benjamin's monad can be interpreted as a revolutionary conceptual form, for it is constituted by "lived", "full" time, as opposed to the category of totality. Benjamin's monad is not a totality which confronts another as a result of the movement of reality's objective contradictions. On the contrary, the monad expresses the temporality of rebellion, the breaking with the abstract temporality of totality. In other words, the monad is class in struggle as a heterogeneous, multiple subject that interrupts history like a thunderbolt. For *the revolutionary class is not a synthesis, as the bourgeoisie*, but the constellation of struggles against the synthesis of capital.

Class can then be thought of as a community of struggles, different modes of collective resistance. This position moves against the idea of class as a homogeneous and synthetic social form. The unity of the monad is not homogeneity, but, one could argue, the *specific community*. So, the specific community is the irruption of "messianic time" in the *continuum* of the abstract community. In this sense, the concepts monad and constellation are a rebellion against the unity based on the preservation of material and conceptual abstraction as a form of rule, i.e. against the abstract subject: capital, state, nation, history.

Now, it would be difficult, if not impossible, to find in Adorno an explicit nexus between class-struggle–constellation, as in Benjamin. However, the category of particularity that, as mentioned, is the main critical category in Adorno feeds abundantly on Benjaminian thought as a conceptual form of rebellion against totality and abstraction, both conceived as a texture of social domination.

VI

If these insights are linked to the issue of class struggle, one can conclude that the latter in its dominant, orthodox, conceptual form has been a prisoner of the fetishism of totality, an identitarian concept: in any case, an insufficiently elaborated concept which, as such, became a prisoner of dominant epistemology: "The remaining theoretical inadequacies in Hegel and Marx became part of historical practice" (Adorno 1990: 144).

So, can class struggle be thought of in non-reified terms, having recourse to the Adornian category of particularity? The answer is not straightforward, especially if one considers that, in Adorno, the issue of exploitation seems to be absent or blurred; in any case, it is not at the heart of critical reflection. That is one of the reasons why, with Adorno's micro-logical method, inherited from Kracauer and Benjamin (Jay 1984b: 87–8), one risks transforming particularity into a fetish (Eagleton 1998: 145) and producing a slippage towards the complete indetermination of the subject in the theory of revolutionary change and class struggle. However, if we are paralysed by this danger, we risk missing the revolutionary force of Adorno's insights and excluding ourselves from the possibility of thinking class struggle from the perspective of non-identity.

How can we proceed? We believe our theoretical path has taken us to a point where we must turn to Marx, not as a drowning man to a piece of wood, but as a possibility of reading Marx from the perspective of critical theory and, in particular, negative dialectics. We believe that Adorno's insights allow for a deeper and more radical reading of Marx, and that this possibility of interpretation had been frozen by the dominant mode of conceptual organisation surrounding class struggle. As we have seen, one of Adorno's greatest achievements is to have exposed the conceptual and class limitations of that mode of organisation, an issue which has not yet been fully understood and has resulted in an interpretation of Marx starting from the epistemic texture of the value form.

VII

Marx's critique of political economy centres on the unveiling of capital as a specific social relation which entails an historic form of exploitation and the corresponding relations of domination. Exploitation and domination have the characteristic of being impersonal, which implies a form of power that is historically specific and based on functional rationality and material abstraction.

Capital is a real domination founded in that type of abstraction. At its centre lies general or abstract labour, a social metabolism that transforms the constitutive heterogeneity of the natural form of labour into homogeneous units of time. Thus, capital is a social relation that produces a specific temporality, whose rationality is, at the same time, marked by the private appropriation of general time. Rather than a logic of appropriating things, capital is an appropriation of time through things, because all that things have in common in this social form is that they are the result of human activity distilled as general labour or homogeneous time. Exploitation is not only the appropriation of products snatched from their producers. A specific characteristic of exploitation is that it is based on the organisation of time according to the appropriation of time: the labour-power of the labourer is not an object appropriated by capital, but a time that belongs to capital. However, in order for capital to appropriate this time, the latter must be objectified in things, in useful products. Now, these products are not directly related to the natural form of labour, the satisfaction of necessities; rather, they are like ghosts that wish to abandon their bodily form because it will not let them rest: a true schizophrenia.

The commodity is this social form of schizophrenia. On the one hand, it is a useful object, but this characteristic is subordinated to a *social substance* which is radically different from its bodily form: value or abstract labour. This social substance, capital, moves on its own feet. Thus wealth, whose fundamental source is labour, is transformed into an objectification which adopts the form of fetishism. Things move according to the apparent logic of an autonomous system, precisely because the heterogeneous nature of their bodies is dominated by the homogeneous nature of that social substance, which is an abstraction; not a formal, logical abstraction, but the abstraction of a social logic. Thus, as we have seen, the autonomisation of the concept entails the social logic of abstraction as a specifically bourgeois form of exploitation and domination: i.e. abstraction as a totalising social power which is expressed in the figure of the system. As Stavros Tombazos writes: "Capital is precisely a conceptual organisation of time. It is neither a thing, nor a simple social relation, but a living rationality, an active concept, abstraction *in actu*" (Bensaid 2002: 86).

From this whole argument it becomes clear that the issue of homogeneity and abstraction as a formal and social logic is at the centre of Adorno's critique of the concepts of system and positive totality. One could say that Adorno centres his critique on the positive category of totality, precisely revealing the totalitarian nature of the bourgeois rationalisation of the world.

In Marx, however, we find much more clearly the core of the totalitarian rationalisation of the world: abstract labour, the *social substance* which rules the world, a radically new, perverse and apparently autonomous type of objectivity which has its own subjectivity: fetishism. The latter is the appearance of the autonomy of objectivity, for that appearance is no more than objectivity reified in a *negated us*. In Marx, the negated us can be found in the figure of *living labour*,[13] the *use value*[14] of the worker who is subordinated and confronted with the homogenising metabolism of the valorisation of capital (see Tischler 2006).

Keeping Adorno's contribution in mind, one could say that Marx's insight into capital is not suspended in the *value form*; rather, it is the value form which is approached from its negation. The value form is a negation of the natural form of labour but, at the same time, labour in this negation is not transformed into a fully dominated object. On the contrary, labour appears as a subject against its objectification in an objective, abstract and homogeneous materiality.

In this sense, Marx's theory of the subject does not derive from the value form; it is rather the value form which constitutes its process of negation. In other words, the subject is thought of in terms of the crisis of the value form. So, class struggle is not something that has to be derived from a specific independent objectivity or structure of the subject; class struggle is inscribed in objectivity itself, for such objectivity is class struggle. Thus, the subject is the overflowing of objectivity as exploitation and as form of domination by the crisis of objectivity, the contradiction *in actu*.

VIII

One can say that, in Marx, class struggle is conceptualised on the basis of the *antagonistic form* which the capitalist relation entails. *Capital* is, precisely, the most conspicuous thinking of antagonism as a form of social existence. That can certainly be formulated in a regulationist sense: capital as open and dynamic antagonism in the figure of reproduction. However, in Marx, antagonism is always a surplus in relation to the capitalist form: the figure of the rebel subject and the going beyond, as Bloch (1995) put it. Antagonism as a subject is always an opening of the world, an opening that moves from the negativity of the subject: the No exists in all actions of resistance. This No is understood as We insofar as the struggle defetishises reality (see Holloway 2002) and the *general substance* (value) which dominates it loses autonomy and power.

Thus, the movement of class struggle is a movement against the autonomous power of objectivity, against the abstract material form of domination which produces a specific social form, capital, at the heart of which is the metabolism of abstract labour. The production of a non-reified objectification, of a We as a subject, goes hand in hand with the overcoming of totality as a form of command. In this sense, we can think of a concept of class struggle that goes against synthesis. The breaking of abstract labour is not a matter of a new synthesis, but of the dissolution of synthesis as a form of power. To think of the concept on the basis of the critical category of use value entails a movement of emancipation which amounts to the construction of a We that brings into crisis the category of homogeneity, for it is the consciousness that the figures of homogeneity deny the true universality which is based on emancipated labour.

So, class struggle can be thought of as a struggle against material abstractions as forms of rule and power. The category of use value, living labour, allows us to avoid the metaphysical burden which stalks the categories of particularity and constellation. However, at the same time, the category of particularity as crisis of totality allows us to think of class struggle in anti-identitarian terms and approach use value as a fundamental critical category.

This perspective helps us to see, among other things, the cognitive limitations of new forms of thinking about class in today's world, especially in Hardt and Negri's (2004) category of *multitude*. This category clearly unfolds from the value form. That is why, while recognising the primacy of the principle of struggle, they end up deriving the category from the actual form of capitalism. It is not struggle which opens up forms, but struggle conceived in terms of a new positive political figure. In this sense, the *multitude* is seen as a new, emerging synthesis, with the characteristic features of the current form of valorisation. In Virno (2004), despite the fact that the category of multitude encounters a different line of argument, there is also an effort to derive it from the form of post-Fordist capitalism.

A different procedure is expressed in the Zapatista method of *preguntando caminamos* (asking we walk), which opens up a new form of class struggle through the reinforcement of use value (Tischler 2006) and can be appreciated in the new type of political action which distinguishes them.

One of the crucial points which differentiate Zapatismo from any other form of revolutionary organisation is that they know how to distinguish between the movement of insubordination and the specific forms of organisation. They move in the contradiction between the verticalism which defines a political-military structure and the unfolding of a policy of autonomy in the indigenous communities as a form of struggle against capital, as well as the respect and empowerment of the diverse modes of organising resistance in different social and geographic spaces.

The Zapatistas are, and wish to be, conscious of the fact that the military aspect must be dissolved by the autonomous organisation of subjects in struggle. They do not promote a policy of homogenisation and centralisation of political action; that is, they do not hope to be a synthesis. In other words, Zapatismo does not reduce the No of resistance and insubordination to a positive political figure. The No goes beyond this figure and the strategy of its capture in an organisational synthesis is consciously rejected, for such a reduction amounts to the mutilation of the emancipating movement: the revolutionary history that must be overcome.

* Translated by Anna-Maeve Holloway

NOTES

1. The Marxism of Lukács forms part of the 1917 Russian Revolution. Its postulates can be considered to represent the sharpest philosophical edge of this event.
2. It must be pointed out that the issue of totality and class consciousness is, in Lukács, formulated at different levels. At the level of the knowledge of reality, it is argued that totality can be conceived only from the standpoint of the proletariat (a proletariat with class consciousness). The concept of capital as a social antagonistic

relation, that is, as a historic totality, is something that can become visible from the perspective of the proletariat. On the contrary, the bourgeoisie would be a blind class in relation to this issue, and its *organic intellectuals*, in Gramsci's words, would produce the notion of a spiritualised totality, that is, a unity in the field of discourse and philosophy. But never as a vision of totality as antagonism that must be overcome by another, non-antagonistic, totality. That is, the experience and consciousness of antagonism are fundamental if one wants to open up thought to totality as a critical category. In Lukács, the cognitive aspect is inscribed in antagonism, so that even to name totality as part of the antagonism is already a critical starting point.

3. Among others, this concept of totality was a critique of the typically sociological dichotomy between the structure and action of the objectivist concept of class struggle, a concept that reproduced the modern epistemology of the subject/object divide.

4. Adorno questioned the possibility of a full identity between subject and object. See Jay (1984a; 1988b).

5. "The system, the form of presenting a totality to which nothing remains extraneous, absolutises the thought against each of its contents and evaporates the content in thoughts. It proceeds idealistically before advancing any arguments for idealism" (Adorno 1990: 24).

6. In discussion with Karl Popper and his disciples, Adorno said: "Totality is not an affirmative but rather a critical category. Dialectical critique seeks to salvage or help to establish what does not obey totality, what opposes it or what first forms itself as the potential of a not yet existent individualization ... A liberated mankind would by no means be a totality" (quoted in Jay 1984a: 266–7).

7. It must be added that, in Adorno, totality is part of the issue of identity. One could say, following his line of argument, that totality is identity because in its centre can be found a nucleus of power and rule which determines the form of reality and the form of the concept. Partly because of this, totality is identified with the system.

8. Hegel was never able to give the category of particularity a content of its own, for it was always subordinated to the universal: "We are not to philosophize about concrete things; we are to philosophize, rather, out of these things" (Adorno 1990: 33). One could say: one must not think *about* particularity but *out of it*.

9. The theoretical effort to overcome the Hegelian notion of the concept can also be found in Benjamin and Bloch – in Benjamin, in his critique of a dialectics whose prerequisite is homogeneous temporality, to which he opposes *messianic time*; in Bloch (1995,

Prologue), this critique is more open. When the latter argues that
"to think is to break through" and that the concept has been part of
what is "given," that is, of an already completed reality, he is saying
that Hegelian dialectics looks towards the past and one cannot think
of the future with such a concept.

10. According to Benjamin, Marxism suffered from a dialectical theo-
retisation surrounding the relation between concept and time, whose
solution was essential. "Resolute refusal of the concept of 'timeless
truth' is in order. Nevertheless, truth is not – as Marxism would
have it – a merely contingent function of knowing, but is bound to
a nucleus of time lying hidden within the knower and the known
alike. This is so true that the eternal, in any case, is far more the
ruffle on a dress than some idea" (1999: 463).

11. We have in mind the historical process of perversion and bureau-
cratisation of the Russian Revolution and the reformism of social
democracy.

12. This observation does not apply to Lukács, whose theory of totality
aims at the critique of objectivist reductionism and economism.
In this sense, Lukács represents the most important philosophical
contribution in relation to the Russian Revolution. However, this
critique, which brought Stalinist censorship upon the Hungarian
philosopher, is formulated under the spell of the Hegelian concept.
One could say that the Russian experience was not radical enough
to produce historical material on which to elaborate a theory of
the subject which is not contaminated by the existing traditional
philosophical material. On this, see Lukács's defence of *History and
Class Consciousness* in *A Defence of History and Class Consciousness.
Tailism and the Dialectic*, as well as the Postface by Žižek.

13. A central part of our argument has a lot in common with the insights
of John Holloway on this issue, which can be found in a draught of
a book not yet published.

14. From our point of view, one could say that living labour as a general
capacity for labour can be found in capitalist form in the form of the
use value of labour, which entails the contradiction capital/labour
and the possibility of liberating living labour from the value form
of subordination. So, it implies the possibility of the emancipated
form of labour.

REFERENCES

Adorno, T. W. (1990) *Negative Dialectics*. London, Routledge.
Adorno, T. W. and Horkheimer, M. (1972) *Dialectic of Enlightenment*,
New York, Herder and Herder.

Bakhtin, M. (1984) *Problems of Dostoevsky's Poetics*, Minneapolis, University of Michigan Press.

Benjamin, W. (1968) *Illuminations. Essays and Reflections*, New York, Schocken.

Benjamin, W. (1999) *The Arcades Project*, London and Cambridge, MA, Belknap Press.

Bensaid, D. (2002) *Marx for our Time*, London, Verso.

Bloch, E. (1995) *The Principle of Hope*, Cambridge, MA, MIT Press.

Eagleton, T. (1981) *Walter Benjamin: Or, Towards a Revolutionary Criticism*, London, Verso.

Holloway, J. (2002) *Change the World Without Taking Power*. London, Pluto Press.

Holloway, J. this volume, Chapter 2.

Hardt, M. and Negri, A. (2004) *Multitude. War and Democracy in the Age of Empire*, New York, Penguin Press.

Jay, M. (1984a) *Marxism & Totality. The Adventure of a Concept from Lukács to Habermas*, Berkeley and Los Angeles, CA, University of California Press.

Jay, M. (1984b) *Adorno*. London, Fontana.

Lenin, V. I. (1966) "What is to Be Done?" in *Essential Works of Lenin*, London, Bantam Books.

Lukács, G. (1999) *History and Class Consciousness*, London, Merlin Press.

Lukács, G. (2000) *A Defence of History and Class Consciousness. Tailism and the Dialectic*, London, Verso.

Tischler, S. (2006) "Valor de uso y política. Notas teóricas sobre la *Otra Campaña* Zapatista," in *Bajo el Volcán*, No. 10. Postgrado de Sociología, México, Benemérita Universidad Autónoma de Puebla.

Virno, P. (2004) *A Grammar of the Multitude*. New York, Semiotext(e) Foreign Agent Series.

Žižek, S., Postface to Georg Lukács (2000) *A Defence of History and Class Consciousness. Tailism and the Dialectic*, London, Verso.

8

EMANCIPATORY PRAXIS AND CONCEPTUALITY IN ADORNO

Werner Bonefeld[1]

They [the adherents of dialectical materialism] did not challenge the ideas of humanity, liberty, justice as such, but merely denied the claim of our society to represent the realization of these ideas. Though they treated the ideologies as illusions, they still found them illusions of truth itself. This lent a conciliatory splendour, if not to the existent at least to its 'objective tendencies' ... Ideologies were unmasked as apologetic concealments ... [and] were rarely conceived as powerful instruments functioning in order to change liberal competitive society into a system of immediate oppression ... Above all the leftist critics failed to notice that the "ideas" themselves in their abstract form, are not merely images of the truth that will later materialize but that they are ailing themselves, afflicted with the same injustice under which they are conceived and bound up with the world against which they are set. (Adorno 1941: 318f)

INTRODUCTION

In the context of war and terror, globalisation and anti-globalisation movements, a discussion of Adorno's conception of praxis might appear quaint. Here we have modern forms of barbarism and a movement of movements that demands an end to poverty and war. And there we have the theoretician who despaired in the face of barbarism and who denounced 1968 as a "pseudo-movement" (Adorno 1969). Nevertheless, Adorno's negative dialectics is important. It challenges us to think what it means to say "no" in the false totality of bourgeois society.

The demand for the unity of theory and practice does not entail a concession to the weakness of thought. Nor does it give dispensation to a practice to engage in battle for the sake of battle, indifferent to social content. What sort of praxis is needed to fight barbarism? Can this fight be reduced to This course of action against That outrage, or vice versa? And who negates the social preconditions that constitute the possibility of This and That (see Psychopedis 2005)? Further, can barbarism be fought, say, in alliance with Islamo-fascists, who repeating the paradigmatic Fascist gesture, demand a "capitalism without capitalism"?[2]

Only a reified consciousness can declare that the enemy of my enemy is my friend. Critical thought is not an "expression" of social forces whose "real" interests it pretends to represent in theoretical terms. Instead, it aims at these forces themselves, seeking their dissolution.

In the quotation that opens this chapter, Adorno also praises Georg Lukács as the dialectician who asked how society can be changed by those who are its victims. Adorno's endorsement is surprising. Lukács's Leninist conception of the vanguard party as the locus of revolutionary practice was anathema to Adorno. For Adorno, Lukács was important because of his theory of reification. One could argue, as indeed Fracchia (2005) does, that Lukács's theory of reification provided Adorno (and Horkheimer) with a research programme that led them to uncover reification in every aspect of social life. In distinction to Lukács's conception of the vanguard party as the locus of non-reified proletarian class-consciousness (1970: 172), Adorno (and Horkheimer) retreated into theory and argued that it was the locus that preserved the promise of a human world whose moment of realisation had passed. Indeed, Adorno argued that "the metamorphosis of labour-power into a commodity has permeated men through and through and objectified each of their impulses as formally commensurable variations of the exchange relations." Social reproduction, he argues, is possible only on the condition that the living have been replaced by the dead, that is, every social activity is always already what Marx called the activity of character-masks or personifications of economic categories (Adorno 1974: 229). He seems to suggest that the reified world allows only reified activity and that there can therefore be no such thing as emancipatory praxis. Although it was "time for a praxis that fights barbarism," such praxis is impossible since "whatever one does, it is false" (quoted in Böckelmann 1969: 31).[3] In the end, "everything is the same" (Adorno 1972: 369), but not quite: when the students occupied the Institute of Social Research, Adorno called in the police to have them removed by force.

In my view, Johannes Agnoli's take on Adorno's action is apposite. As he put it, "the Adorno who called in the police was already his successor" (Agnoli 1969: 202). Hans-Jürgen Krahl (1971) argues in similar vein. Both Agnoli and Krahl liken his negative dialectics to the workings of a mole that burrows away underground and whose efforts thus prepare the insurrection at a time of its enforced retreat. Krahl (1971: 292) rightly points out that conceptuality [Begrifflichkeit] is one of the most important elements of Adorno's negative dialectics. Better: it is key. What is the concept of the concept [Begriff]?

Chris Arthur (2004: 243) rightly commends Adorno for having understood that capitalism has a specific conceptuality, and that therefore conceptuality "'holds sway in reality (Sache) itself.'" Conceptual thinking is thus not external to reality in the sense that it requires validation by means of empirical corroboration (see Callinicos 2005: 58–9). The presumption of such externality lies at the heart of traditional theory. Contrary to Callinicos's suggestion, a Marxist inspired realist epistemology does not alter tradition, it merely radicalises traditional theory from the standpoint of traditional theory. That is to say, theory does not possess photographs of the empirical world. In contrast to traditional theory, critical theory aims to penetrate reality – thought "aims at the thing itself" (Adorno 1973: 205). Adorno thus holds that the categories of bourgeois political economy are finite, transient products of the finite and transient reality of capitalism. For him, a dialectics that deciphers the social constitution of things "extinguishes the autarky of the concept, strips the blindfold from our eyes. That the concept is a concept even when dealing with things in being does not change the fact that on its part it is entwined with a non-conceptual whole" (1973: 12). History does not make history. Man makes history.[4] "History does nothing, does not 'possess vast wealth', does not 'fight battles'! It is Man, rather, the real, living Man who does all that, who does possess and fight, it is not 'history' that uses Man as a means to pursue its ends, as if it were a person apart. History is nothing but the activity of Man pursuing its ends" (Marx and Engels 1980: 98). If anything, historical materialism is the critique of things understood as dogmatic. It melts and dissolves all that appears solid. Adorno's negative dialectics is such historical materialism. It penetrates reality and dissolves its dogmatic posture by turning towards the non-identical in the identical, the non-conceptual in the conceptual. Especially in miserable times, it thus makes sense to look at Adorno's negative dialectics to see the mole at work, to appreciate its philosophical destruction and subversive cunning, and to ask about the (non-)conceptuality of human social practice in a world governed by things.

The chapter develops aspects of Adorno's "concept of the concept" in broad terms. The aim is not to regurgitate Adorno's argument, but to map it out. The conclusion returns to the difficulty of saying no.

I

> Concepts are moments of the reality that requires their formation. All concepts refer to non-conceptualities. (Adorno 1973: 11)

The task of a critical social theory is to demystify rigidified, thing-like, congealed relationships, rendering their immediacy transparent. For example, Marx (1973: 239) writes that in the money fetish, "a social relation, a definite relation between individuals ... appears as a metal, a stone, as a purely physical external thing which can be found, as such, in nature, and which is indistinguishable in form from its natural existence." There is only one world, and that is the world of appearance. This world has to be deciphered to reveal its social constitution in social relations.

In the critical tradition, conceptualisation therefore does not mean the expounding of meta-theories, which, by means of infinite regress, finishes up akin to the doctrine of the Invisible Hand with deist conceptions of social existence, whether in their religious or secularised forms – the so-called logic of things. Instead, it grounds the existence of invisible principles in human social relations and argues that it is these that produce their own enslavement to the invisible, whether in its religious or secularised forms. Conceptuality does also not entail the explanation of one thing by reference to another. Such thought moves from one thing to another in an attempt to render its term coherent by means of external reference. The state is explained by reference to the economic, and the economic by reference to the state. Similarly, demand is explained by supply and supply by demand. By means of vicious circularity, then, explanation becomes tautological. Further, conceptuality does not mean the discovery of natural laws, like, for example, the natural tendency of Man to barter, as Adam Smith alleged. That Man has to eat says nothing about his mode of subsistence and the social necessities that a mode of subsistence entails – so-called social laws.

To conceptualise means to bring the thing to its concept [*die Sache auf den Begriff bringen, der Begriff der Sache*]. Conceptuality has to do with the recognition of reality – not with the analysis of concepts. Concepts are required to recognise reality. Conceptualisation goes beyond the immediate perception of reality in order to comprehend what is hidden in its immediacy or immediate appearance. What is appearance an appearance of, and what appears in appearance? Concepts belong to reality and exist through reality. They do not live a life of their own, detached from reality. A concept that has no content is a concept of no-thing. Conceptuality is thus the way in which reality is rendered concrete – it is our way of comprehending reality by means of thought and experience. It focuses the experience of reality and thinks from within reality. Concepts are thus moments of a reality that requires their formation, and it is the business of conceptual thinking to subvert the critical subject by denouncing its deceitful publicity according to which its thing-hood is either self-constituted or a natural phenomenon. It denounces by asking, "why does this content (human social relations) take that form (the form of capital)" (Marx 1979: 95). This also means that thought's critical quality does not rest on the answers it gives, but on the question it asks.

The comprehension of things is not the same as their definition *qua* identification, or indeed "registration in a system governed by, for example, ideal-types" (Adorno 1973: 25). Conceptual comprehension of a thing means to perceive its individual moment in its connection *not* with other things but *in and through* them (see Adorno 1973: 149). Thinking by means of definition or identification is quite able to say what something comes under, what it illustrates, exemplifies or represents. It does not, however, say what it is. Thinking, as Adorno saw it (1997: 204), is essentially the negation of things in their immediacy, of something immediately perceptible. Conceptualisation thus means to dissolve the immediate appearance of things in order to recognise the thing in its now pregnant immediacy – a mediated immediacy [*vermittelte Unmittelbarkeit*]. It melts what appeared at first hard and solid. Every act of conceptualisation implies this effort. Conceptualisation is an act of revolt against immediacy. It does not bow to things. It wants to know what they are, and what they are is within them. It thus does not pretend that the immediate appearance of things is unreal; nor does it simply negate the world of appearances as if it were no more than a veil that hides the real human being in his social relations. Rather it recognises "the existent" (Adorno 1941: 318) for what it is: "the human being itself in its social relations" (Marx 1973: 712). That these social relations are reified does not make them less "human," as if the reified world is a world apart. Reification is not something objectively "given." It is a social product. However reified the world of things, it remains a human world. The immediacy of things is thus real as objective illusion [*gegenständlicher Schein*] (Reichelt 2005). Conceptualisation is required to decipher this illusion, that is, to reveal its social genesis, or social constitution, in human social practice.

Conceptualisation does thus not mean "thinking" *about* things. Rather, it means thinking *out of* things (Adorno 1973: 33). If it were really *about* things, then conceptualisation would be external to its subject matter – thought would be applied to something presupposed as fact. Thought would thus relate to its world as a tool that can be applied to society like an instrument. The thing or reality is here presupposed as something external to thought, and vice versa, as if they really belonged to different worlds. Thought that does not go into its object does not recognise its object. Instead, it hypothesises its object and, by doing so, analyses it as an "as if." That is, by hypothesising the objective world it hypothesises itself as a derivative of objects. Such thought is able to name and order things but cannot recognise them. In its vulgar version it operates an ethics akin to a cash register – indifferent to its own substance, eager to calculate.

Thinking *out of* things aims at discovering their social constitution. For instance, does "price of labour amount to a yellow logarithm" (Marx 1966: 818) or is £5 an hour just and fair? Whatever the fairness or unfairness of a £5 an hour wage, analytical thinking does not bring the thing to its concept. It presupposes the thing and describes it in analytical terms, but does not recognise it. Why has human social existence acquired the form of a commodity? And what laws of necessity exist in a society whose labour power is saleable? Do the interests of the sellers and buyers of labour power coincide? These questions suggest that reification is really just an "epiphenomenon" (Adorno 1973: 190). What is reified and what is reification a reification of? Marx's critique of religion argues that God requires no explanation. This is not because God cannot be explained but because the explanation of God rests on the comprehension of the social relations that bring God to the fore as an objective abstraction that controls and cows those same social relations from which it springs. Equally, reified things do not require explanation by and of themselves. Their comprehension rests on the understanding of the social relations that exist in the mode of the object, and disappear in the appearance [*Schein*] of reality's objective [*gegenständlicher*] character. What is it about the particular mode of human practice that requires it to exist against itself in the mode of the object?

The *reductio ad hominem* that for Adorno (1993: 143) characterises the critical intent of Marx's work does not entail the replacement of the object by the subject. It means the comprehension of the object as a mode of existence of the subject. Just as objectivity without the subject is nonsense, subjectivity without the object is nothing. Human practice is not only constitutive of the social world. Human practice also constitutes Man as a social being. Man is a social concept – Man is neither a biological fact nor is society the result of instinct; Man is not made by God, nor is society regulated by a total social subject [*gesamtgesellschaftliches Subjekt*] that governs social reproduction through invisible means. In order to understand things, one has to be within them. Hegel's notion of the work of the concept [*die Arbeit des Begriffs*] entails an internal connection between concept and thing, experience and substance. The concept, of course, does not work. We do. The work of the concept thus means to be led by thought without fear of where it might take us. The work of the concept means recognising the interior life of the thing-hood of society, to engage in its contradictions, and thus to understand not only the necessity of its movement, but also its capacity. What belongs to the constituted conceptuality of, say, the state? What is it capable of? What lies within its concept? Revealing the constituted conceptuality of things entails discovery of their internal life; it entails understanding the necessity of their mode of motion [*Bewegungsweise*], capacity and power [*Macht*], means and ends. Conceptualisation thus means articulating what is active in things, revealing their contradictory constitution and movement, and comprehending the violence that is hidden in and sustains the civilised appearance of equal and fair exchange relations. This, however, also means that conceptualisation – the work of the concept – works against its own tendency. Its critical intent is to demystify the fetish. However, to conceptualise means to identify. Identification does not crush the fetish; it affirms it. Conceptualisation is thus itself contradictory – it has to think against itself. In order to bring the thing to its concept [*die Sache auf den Begriff bringen*] the concept cannot encompass the thing [*aufgehen in der Sache*]. It has to be more than the thing, and this "more" has also to be within the thing. If thing and concept were to coincide, a critical theory of society would be superfluous. In short, the conceptualisation of things entails recognising their contradictory existence.

II

"All social life is essentially practical." This, from Marx's *8th Feuerbach* thesis, includes thinking. Thinking is part of social life and all social life is essentially practical. The thesis continues: "All mysteries which lead theory to mysticism find their rational explanation in human practice and in the comprehension of this practice." The thesis is clear and at the same time most difficult. Thought is able to reveal reality *qua* demystification, and demystification depends on the comprehension of human practice. Human practice is thus deemed essential, and thought's purpose is a subversive one: it reveals the hidden essence of things in human practice. The difficult aspect is this: like the reality through which it exists, thought can reinforce the mysticism against which it ostensibly, as thought, operates. For thought to be thought it needs to comprehend human practice. Its comprehension demystifies. And here the difficulties start. What human practice has Marx in mind? How can it be revealed and where might it be found? The appearance of human practice in the world as we know it does not show the human practice whose comprehension alone is said to explain the appearance of the world. If it were, there would be no need for demystification as essence and appearance would coincide. Marx's thesis suggests that human practice needs to be discovered by thought in order to comprehend the mysticism of its own appearance in forms that deny it. In short, the comprehension of human practice demystifies, but human practice is not immediately given in its appearance. What sort of human practice do we have to comprehend for demystification to occur in a valid sense? Can its validity be tested by means of verification or falsification, or is a different "test" required? Is it valid on the condition that it is true in practice, as a conceptuality that holds sway in reality itself (Reichelt 2005)? What does it mean to say that something is true in practice? Which practice is the valid one? And this in a society where the "living have been replaced by the dead" and where the "denial of all will to live" is the condition of existence (Adorno 1974: 229).

The problem analysed here is well focused by Helmut Reichelt (2002: 143). Expounding on Marx's critique of fetishism – human social relations appear contradictorily as relations between things and this appearance is real – he argues that capitalist exchange relations suggest that rationally acting subjects meet freely in the marketplace to realise their rational interests, whereas in fact they act as executives of abstract social laws which they themselves have generated historically and reproduce through their rational behaviour, and over which they have no control. In this context, Marx speaks of Man as a personification of economic category: a real abstraction of sensuous activity, an activity that vanishes in its own social world and appears as a mere derivative of the logic of things. Man is ruled by abstractions, yet receives from them only what he has put into them.

The circumstance that subjective rational behaviour subsists through a context of objective irrationality, that is, beyond the control of human reason, is often taken to mean that human social praxis moves within an objective framework of apparently extra-mundane structures. These structures are thus not seen as inverted [verkehrte] and perverted [verrückte] forms of human practice. Rather, they are posited as the objective framework within which human action unfolds. It is their objective laws of development that structure the behaviour and actions of social groups (see Hirsch and Roth 1986). Human action thus derives from presupposed structures, takes place within them and actualises their objective force in concrete settings. This view is widely shared, from Hayek's praise of the logic of the market as the best possible framework for the pursuit of individual autonomy, to Althusser's theory of the unintended consequences of class struggle and Habermas's dualist differentiation of reality into life-world and system.[5] If, as Marx claims, the comprehension of human practice really is key to the comprehension of social existence, can this same human practice be derived from those things whose comprehension is said to depend on the understanding of human practice? Instead of being demystified, the world of things would be affirmed in every conceivable way. The mythological idea of fate becomes no less mythical when it is demythologised "into a secular 'logic of things'" (Adorno 1973: 319) or into a system-logic that constantly threatens the colonisation of the life-world.

The derivation of human social practice from presupposed, that is, from hypothesised social structures, accepts what the critical tradition sets out to subvert *qua* demystification: it accepts commodity fetishism as something that is both immediately valid and beyond comprehension; and seeks demystification not by comprehending human practice in its form of appearance but by deriving human practice from presupposed social structures (see Bonefeld 2004). By hypothesising the constituted world of things as an already existing and given "anatomy" or objective framework of action, the understanding that society has to do with human beings in their social relations is cut short to the notion that the human being is a mere derivative of things (see Adorno 1975: 32). What, then, is the social practice that Marx has in mind when he argues that its comprehension demystifies the social world? Surely, it cannot be the action of economic categories and attendant human agents – it cannot be the action of a human subject that operates, as it has to, as a personification or character-mask of those same categories. The much praised dialectics between structure and agency is not helpful. It presupposes what it sets out to explain. It presupposes human practice in the form of an object and supposes the object as an active extramundane thing. The dialectics of structure and agency gives dialectics a bad name. It depends on dogmatic immediacies and moves in vicious circles as it hops from structure to agency, and back again, from agency to structure; and instead of comprehending what they are, each is presupposed in a tautological movement of thought; none is explained.

Marx's thesis that the understanding of the world of things has to comprehend human practice implies that this practice is constitutive. However, this formulation is full of dangers, too. It presupposes a definite resolution to the stated problem: If social practice constitutes, is it *ursprünglich*, be it primitive or original? If it constitutes, does it remain external to its creation? Can it remain innocent in the perverted world that it has created? Negri (1992: 89) says that capital is a "bewitching force" whose power is such that the constitutive subject is, as it were, sucked into capital. The constitutive subject is merely an alleged subject. The real power, it seems, is not the constitutive but the constituted subject. Better: the mythical subject (see Bonefeld 2003). Concepts do indeed live a dangerous life. As Debord (1987, para. 9) puts it: "in a world which really is topsy-turvy, the true is a moment of the false." Truth appears thus to exist in the mode of being denied – an existing untruth. Yet, it is true all the same.

III

All science would be superfluous if the outward appearance of things and the essence of things directly coincided. (Marx 1966: 817)

Nor do essence and appearance coincide directly, or belong to distinct realities. As Marx (1981: 265) put it in an earlier work, the "separation between in-itself and for-itself, the substance of the subject, is abstract mysticism." In contrast, then, to the traditional acceptance that social theory is either a theory of structures or of social action (Vanberg 1975), the conceptualisation of things amounts to a process of deciphering their essence. But the essence of things can only be human practice in the mode of the object. Better: in the "mode of being denied" (see Gunn 1992). Essence must appear. If it does not, then it is not essence; conversely, appearance must be the appearance of essence or it is nothing. There is only one reality – a reality of disunion, contradiction, fissures and antagonism; and thus a reality where subject and object are inverted in a topsy-turvy way (see Backhaus 2005). The distinction between essence and appearance exists within the things by means of an irreconcilable, antagonistic, restless unity. Disunity subsists against itself in the form of unity. Disunity in the form of unity entails coercion as the condition of unity – a coerced and coercive unity. The bourgeois relations of abstract equality render difference commensurable in the form of an abstract identity where everything is indifferent to its social content as mere variations of exchange relations. Abstract identity is indifferent to human distinctiveness; it is an identity of death (see Adorno 1973). Difference exists in the form of unity; that is, difference is coerced to appear indifferent to itself in the form of value – "the actual mask of death" (Adorno 1975: 60). Disunity in the form of unity entails a social reality that is not reconciled with itself and whose concept is not at peace with itself. For this reality to be conceived conceptually, antagonism has to be a moment of the concept itself – a concept torn by contradiction and in antagonistic battle. It is within the concept, in its internality and immanence, that the non-coincidence of essence and appearance exists in the form of unity. This non-coincidence strains the concept, forcing it to operate against itself.

Essence and appearance thus form an "inner connexion" (Marx 1983: 28) of an antagonistic kind. "Already the simple forms of exchange-value and of money latently contain the opposition between labour and capital" (Marx 1973: 248). Antagonism is, however, not only a relationship of battle; it is also a relationship of mutual dependency, of social unity. Thus, the concept of reality is divided within itself: mutual dependency exists *qua* antagonism, and unity exists *qua* disunity. Its content is suppressed in its forms. These deny their substance and yet contain within themselves what they deny, that is, the antagonistic struggle that threatens to force reality apart, beyond itself. And yet the concept is not one of antagonism but of unity. It is as if its revolutionary march into the world is forced underground in order for the concept to retain its air of civilised normality and bourgeois respectability.

Hegel's notion that essence has to appear does not mean that the human subject makes an appearance by asserting itself against the world of things – say, in terms of a conception of class struggle as a force that, from the outside, breaks into the capital relation during periods of crisis (see Bonefeld 1995). Hegel's notion that essence has to appear means that essence cannot choose not to appear. It is forced to appear – it is as if essence is coerced to appear in its own inhospitable world, that what makes essence essential, subsists in appearance. Its appearance is thus at the same time its disappearance. It is forced to appear and the necessity of its appearance entails that it vanishes. Essence vanishes in its appearance. The law of essence is its disappearance *qua* appearance. In the "enchanted and perverted" world of capital (Marx 1966: 830) essence appears in the form of its denial "as a thing" (Marx 1973: 157). The circumstance that essence disappears in its appearance is as real as the fact that, on the other hand, there would be "nothing without individuals and their spontaneities" (Adorno 1973: 304). Reification, then, "finds its limitation in reified Man" (Adorno 1975: 25). The reality in which the social individual moves day in and day out has no invariant character, that is, something which exists independently from Man. Horkheimer's (1992) characterisation of Marx's critique of political economy as a "judgment on existence" expresses the same fundamental idea, that is, capitalist social relations render the human being invisible. Yet, however invisible, the world of things has no independent existence from human social practice. In its entirety, it is a world of human practice (see Adorno 1975: 173) and thus a human world. For the critical tradition, the critique of political economy amounts, therefore, to a conceptualised praxis [*begriffene Praxis*] (see Schmidt 1974), that is, an understanding of the totality of human social practice, which constitutes and contradicts the world of capital. In short, "the constitution of the world occurs behind the backs of the individuals; yet it is their work" (Marcuse 1988: 151).

Human practice, in sum, exists in appearance and it does so in the mode of being denied. The conceptuality of things obtains through what they deny. That is, "essence passes into that which lies concealed beneath the façade of immediacy, of the supposed facts, and which makes the facts what they are" (Adorno 1973: 167), that what is hidden in facts gives them their meaning. The positivity of facts is deceitful. It hides what they are, and when confronted with what they are, their positivity becomes comprehensible and for this reason, dissolves – but not without a fight. Truth has not harmed anyone, except the messenger.

The circumstance that the "appearance of things hides their genesis" (see Adorno 1993: 25) in human practice, entails a programme of critique that deciphers the "puzzling forms" of value as forms "assumed by social relations between Man and Man" (Marx 1983: 94) and reveals their social constitution in the peculiar social character of labour that "becomes productive only by producing its opposite," that is, capital (Marx 1973: 305). That is, essence appears at the same time as it remains hidden in its appearance. Critique's enlightening intent is to make visible what is hidden in things. It comprehends essence in its appearance, that is, as a disappeared essence. Adorno captures this appearance *qua* disappearance when he argues that essence [*Wesen*] is first of all the fatal mischief [*Unwesen*] of a world that degrades men to means of real abstractions that rule over them (see Adorno 1973: 167). Essence [*Wesen*] exists in the mode of being denied – as mischief [*Unwesen*]. That is to say, sensuous human practice subsists against itself in the form of, say, freedom as wage slavery.

Neither are social structures external to human practice, nor is human practice external to social structures. Man is a social being and therewith a being *qua* objectification [*Vergegenständlichung*]. Man is always objectified Man. The issue that reification or alienation, or indeed fetishism, brings to the fore is not objectification but its alienated or reified mode. Therefore, the immediacy of the objective world is not really an immediacy of things. It is the immediacy of things in the mode of an objective illusion [*gegenständlicher Schein*]: the subject's objectification exists in inverted form where the thing subjectifies itself in the person, and the person objectifies himself in the thing. That is to say, the apparent immediacy of the objective world is in fact always already a mediated whole [*vermitteltes Ganzes*]. Mediation does not entail an external relationship between subject and object – mediation is not the point of collision between subject and object. Nor is mediation the middle point between two extremes; or a point of reconciliation between subject and object. Mediation means mediation of subject and object in their topsy-turvy movement where both exist *qua* the other, where both are identical with the other, and where identity exists only against itself as contradiction and disunity, that is, as non-identity. Every category is at the same time a denied category. Mediation thus means that the world of things is the mode of existence of the subject that exists *qua* things in the mode of being denied. There is thus a continuing change of form between object and subject, where both are "inverted" forms of a social reality that renders Man in his social relations "invisible." The "perverted [*verrückte*] form" of value (Marx 1979: 90), in other words, presents the mode of existence of human purposeful activity in the form of impersonal relations, including wage labour and capital.[6] Capital finds its conceptuality in labour and in the denial of this labour. It posits itself as the restless expansion of wealth only on the condition that it maintains its relationship to labour at the same time as it goes beyond labour: it is movement of restless positing *qua* destruction. Concealed in the concept of capital as self-valorising value lies the conceptuality of social labour. The necessity of its affirmation *qua* destruction – discussed by Marx at times as the dialectic between the forces and the relations of production – belongs to the constituted existence of social labour in the form of capital.

Destruction is the constituted nightmare of the capitalist mode of social reproduction:

> Society suddenly finds itself put back into a state of momentary barbarism; it appears as if famine, a universal war of devastation had cut off the supply of every means of subsistence; industry and commerce seem to be destroyed; and why? Because there is too much civilisation, too much means of subsistence; too much industry, too much commerce. The productive forces at the disposal of society no longer tend to further the development of the conditions of bourgeois property; on the contrary, they have become too powerful for these conditions, by which they are fettered, and so soon as they overcome these fetters, they bring disorder into the whole of bourgeois society, endanger the existence of bourgeois property. The conditions of bourgeois society are too narrow to comprise the wealth created by them. And how does bourgeois society get over these crises? On the one hand by enforced destruction of a mass of productive forces; on the other, by the conquest of new markets, and by the more thorough exploitation of the old ones. (Marx and Engels 1997: 18–19)

This commentary on globalisation by the 29-year-old Marx is not a brilliant anticipation, which after all turned out to be far too optimistic. Rather, it conceptualises the critical subject and, in doing so, shows what lies within it. What lies within the concept are its determinate necessities. These belong to the critical subject and constitute its conceptuality. Creation *qua* destruction is a valid necessity of capitalist social relations – it belongs to its conceptuality [*Begrifflichkeit*]. "Conceptuality expresses the fact that, no matter how much blame may attach to the subject's contribution, the conceived world is not its own but a world hostile to the subject" (Adorno 1973: 167). Man vanishes in her own world and exists against herself as a personification of economic categories – an "alienated subject" (see Backhaus 1992) that constitutes the world of things and is invisible, lost and denied in its own world.

In sum, the meaning of objectivity excludes the possibility that it can also be a subject. However, to be an object is part of the meaning of subjectivity. Subjectivity means objectification. In its capitalist form it appears in the logic of things. Appearance [*Schein*] "is the enchantment of the subject in its own world" (Adorno 1969: 159). The circumstance that objectification [*Gegenständlichkeit*] exists as alienation thus does not imply that there is an as yet undiscovered, and indeed undiscoverable, logic that lies solely within the thing itself. Only as a socially determinate object can the object be an object (see Adorno 1969: 157). Reason exists – but in irrational form. The irrational world is a rational world.

IV

The circumstance that human beings enter into relationships with one another as personifications of things says that the subject vanishes in the mode of its appearance. Thus, the demand that thought is adequate to its subject matter entails more than it bargains for. Its adequacy cannot be established by means of falsification or verification. There is no verifiable "it is." To say that something "is" already casts doubt on the proclaimed identification of the "it." To bring things to their concept requires that concepts are open to the experience of the thing. The freedom of the wage contract challenges the concept of freedom in its experience. Dialectics opens concepts.

Dialectics is not a formal procedure or method applied to reality. Instead, it focuses on social contents and does so by moving within their social forms. Dialectics is immanent to its social context. It knows that there is no second reality. Dialectics does not practise self-deception by pretending that appearance is distinct from essence as if reality comprises the interplay between structural laws of development and the social action of human agents. Dialectics is also not a self-perpetuating triad where the thesis confronts its anti-thesis, reconciling the two by means of synthesis, only for the synthesis to result in a new thesis. Dialectics concretises reality by means of a determinate negation. Dialectics thinks the disunited unity of things, moves within reality's contradictory constitution and deciphers the reality of things by revealing human practice as the "form-giving fire" (Marx 1973: 361) of things. Dialectics says "no more, to begin with, than that objects do not go into their concepts without leaving a remainder" (Adorno 1973: 5). Dialectics is thus a sort of "cogitative confrontation of concept and thing" (Adorno 1973: 144). As the disappeared essence of things, human practice is the non-conceptual content of things. Confronting the thing means deciphering the non-conceptual in the act of conceptualising it. For example, the conceptuality of the wage-labourer as a personification of variable capital confronts what it denies – human sensuous being – and this non-conceptuality belongs to the concept wage-labour and therefore haunts and contradicts it. Sensuous being exists within the concept of variable capital in the mode of being denied. Further, for variable capital to function, it requires the ingenuity and spontaneity of human purposeful practice. Yet, this too is denied in its posited concept. That what is denied in the concept has no separate existence from the concept. It lives not only within and through the concept, but also against it. Dialectics is thus not a form of thought that pacifies the contradiction, be it by means of reconciliation, integration, incorporation or simply formalistic indifference to social contents.

Dialectics recognises the non-conceptual in the concept and so illuminates the contradiction, follows its movement and reveals the secrets of its perverted mode of existence. Demythologisation is dialectics' enlightening intent.

Adorno's notion that "dialectics is the consistent sense of non-identity" (1973: 5) does not report on something that is external to things. It is an internal non-identity. Better: "it is nonidentity through identity" (1973: 189). To think dialectically means to think "in contradictions, for the sake of the contradiction once experienced in the thing, and against that contradiction" (1973: 145). What appears identical in exchange is non-identity under the aspect of identity. Although no atom of matter goes into the determination of value, use value "constitutes the substance of all wealth," whatever the social form of that wealth (Marx 1983: 44). Non-identity is immanent in identity. Its recognition makes dialectics negative. Negative dialectics is "suspicious of all identity" and hinges on this "turn towards nonidentity" within the concept (Adorno 1973: 12).

Althusser was right to argue that Man does not exist. In the topsy-turvy world of capital, Man is indeed a non-conceptuality. However, does it therefore follow that the critique of political economy is really no more than a secularised myth of the "logic of things"? *Pace* Althusser's idea that capital contradicts itself in the form of structural contradictions, it is

Man, who, as a single individual, as a group, or as a mass, understands himself as subject and who defends himself against a merely objective existence – in politics, in religion, in philosophy. One can say that subversion is a truly human phenomenon. Man objects to be a mere football of the almighty. Here he is mere object. Similarly, as a servant of the master he is mere object, regardless of whether we conceive this in social or religious terms. Man is never at the centre of politics (as the political parties say), but he is a means of politics...And an object he remains most of all when he is kept in a state of ignorance...Subversion operates against systems of thought, against political and economic systems, that threaten nature and therewith always also Man. (Agnoli 1996: 29)

In other words, the non-conceptual is the negative force of the concept. Reality develops by force of its negation (Agnoli 2001: 169). Thus, variable capital does not go on strike, humans do, and they do so at the same time that they really exist as personifications of variable capital. Fetishism is real, but its concept contains more than it reveals; that what is non-identical to the concept drives the concept. There is no secret reality beyond its concept, nor is there an external vantage point from which to launch the assault. Reality is divided within itself. The resolution to the dialectical context of immanence is that context itself. "The whole is false" (Adorno 1974: 50). Thus the whole has to go.

In conclusion, the "constitutive character of the non-conceptual in the concept" (Adorno 1973: 12) entails the recognition of reality by means of determinate negation. Determinate negation entails the deciphering of things as "relations between humans" (Marx 1972: 147). The foundation of human existence can only be Man herself. Critique, then, has to decipher the world of things on a human basis and does so by showing that the forms of capital are constituted by and subsist through the social practice of "active humanity" (Marx 1973: 489). Their conceptualisation as forms of social relations does not entail Man as an abstract individual but as a member of a definite form of society. Determinate critique seeks to decipher the human content of reified things and thus to recognise Man in his social relations. It resists suppression of this human content, and instead of deriving human practice from presupposed, hypothesised things, it recognises these things as forms of human practice, however perverted this practice might be in the form of the object (see Backhaus 2005).

CONCLUSION

Adorno's negative dialectics detests reconciliation with negative conditions. The idea that the negation of the negation is positive makes no sense. This idea "can only be upheld by one who presupposes positivity" (Adorno 1973: 160). Refusal to sanction things as they are entails irreconcilability: the negation of the negation does not negate what it has negated. It negates the negative human condition – a condition governed by things. In short, "what is negative is negative until it has passed" (Adorno 1973: 160). What is false is false. The whole is false – the whole has to go. If, however, the whole is false, then whatever one does is false. Irreconcilability of negative dialectics with negative conditions appears thus to render impotent its practical dimension.

Adorno's concept of the concept is emphatically practical. It holds that however much the forms of human practice have autonomised themselves from the individual, they remain forms of human practice. Reichelt (2005: 65) expresses this well when he argues that "human sensuous practice subsists through its supersensible existence in the autonomization of society as both the object and subject of its perverted social practice." From within economic categories, the human subject is a mere metaphysical nuisance. Adorno's critique shows that this nuisance is in fact the essence of things. His "concept of the concept" is thus distinct. According to Lukács the worker can resist reification because, as long as he rebels against it consciously, "his humanity and his soul are not changed into commodities" (1970: 172). That the soul of the worker-in-resistance is the party is of no interest here. What is important, however, is that reification does not affect the soul of the worker, as if the soul is not of this world but of divine issue. Lukács's position is a paradox. He derives the revolutionary subject, he calls it the totality of the proletarian subject represented by the party, from something that is and remains external to its reified existence. Bloch (2000) conceived of the unreified within reification as the "inner transcendence of matter"; and Negt and Kluge (1993) conceived of it as "materialist instinct." And Adorno? He would have none of this. The very idea that there is a world out there that has not yet been colonised by the logic of things is nonsensical. Instead of a concept of society, their differentiation of society into system and soul or transcendent matter or materialist instinct, separates what belongs together. Indeed, whichever formulation is favoured, they all insist on a subject that is conceived in contradistinction to society. The insisted subject is not a social subject; it is an asserted subject. It is meant to do what the antagonistic society is no longer assumed to be able to do, that is, realise the social subject in battle against its own perverted mode of existence.

Leaving aside Adorno's despair – "he allows himself to hope only on the condition that all hope has disappeared" (Böckelmann 1969: 22) – his conception of bourgeois society does not allow for externalities. There is only one world. Human practice ensues in and through perverted social forms. Like Marx, Adorno's work mocks those who depict socialism as the realisation of the ideals of bourgeois society. As Marx put it:

> what divides these gentlemen from the bourgeois apologist is, on the one side, their sensitivity to the contradictions included in the system; on the other, the utopian inability to grasp the necessary difference between the real and the ideal form of bourgeois society, which is the cause of their desire to undertake the superfluous business of realizing the ideal expression again, which is in fact only the inverted projection [*Lichtbild*] of this reality. (Marx 1973: 248–9)

Or in Adorno's words, "the whole is false" (1974: 50; see also Adorno 1941: 318f). Since, however, the whole is false, everything is false, that is, a "wrong life cannot be lived rightly" (Adorno 1974: 39). Adorno's conception of bourgeois society does indeed force us to think about what it means to say no in a negative world.

To say no to something is simple. But to say what the no is is difficult. For one, the no is not external to but operates within society's false totality. Like Marx's summons of class struggle as the motor of history, the no drives the negative world forward. It is its dynamic force (see Heinrich 1982). Furthermore, to say what the no is compromises the no insofar as it becomes positive in its affirmative yes to something that has no valid content except the false totality of bourgeois society itself. The no is immanent to the false society; it belongs to its concept. Horkheimer's (1981: 150) statement "I can say what is wrong, but I cannot say what is right" is thus apt. The no not only drives the negative world forward, it also posits uncertainty. Adorno's negative dialectics ponders the practical dimension of this uncertainty, cannot accept it and rejects it as pseudo-activity – the collapse of working-class politics in the face of Fascism and Nazism has left a permanent imprint. Adorno's conception of bourgeois society entails the experience of the concept. The experience of the concept is Auschwitz.

In conclusion, Adorno's negative dialectics has to be studied, especially in miserable times. Its courageous delivery of the concept of bourgeois society operates like the proverbial mole which, according to Marx, prepares for the revolution by tunnelling through the defences. The mole is a philosophical mole. Once its work is done, the mole departs. Its departure demands that Adorno's confrontation of the concept of reality with its experience be brought down to "the real life-activity" (see Marx 1978: 154) of the unhappy consciousness in struggle. Man's existence as an economic category does not entail reduction of consciousness to economic consciousness. It entails the concept of economy as an experienced concept, and economic consciousness as an experienced consciousness. At the very least, economic consciousness is an unhappy consciousness. It is this consciousness that demands reconciliation: "freedom turns concrete in the changing forms of repression as resistance to repression. There has been as much free will as there were men with the will to be free" (Adorno 1973: 265). That is to say, Adorno's (1974: 39) statement that one cannot live honestly in the false totality of bourgeois society is only partially correct – an honest life begins already in the struggle against the falsehood of bourgeois society. In distinction to Adorno, then, those who claim to want freedom but refrain from struggling against bourgeois society contradict themselves.

NOTES

1. An earlier version of this chapter was presented at the conference "Philosophy Today," held at the Department of Philosophy, University of Crete, November 2005. The conference was organised in memory of Kosmas Psychopedis. Many participants commented on the paper and I am grateful to them all. I want to thank Joe Fracchia, Helmut Reichelt, John Roberts, Marcel Stoetzler, Stavroula Tsinorema and Chris Wright for their helpful advice and comments. The usual disclaimers apply.

2. "We say we have to work with the Muslim Brotherhood over specific issue [Palestine or Iraq]" (IS, 2005, p. 31). For an assessment of such a position, see Bonefeld (2005) and Žižek (2002).
3. Quotations from German have been translated by the author.
4. "Man" with a capital "M" is used here and throughout in the sense of *Mensch*. *Mensch* can be feminine, masculine and even neutral as in *das Menschlein*. *Die Menscheit* is a universal – is everybody.
5. For critical assessments, see Bonefeld (1993), Clarke (1980), Schmidt (1983) and Reichelt (2000).
6. The quotation is from the German edition of *Capital*. The English edition translates *verrückte Form* as "absurd form." This translation fails to express the double meaning of *"verrückt"*: mad (*verrückt*) and displaced (*ver-rückt*). I use the word "perverted" to indicate this double meaning, and "perverted" is used throughout in this double sense. Thus, the notion of "perverted forms," "perverted" and "perversion" means that these forms are both mad and displaced. The phrase thus expresses the idea of a continuing change of form between object and subject, where both, subject and object, are "inverted" forms of a social reality that renders Man in his social relations "invisible." On this, see Backhaus (1992).

REFERENCES

Adorno, T. W. (1941) "Spengler Today," in *Zeitschrift für Sozialforschung*, vol. 9.
Adorno, T. W. (1969) *Stichworte Kritische Modelle 2*, Frankfurt, Suhrkamp.
Adorno, T. W. (1972) *Soziologische Schriften* in *Gesammelte Werke*, vol. 8, Frankfurt, Suhrkamp.
Adorno, T. W. (1973) *Negative Dialectics*, London, Verso.
Adorno, T. W. (1974) *Minima Moralia*, London, New Left Books.
Adorno, T. W. (1975) *Gesellschaftstheorie und Kulturkritik*, Frankfurt, Suhrkamp.
Adorno, T. W. (1993) "Einleitung," *Der Positivismusstreit in der deutschen Soziologie*. Munich, dtv.
Adorno, T. W. (1997) *Drei Studien zu Hegel* in *Gesammelte Schriften*, vol. 5, Frankfurt, Suhrkamp.
Agnoli, J. (1969) "Die Schnelligkeit der realen Prozesse. Vorläufige Skizze eines Versuchs über Adornos historisches Ende," in W. F. Schoeller (ed.), *Die neue Linke nach Adorno*, München, Kindl.
Agnoli, J. (1996) *Subversive Theorie*, Freiburg, Ça ira.
Agnoli, J. (2001) *Geschichte und Theorie*. Freiburg, Ça ira.

Arthur, C. (2004) *The New Dialectic and Marx's Capital*, Leiden, Brill.

Backhaus, HG. (1992) "Between Philosophy and Science: Marxian Social Economy as Critical Theory," in W. Bonefeld, R. Gunn and K. Psychopedis (eds.), *Open Marxism*, vol. I, London, Pluto.

Backhaus, H. G. (2005) "Some Aspects of Marx's Concept of Critique in the Context of his Economic-Philosophical Theory," in W. Bonefeld and K. Psychopedis (eds.), *Human Dignity*, Aldershot, Ashgate.

Bloch, E. (2000) *Logos der Materie*, Frankfurt, Suhrkamp.

Böckelmann, F. (1969) "Die Möglichglichkeit ist die Unmöglichkeit. Die Unmöglichkeit ist die Möglichkeit. Bermerkungen zur Autarkie der Negativen Dialektik," in W. F. Schoeller (ed.), *Die neue Linke nach Adorno*, München, Kindl.

Bonefeld, W. (1993) "Crisis of Theory," in *Capital and Class*, no. 50.

Bonefeld, W. (1995) "Capital as Subject and the Existence of Labour," in W. Bonefeld, , R. Gunn, and K. Psychopedis (eds.), *Open Marxism*, vol. III, London, Pluto.

Bonefeld, W. (2003) "Human Practice and Perversion: Beyond Autonomy and Structure," in W. Bonefeld (ed.), *Revolutionary Writing*. New York, Autonomedia.

Bonefeld, W. (2004) "Anmerkungen zur Kritik der Vorrausetzungen," in C. Kirchoff et al. (eds.), *Gesellschaft als Verkehrung*, Freiburg, Ça ira.

Bonefeld, W. (2005) "Nationalism and Anti-Semitism in Anti-Globalization Perspective," in W. Bonefeld and K. Psychopedis (eds.), *Human Dignity*, Aldershot, Ashgate.

Callinicos, A. (2005) "Against the New Dialectic," *Historical Materialism*, vol. 13, no. 2, 41–59.

Clarke, S. (1980) "Althusserian Marxism," in S. Clarke et al., *One Dimensional Marxism*, London, Allison & Busby.

Debord, G. (1987) *Society of the Spectacle*, London, Rebel Press.

Fracchia, J. (2005) "The Untimely Timeliness of Rosa Luxemburg," in W. Bonefeld and K. Psychopedis (eds.), *Human Dignity: Social Autonomy and the Critique of Capitalism*, Aldershot, Ashgate.

Gunn, R. (1992) "Against Historical Materialism," in W. Bonefeld, R. Gunn, and K. Psychopedis (eds.), *Open Marxism*, vol. II, London, Pluto.

Heinrich, K. (1982) *Versuch über die Schwierigkeit nein zu sagen*, Marburg, Stroemfeld/Roter Stern.

Hirsch, J. and R. Roth (1986) *Das neue Gesicht des Kapitalismus*, Hamburg, VSA.

Horkheimer, M. (1981) *Gesellschaft im Übergang. Aufsätze, Rede und Vorträge 1942–1970*, Frankfurt, Fischer.

Horkheimer, M. (1992) *Kritische und traditionelle Theory*, Frankfurt, Fischer.

IS (2005) "Egypt: The Pressure Builds Up," *International Socialism*, no. 106.

Krahl, H. J. (1971) *Konstitution und Klassenkampf*, Frankfurt, Verlag Neue Kritik.

Lukács, G. (1970) *History and Class Consciousness*, London, Merlin.

Marcuse, H. (1988) *Negations*, London, Free Association Books.

Marx, K. (1966) *Capital*, vol. III, London, Lawrence & Wishart.

Marx, K. (1972) *Theories of Surplus Value Part III*, London, Lawrence & Wishart.

Marx, K. (1973) *Grundrisse*, London, Penguin Books.

Marx, K. (1978) "The German Ideology," in R. Tucker (ed.), *The Marx–Engels Reader*, New York, Norton.

Marx, K. (1979), *Kapital*, vol. I, Dietz, Berlin.

Marx, K. (1981) "Kritik des Hegelschen Staatsrechts," in *MEW I*, Berlin, Dietz.

Marx, K. (1983) *Capital*, vol. I, London, Lawrence & Wishart.

Marx, K. and F. Engels (1980) *Die heilige Familie, MEW 2*, Berlin, Dietz.

Marx, K. and F. Engels (1997) *Communist Manifesto*, London, Pluto.

Negri, A. (1992) "Interpretation of the Class Situation Today," in W. Bonefeld, R. Gunn and K. Psychopedis (eds.), *Open Marxism*, vol. II, London: Pluto Press.

Negt, O. and A. Kluge, (1993) *Public Sphere and Experience*, Minneapolis, MN, University of Minnesota Press.

Psychopedis, K. (2005) "Social Critique and the Logic of Revolution," in W. Bonefeld and K. Psychopedis (eds.), *Human Dignity*, Aldershot, Ashgate.

Reichelt, H. (2000) "Jürgen Habermas' Reconstruction of Historical Materialism," in W. Bonefeld and K. Psychopedis (eds.), *The Politics of Change*, London, Palgrave.

Reichelt, H. (2002) "Die Marxsche Kritik der ökonomische Kategorien. Überlegungen zum Problem der Geltung in der dialektischen Darstellungsmethode im 'Kapital'," in I. Fetscher and A. Schmidt (eds.), *Emanzipation als Versöhnung*, Frankfurt, Neue Kritik.

Reichelt, H. (2005) "Social Reality as Appearance: Some Notes on Marx's Concept of Reality," in W. Bonefeld and K. Psychopedis (eds.), *Human Dignity*, Aldershot, Ashgate.

Schmidt, A. (1974) "Praxis," in *Gesellschaft: Beiträge zur Marxschen Theorie 2*, Frankfurt, Suhrkamp.

Schmidt, A. (1983) *History and Structure*, Cambridge, MA, MIT Press.

Vanberg, V. (1975) *Die beiden Soziologien*, Tübingen, Mohr.

Žižek, S. (2002) *Welcome to the Desert of the Real*, London, Verso.

IV

The Politics of Sexuality and Art

9

ADORNO, NON-IDENTITY, SEXUALITY

Marcel Stoetzler

This chapter explores some of Adorno's scattered remarks on love, on the gender relation between men and women, as well as on homosexuality, and how these relate to modern individuality, subjectivity and the capitalist mode of production. Its focus is on the modernity of the idea that there are exactly two sexes, understood as two distinct species or essences, and some of the implications and reverberations of this idea. It proceeds by way of arranging (juxtaposing perhaps) a number of related arguments taken from a body of Marxist writing mostly from the 1970s and 1980s that seems, if not influenced by, then at least compatible with, Adorno's theorising. The guiding idea is that strict sexual dimorphism is an aspect, or expression, of the increasingly genital organisation of sexuality on the one hand, and on the other, the sublimation of Eros in the service of capitalist real subsumption. Both have been, and still are, part of the same historical process.

ECHO; ABANDON

"There is no love that is not an echo"; happiness is "what is not exchangeable, not open to complaint" (Adorno 1974, 1994, s.139). "It is a piece of sexual utopia not to be oneself, and to love more in the beloved than only her" (Adorno 1964: 104–5; 1998: 75). Love suggests "the negation of the ego principle," the negation of "the demand for identity" (1998: 75). "The genital fixation on the I and on the other, who is thought of as equally consistent in her/himself, harbours narcissism" (Adorno 1964: 105).

When bourgeois love and marriage in their initial stages seemed to promise freedom, the exit from "servitude in the father's house,"[1] in the period of "big industry" conditions have changed to such an extent that "[d]efiance of the family is no more an act of daring than the leisure-time relationship with the *boyfriend*[2] is the gateway to heaven" (Adorno and Horkheimer 1971: 97; 1997: 107; 2002: 84). People adopt a "rational, calculating attitude to their own sexuality" based on a more casual but all the more effective version of the radical separation of mind and body that underlies the libertinage celebrated by de Sade in the short summer of bourgeois radicalism, the period of the French Revolution: "Love and pleasure are very different things ... for the sentiments of tenderness correspond to the conditions of humor and convenience, but are in no way dependent on the beauty of a neck or a handsomely curved hip" (de Sade, quoted in Adorno and Horkheimer 1997: 108). De Sade's reasoning – a Cartesianism carried to absurd extremes, and indeed turned against its own emancipatory intent – is wrong, as Adorno and Horkheimer show (and as Adorno, 1973: 97–122, 2006: 61–72, would later develop in his discussion of "natural beauty" in *Aesthetic Theory*), de Sade's Cartesianism "diminishes not only the utopian exuberance of love but its physical pleasure" (Adorno and Horkheimer 1997: 109):

> The beauty of a neck and the curve of a hip do not act on sexuality as a-historical, purely natural facts, but as images which comprise all social experience. In this experience there survives an intention of something other than nature, of love which is not restricted to sex. (Adorno and Horkheimer 1971: 98; 1997: 108; 2002: 85)

Not even physical pleasure is actually *physis*, but its actual, namely social, content is congealed historical experience, including a moment of intimation of utopia, the better state of things, projected by the beholder onto the "beautifully" curved hip. Adorno and Horkheimer may have had in mind here the Shakespeare quote with which Marx concluded the chapter on fetishism in the first volume of *Capital*: to be good-looking is a matter of circumstance, while reading and writing come by nature (Marx 1990: 177).[3]

"Nothing pleased Adorno more than when a friend came to similar insights independently, for he considered it a validation of their correctness" (Buck-Morss 1977: 85). Adorno might have been pleased to read, then, that Mario Mieli, one of the founders of the radical gay movement in England and Italy in the 1970s and advocate of "gay communism," came – by a different route – to the similar conclusion that "love is the tendency to annihilate the outworn neurotic and egoistic categories of 'subject' and 'object'" (Mieli 1980: 56).[4] Or the French communist Dominique Karamazov's demand (published in French in the same year as Mieli's Italian text, 1977) that "the sexual" be dissolved in loving relationships rather than conceptually separated from "love". In capitalist society, "tenderness and esteem only prepare for or accompany sex and even constitute a form of barter" on the terms of x amount of tenderness for y amount of sexual availability (Karamazov 1998: 31). "Abandon, the submission which a loving relationship implies, unaccepted because it is in contradiction with a whole way of life" – the everyday reality of ubiquitous exchange of equivalents – "returns in the form of an exterior domination that is violent, imposed, feared and desired at the same time" (1983: 33):

> For Hite & Co., sexual relations are reduced to helping each other towards pleasure, to rendering each other a service, naturally blending the sauce with the indispensable tenderness. Reciprocal masturbation would be the ideal. What escapes them is the possibility of self-abandonment in the other .... If it is just a matter of the intensity of pleasure, then there can be no doubt that the electronic feeling and sucking machine will win out over masturbation nine times out of ten. (1983: 40)[5]

On this account, all late-bourgeois subjects seem to be dreaming of being so many de Sades, but – due to the reality principle of exchange of equivalents – have to take some limited amount of tenderness into the bargain: an instance of bourgeois society's celebrated capacity to civilise and domesticate the barbarisms that it produces in the first place. Karamazov, like Adorno, defends, in Marxian language, the revolutionary dimension of romanticism against the instrumental logic of left-liberal utilitarianism, which suggests the quantification and accumulation of pleasure and the exchange of equivalent portions of it, based on the calculus of mutual benefit. For Adorno, the "misshapen bourgeois form of sex, murkily enmeshed with every kind of material interest," "marriage as an ignoble compromise," "the institutional, permitted, assimilated character of pleasure, its false immanence in an order that cuts it to shape and imparts to it in the very moment of ordaining it a deathly melancholy," creates "repugnance" which may even lead ecstasy "to withdraw completely into renunciation, rather than sin by realization against its own principle." Although, however, "fidelity exacted by society is a means to unfreedom," "only through fidelity can freedom achieve insubordination to society's command" (Adorno 1974, s.113).

Developed capitalism is bad news for romantic love. The "integration of society ... designates subjects more and more exclusively as partial moments in the network of material production" to the effect that "the organic composition of man is growing" (1974, s.147): "that which determines subjects as means of production and not as living purposes, increases with the proportion of machines to variable capital." The "process that begins with the metamorphosis of labour-power into a commodity has permeated men through and through and objectified each of their impulses as formally commensurable variations of the exchange relationship."

> Under the a priori demand for saleability the living has made itself, as something living, a thing, equipment. The ego consciously takes the whole man into its service as a piece of apparatus. In this re-organization the ego as business-manager delegates so much of itself to the ego as business-mechanism, that it becomes quite abstract, a mere reference-point: self-preservation forfeits its self. Character traits ... are no longer the subject; rather, the subject responds to them as to his internal object. ... This is the social pathogenesis of schizophrenia. The severance of character traits both from their instinctual basis and from the self, which commands

them where it formerly merely held them together, causes man to pay for his increasing inner organization with increasing disintegration. The consummation of the division of labour within the individual, his radical objectification, leads to his morbid scission. Hence the 'psychotic character', the anthropological pre-condition of all totalitarian mass-movements. Precisely this transition from firm characteristics to push-button behaviour-patterns ... is an expression of the rising organic composition of man. ... in the prompt, unresistant reflexes the subject is entirely extinguished. (Adorno 1974, s.147)

Adorno holds that love "partially withstood throughout the bourgeois age" the principle of exchange of equivalents, until the present time (writing in 1945) (1974, s.107). "The exchange relationship ... has completely absorbed" love; if love was "the last immediacy," it has fallen "victim to the distance of all the contracting parties from all others. Love is chilled by the value that the ego places on itself." The more libido is being celebrated in society's shop windows, the less it is really able to undergird actual relationships: "The objective dissolution of society is subjectively manifested in the weakening of the erotic urge, no longer able to bind together self-preserving monads" (1974, s.107):

When Casanova [in the eighteenth century] called a woman unprejudiced, he meant that no religious convention prevented her from giving herself; today the unprejudiced woman is the one who no longer believes in love, who will not be hoodwinked into investing more than she can expect in return. ... As the arrangements of life no longer allow time for pleasure conscious of itself, replacing it by the performance of physiological functions, de-inhibited sex is itself de-sexualized. (1974, s.107)[6]

The presence of continuing an ever-renewed exploitation (sexual and otherwise) keeps alive and actualises the memory of violence and forces the individual to adopt the self-protective, calculating utilitarianism of fair and equal exchange of pleasure units. The reality of love under such social conditions destroys love's own basis, abandon:

The experience of pleasure presupposes a limitless readiness to throw oneself away, which is as much beyond women in their fear as men in their arrogance. Not merely the objective possibility, but also the subjective capacity for happiness, can only be achieved in freedom. (1974, s.55).

In a typical move, acknowledging the relevance of bodily history, including our pre-history as animals, Adorno introduces this statement with the observation, or rather the claim, that female animals undergo copulation "in unfreedom, as objects of violence":

> Women have retained a consciousness of this, particularly among the petty bourgeoisie, down to the late industrial era. ... Society constantly casts woman's self-abandon back into the sacrificial situation from which it freed her.

We are thrown back here to the familiar dialectic of bourgeois society: according to its own standards, it makes possible the ability for loving echo and abandon for the first time in human history, but, as it denies these possibilities in the same breath, it destroys not only the potential for transcendence that it provides, but even the basis of actual "experience of pleasure" *tout court*.[7] "No emancipation without that of society" (1974, s.111).

GENITALITY; NATURE

Adorno observed, apparently in the male environs of an English club, that whisky-drinking, cigar-smoking "he-men" despise women because they do not smell of smoke, leather and shaving cream: "In the process of its disintegration, the subject negates everything which is not of its own kind" [*Während das Subjekt zugrunde geht, negiert es alles, was nicht seiner eigenen Art ist*]. To these masochistic men, "repressed homosexuality present[s] itself as the only approved form of heterosexuality" (1974, s. 24).[8] "He-men" are not capable of either.

It appears that thinking about sexuality has always been fundamentally shaped by the obvious but perplexing way in which the sexual act confounds, or burdens, lust with procreation. It is easy to see that lust would tend to inhabit the realm of freedom and spirit, procreation that of necessity and matter. This cannot but reverberate with the social fact that the concepts "man" and "woman" are similarly charged. The conceptual dichotomy of nature and spirit, matter and form is rooted in "the wish to escape nature on which though, one's life depends" (Krahl 1971: 116).[9] It was formulated in Ancient Greece when human domination over nature was not yet complete and irreversible. Spirit is conceived of as pure and identical with itself out of (wishful) denial of the fact that human life and freedom independent of matter and nature are impossible, i.e. denial of the fact of spirit's non-identity with itself. This strategy of denial is bolstered by the attempt to think of society and culture as "anchored in natural [*naturwüchsige*] relationships between humans in order to make the former appear as irreversible and indestructible as the latter." In Platonic philosophy the pleasure principle [*Lustprinzip*] and the procreational act are radically separated: the latter is part of the material, soul-less, non-identical world. In the context of still insecure bourgeois domination, "loving women is a disgrace" (Krahl 1971: 117), a procreational necessity, imposed by the "reality principle," while true love is only homosexual, pederastic love which is not part of the banal procreation of matter. (That men could have non-procreational sex with women did not seem to occur to Plato. The reduction of women to instruments of procreation, and thus their distance from spirit is silently presupposed in this train of thought.) Aristotle, who is more prepared to acknowledge that culture and society need to be mediated with nature, is "well disposed towards heterosexuality." This seems to reflect increased confidence in culture's domination of nature: culture (spirit; men) is now confident enough to admit its dependence on nature (matter; women). Krahl writes that only in the nineteenth century did the equation of truth with identity (the notion of spirit's self-identity as its purity from matter) lose its grip on philosophy. Developed bourgeois society had grown so confident of its domination of nature that it found it safe now to admit (in political economy) that human existence can only be produced in mediation with nature. Paulinian Christianity offered an alternative way of revising the Platonic conception: flesh is "sinful matter" opposed to God's "pure identity in his trinity," the sexual act is "mere duty," a concession to natural necessity that must not provide pleasure. Non-procreational sexuality (i.e. sex for pleasure) is forbidden; in the Christian framework, differing from the Platonic, only God and Jesus (God's son) are entitled to (spiritualised) homosexual as well as pederastic, incestuous embrace in love (not to mention the Holy Spirit, who completes the Trinity). "Through this reorientation ... all eroticism turns in Europe into neurosis, repressed homosexuality"; homosexuality is repressed because it is thought to be pure bliss and is therefore illicit. We mortal sinners don't deserve it.

The crucial contribution of homosexuality to human civilisation lies in its unequivocal assertion of the purposelessness of sexuality. In spite of knowing, it seems to recapture some of the innocence, or naivety, that must have reigned in human sexuality before humans discovered that there was a causal relationship between intercourse and pregnancy. Adorno writes that the homosexual becomes "the portent of a sexuality alienated from its proper purpose" [*Menetekel zweckentfremdeter Sexualität*] (Adorno 1964: 111, 1998: 80). To "alienate" sexuality from its alleged purpose – procreation – is, however, the whole point of its emancipation, and being its "portent" is what gives homosexuality such a prominent place in the debates and struggles about sexuality's "liberation" and "alienation." If, however, the emancipation of sexuality can only mean its alienation from what society claims is its purpose, gender dimorphism, too, loses in the process its real basis.

"Woman as an alleged natural being is a product of history which denaturizes [*denaturiert*] her" (Horkheimer and Adorno 1997: 110–11).[10] "Male logic" (a specific instance of what Adorno describes as "identity logic") refers to women only as representatives of a species that is alleged to represent "nature." Therewith it denies the "naturalness" of any particular woman which consists – to the extent that meaningful use of the term "naturalness" is possible at all – in her individuality, namely any individual's identity against his or her identification (as Adorno would later put it in *Negative Dialectic*). In *Minima Moralia* he writes:

The female character and the ideal of femininity, on which it is modelled, are products of masculine society. ... The female character is a negative imprint of domination. But therefore equally bad. Whatever is in the context of bourgeois delusion called nature, is merely the scar of social mutilation. ... what passes for nature in civilization is by its very substance furthest from all nature... femininity is already the effect of the whip. ... Glorification of the feminine character implies the humiliation of all who bear it. (1974, s. 59)

Oscar Wilde famously remarked in "The Soul of Man under Socialism" that "the only thing that one really knows about human nature is that it changes" (quoted in Weeks 1989: 199); it is in the nature of humans to change their own nature – we are *natura naturans* (active nature) as much as *natura naturata* (nature as created). In the nineteenth-century context, the idea was widespread that what makes human beings human is that they have begun to play with their "natural conditions," "whether one is talking about changing the course of a river or the sexual use of an orifice not naturally 'intended' for the purpose" (Anon. nd: 3). In the modernist context "natural" does not mean "unchangeable" but, on the contrary, the natural may be what humans *can* and *ought* to change, and what they already are in the process of changing. This needs to be kept in mind when reading, for example, Marx's remark, in the *1844 Manuscripts*, that "the most natural relationship between man and man is the relationship between man and woman" (Marx 1992: 347). Marx explains that

the relationship of *man* to *woman* ... *reveals* in a *sensuous* form, reduced to an observable *fact*, the extent to which the human essence has become nature for man or nature has become the human essence for man. It is possible to judge from this relationship the entire level of development of mankind. It follows from the character of this relationship how far *man* as a *species-being*, as *man*, has become himself and grasped himself; ... [it] demonstrates the extent to which man's *natural* behaviour has become *human* or the extent to which his *human* essence has become a *natural* essence for him, the extent to which his *human nature* has become *nature* for him. (Marx 1992: 347)

Marx differentiates here between the *natural* state of "human nature," which is a quasi-pre-civilisational starting point, and the human nature, or human essence that *becomes* in the process of civilisation. He presents the gender relation as its touchstone. This makes clear that the notion that "man" ought to return to an original "human nature" is nothing but reactionary. Human nature – the humane – *ought to become* the nature of the human world, but it exists as yet only as potentiality, and in the pores and interstices of an inhuman reality. The contemporary form of its inhumanity can to a large extent be captured with the concept of the capitalist mode of production. The following remark on the modern concept of nature, made by Marx in an 1862 letter to Engels, is important here:

> It is remarkable how Darwin recognizes among beasts and plants his English society with its divisions of labour, competition, opening up of new markets, "inventions", and the Malthusian "struggle for existence" ... Hobbes's "bellum omnium contra omnes" .... in Darwin the animal kingdom figures as civil society ... (Schmidt 1971: 46)

Darwin reads society into nature, not the other way round. Gilbert Herdt wrote that it has been one of Darwin's basic assumptions "that sexual behaviour served the purposes of reproduction and selective fitness of individuals in evolution" (Herdt 1996: 25). He stresses that "this emphasis on dimorphism reveals a deeper stress on 'reproduction' as a paradigm of science and society." The emphasis on the concept of reproduction points to the predominant role of political economy for nineteenth-century bourgeois thought: "Theorists who followed Darwin's consistent emphasis on reproduction typically viewed sexual selection as an innate and natural property of our own species as well" (Herdt 1966: 26). This view included the idea "that 'male' and 'female' are innate structures in all forms of life, including human beings, and that heterosexuality is the teleologically necessary and highest form of sexual evolution" (Herdt 1966: 27). Even the sex life of flowers was imagined in heterosexual terms.

But the critique of the naturalisation of heterosexuality must avoid the naturalisation of any alternative trajectory. Sartre argued in *Being and Nothingness* that the conception of "libido in need of release" is based on "a category-mistake about human action." Connell paraphrased Sartre's argument as follows:

> We act sexually, we become sexual, but we are not constituted from the start as sexual beings. We are not driven, and we cannot act so as to liberate what is in process of being constituted. The goal of radical politics, therefore, cannot be the 'liberation of sexuality' from social constraint. We can no more liberate libido than we can liberate the square root of minus one. There is no Thing there to liberate. (Connell 1995: 384)

"Sexuality" cannot be liberated, only individuals can liberate themselves from oppression. Connell stresses that such "liberation" would have to be revolutionary, literally, not metaphorically. It requires the overthrow of institutions, it depends on mass actions and it points to a profoundly altered social order. That a real revolution is involved was perfectly clear to women's liberation and gay liberation activists and theorists around 1970, and is exactly what has been lost in the evolution of theory ever since. The early formulas of sexual liberation, which drew their model of power and revolution from a bookish Marxism, were implausible. But they had a sound understanding of the depth of change involved (Connell 1995: 390).[11]

Adorno discussed the connection between the sublimation, integration and genitalisation of sexuality in his essay on "sexual taboos." "[B]ourgeois society coped with the threat posed by the proletariat by integrating it," and likewise it integrated "the sexes," which it institutionalised, domesticated, neutralised and tolerated (Adorno 1964: 100; 1998: 72). "Whatever could not be integrated, the actual spiciness of sex [*das eigentliche sexuelle Aroma*] remains under taboo" (Adorno 1964: 101; 1998: 73). Genital sexuality as the dominant form of sexuality is, according to Freud, the "result of integration" (Adorno 1964: 104). This is an historically specific, impoverished and reduced synthesis of the ensemble of partial libidos and causes the "desexualisation of sexuality" when it makes a taboo, in turn, of the "partial drives" [*Partialtriebe*] (Adorno 1964: 104; 1998: 75). In traditional society, taboos were directed at both the partial drives and genital sexuality. In the context of "formal freedom" taboos take different forms. The most efficient taboo comes in the shape of liberalisation: "sexuality is usurped by an ideal of naturalness, and in a culture of wholesome outdoor living is reduced as much as possible to pure genitality." The liberation in the name of naturalness – nudism is a case in point – "fights back any refinement" (Adorno uses the French *raffinement*) in which the partial drives would have their place (Adorno 1964: 105; 1998: 75–6).

The desublimation of the "partial drives" by the de-genitalisation of sexuality is also central to Mario Mieli's concept of "gay communism." Mieli argued against both the "identities" of hetero- and homosexuality (and also dismissed "bisexuality" as "nothing more than a rather poor conceptual compromise between those"; Mieli 1980: 53ff). If both homo- and heterosexuality are negations of some aspects of life, "gayness" is the negation of the negation. Mieli draws the parallel to communism as the negation of that "automatic monster," capital. The political aim of "gay communism" is general gayness whereby the word flips back into its older and broader meaning: happiness. Gay communism includes "new gay relations between women and men ... different from the traditional couple" (Mieli 1980: 211).[12] The "object of the revolutionary struggle of homosexuals is not that of winning social tolerance for gays, but rather the liberation of the homoerotic desire in every human being" (Mieli 1980: 82). The existence of this desire has most famously been stated by Freud: "in all of us, throughout life, the libido normally oscillates between male and female objects" (Mieli 1980: 23).[13] Repressed homosexual desire is still present, "converted" in many different occasions in which physical contact between members of the same sex is permitted (such as in sport) (Mieli 1980: 123), or where the symbolic more than the actual phallus is celebrated: patriotism and drunkenness, "business partnerships, political rackets, gangs" and the rock star cult, religion ("a universal obsessional neurosis of humanity," partly, to the extent that God-Father figures are being revered, a result of the child's desire for the father) (Mieli 1980: 126, 130, 135).

Like the sons of Freud's mystical primitive father, who after uniting in a homosexual bond find the strength to kill him, but are then overtaken by remorse and establish in memory and substitution for the father the totem, the phallic fetish, so the homosexuals who meet in liberation groups are largely powerless against the attack from the superego that immediately assails them, and find themselves forced to establish in their midst leaders, phallic and charismatic figures who "command" them, personifying the authority of the superego that binds every individual member of the group with a sense of guilt. (Mieli 1980: 111–12)

Mieli's reworking of Freud's "myth" applies to all revolutionary and leftist groups, practically all of which consist mostly of men (unless they consist solely of women) drawn together by some obscure, quasi-Platonic desire (to read, for example) and habitually to kill and reinvent fathers, "phallic and charismatic figures."

The case for revolutionary desublimation is somewhat complicated by the discovery of "repressive desublimation" (Marcuse), by way of which "capital enables the unconscious to 'emerge' in alienated forms, in order to subsume it" (Mieli 1980: 119). Mieli points to voyeurism as "one of the most profitable 'perversions' for capital" (1980: 106).

"Perversion" is sold both wholesale and retail, it is studied, classified, valued, marketed, accepted, discussed. ... It becomes culture, science, printed paper, money ... if for millennia, therefore, societies have repressed the so-called "perverse" components of Eros in order to sublimate them in labour, the present system liberalises these "perversions" with a view to their further exploitation in the economic sphere. (Mieli 1980: 208)

According to Mieli, "perversions" *must* be repressed in order to become liberalised and fetishised into marketable sexual consumer products and liveable "identities."[14]

TWEEDLEDUM; TWEEDLEDEE

"Freedom would be not to choose between black and white but to abjure such prescribed choices," Adorno writes (1974, s. 85). Is there a case for arguing that one could abjure the "prescribed choice" between being male and female? Have "man" and "woman" emerged in history and can they be expected to disappear, too?

The French novelist and theorist Monique Wittig made the probably most powerful claim in that direction, pointing for this purpose to Marx's writing, where dialectical categories

> such as the One and the Other, Master and Slave, were not there to stay and had nothing metaphysical or essential about them, but had to be read and understood in historical terms ... Thus the categories which are today called so solemnly categories of Difference ... were for Marx ... categories of social conflicts – which throughout the class struggle were supposed to destroy each other. (Wittig 1992: 52f)

Failure to question the categories "man" and "woman" impedes the fight for their disappearance. The aim of feminism is to abolish the class "men," thus simultaneously abolishing the class "women," "for there are no slaves without masters" (Wittig 1992: 5). In Wittig's writings, lesbians, "whether they know it or not," are beyond the category of sex, just as the proletariat in Marx's conception is beyond the category of class. Both mean the negation of a negative existence.[15]

> The rise of evangelical religion, Enlightenment political theory, the development of new sorts of public spaces in the eighteenth century, Lockean ideas of marriage as a contract, the cataclysmic possibilities for social change wrought by the French revolution, post-revolutionary conservatism, post-revolutionary feminism, the factory system with its restructuring of the sexual division of labour, the rise of a free market economy in services or commodities, the birth of classes, singly or in combination – none of these things *caused* the making of a new sexed body. Instead, the remaking of the body is itself intrinsic to each of these developments. (Laqueur 1992: 11)

Authors from different backgrounds and persuasions agree that in the late eighteenth century "human sexual nature changed" (in the words of Virginia Woolf, quoted in Laqueur 1992: 3). It was argued that not only were the sexes different, but they were "different in every conceivable aspect of body and soul." Sexual difference was now meant to be a "difference in kind, not degree" (Laqueur 1992: 6).[16] It is in this context that "the discourse on sexual dimorphism begins to shape social theory" (Herdt 1996: 35). Still in the Renaissance context, "no true, deep essential sex ... differentiated cultural man from woman" (Laqueur 1992: 124). The period that developed "claims of the sort that Negroes have stronger, coarser nerves than Europeans because they have smaller brains, and that these facts explain the inferiority of their culture" also came up with the notion that "the uterus naturally disposes woman toward domesticity" (Laqueur 1992: 155).

"Historically, differentiations of gender preceded differentiations of sex" (Laqueur 1992: 62). In pre-eighteenth-century discourses, "the body was far less fixed and far less constrained by categories of biological difference" than thereafter (Laqueur 1992: 106). "In terms of the millennial traditions of western medicine, genitals came to matter as the marks of sexual opposition only last week" (Laqueur 1992: 22). Only the eighteenth century developed the strategy to "escape to a supposed biological substrate" (Laqueur 1992: 8); the teachings of cosmology had no need for biology. The advantage of the older discourse was, though, that it believed that "apart from pleasure nothing of mortal kind comes into existence" (a strange case of wishful thinking). This aphorism (quoted in Laqueur 1992: 3) illustrates the pre-Enlightenment assumption that female orgasm was as necessary for successful conception as the male one. Thanks to this lack of scientific accuracy (subsequently amended by modern medicine), female sexual pleasure still had a place in the logical order of things, although sexuality was (theoretically at least) already subsumed to the notion that its purpose is to produce offspring.[17]

The interpretation of human bodies according to precisely two categories – neither more nor less than two – is logically an outcome of reducing the perception of erogenous zones of the body to those that are functional to reproductive activity: the sexual responsiveness of body areas that are irrelevant for reproduction is denied and may become taboo. These "desexualised" areas are thus made irrelevant to the sexual classification of bodies, too. The concept of "the two sexes," *the one* sex and *the other* sex, is therefore an effect of heterosexuality as a societal norm. In European societies before the modern era, sexuality seems to have been less clearly dichotomised into hetero- and homosexuality. Everybody was assumed – or rather, suspected – to perform homosexual as well as heterosexual acts, the former being variously persecuted and punished. Since the nineteenth century, however, homosexual acts are automatically considered to be expressive of the homosexual nature of the actor, who is no longer considered to be perpetrating sinful homosexual (or rather, "sodomite") acts, but who is "a homosexual", that is, a member of a particular category of human species. The discourse moves from whether, or how, homosexual acts need to be punished to whether the homosexual as such, as a different sort of species, is persecuted, psychiatrised or tolerated.[18] Just as "race" is assumed to determine automatically and spontaneously the racialised individual, "sex" is understood as specific and irreducible urgency. Sex and race are extra-historical essences underlying a species' essence. Whatever the meaning of sex may once have been, in modern society sex, like race, becomes essence.

As Connell writes, the abolition of "the linking of fields of social practice to the reproductive division" would mean that sexual difference would be simply a complementary function in reproduction, not a cosmic division or a social fate. There would be no reason for this to structure emotional relationships, so the categories heterosexual and homosexual would become insignificant (Connell 1987: 287).

What Ernest Renan claimed for nationality is true also for the imposition of dichotomous sex: it has to appear as a "daily plebiscite," but simultaneously as something one has always been, something one has actively forgotten to have become and in how cruel a way one has become so (Renan 1990: 19). The violent history of the shaping of the object "no longer appears with that object. Hence, 'sex' is the reality-effect of a violent process that is concealed by that very effect" (Butler 1987: 135) – in other words, what Adorno, following Marx, would have called a fetish.

In a society based on separation and isolation of atomised individuals who are unhappily chained together only on the basis of a set of neurotic projections (nation, religion, etc.), as well as the practices and institutions that undergird them, it seems unsurprising that Tweedledee will occasionally, perhaps increasingly, have sex without the involvement of Tweedledum, or even of another Tweedledee. Although this tendency must be expected within the dialectic of bourgeois society, it makes its defenders and therapists turn to their Adam Smith problem: masturbation threatens the healthy measure of neurosis that we call social cohesion. It has been vilified by bourgeois society as an anti-social form of subject–object identity[19] that counters heterosexuality and bypasses, or makes irrelevant, the holy cow of sexual dimorphism. The power of the taboo on "the solitary vice" can be read from how strongly it features even in the thinking of bourgeois society's most radical progressives. Richard Carlile, editor of Tom Paine's works and of the "Red Republican," unleashed in *Every Woman's Book or What is Love etc.* (1828) a "sustained attack on conventional sexual morality," advocating birth control and "Temples of Venus" for the "controlled, healthy, extramarital satisfaction of female desire" (Laqueur 1992: 229). In doing so he was, according to Laqueur, motivated by promoting "the natural and healthy commerce between the sexes," which also led him to a particularly "shrill" rejection of masturbation. His concern was a moral one: the "solitary vice" is a vice precisely because it is *solitary*.

> The debate over masturbation that raged from the eighteenth century on might therefore be understood as part of the more general debate about the unleashing of desire in a commercial economy and about the possibilities of human community in these circumstances. (Laqueur 1992)

Laqueur refers to this as a "sexual version" of the classic Adam Smith problem: without actually challenging the principles of the capitalist mode of production, which manifestly produces egoistic, calculating, monadic individuals: how can I make sure that the degree of community necessary for its functioning reproduces itself spontaneously and continuously (that is, without an overtly Hobbesian, Leviathan-type state)? This question which haunted

Smith has never lost anything of its near-universal grip on liberal thought in the widest sense of the word.

A parallel case is the discourse on prostitution, which, like masturbation, was declared to be a core anti-social evil for the first time in the nineteenth century (Laqueur 1992: 230). The modern obsession with campaigning against prostitution is grounded in seeing it as "a confusion between the dangerously asocial world of commercial exchange and the healthy social world of married love" (Laqueur 1992: 231). Laqueur draws a surprising parallel here between the nineteenth-century discourse on prostitution and the twelfth-century papal campaign against usury (which subsequently re-emerged in the various forms of modern anti-Semitism), an early "response to a nascent market economy." The church hierarchy, basing itself on Thomist philosophy, denounced the "usurious" charging of interest because "nothing real is gained by it." In Thomist Catholicism, the usurer's capital is illegitimate because it is generated in the sphere of circulation only: it does not come from productive (which in this context means first of all agricultural) labour. Laqueur points out that the same pattern of argument is directed in the nineteenth century against prostitution: money earned from prostitution is illegitimate money since "nothing is produced." Like usury, prostitution is "pure exchange" (Laqueur 1992: 231–2); like homosexuality, it is unproductive and purposeless. The concern with social cohesion and a clean separation of the sphere of exchange from that of love, privacy, etc. collides in the case of prostitution with the tendency of commodity relations to "really subsume" all aspects of life. Bourgeois society cannot consistently maintain that value-production is the only value it respects; it has to try to maintain values (family life, heterosexual love, parental affection, etc.) that are undermined by the production of value. Laqueur does not make any such references here, nor does he develop the theoretical implications of what he is describing, but his attempt to think antisemitism and sexuality together within the framework of a critique of the concept of production resonates with the thrust of *Dialectic of Enlightenment*.

SUBSTANCE; SUBSUMPTION

Adorno quotes in *Negative Dialectic* a passage from Hegel's *Rechtsphilosophie* in which Hegel gives eloquent expression to one of the fundamental paradoxes at the core of the concept of the modern state:

> It is downright essential that, although the constitution originated in time, it not be viewed as a product; for it is that, rather, which is flatly in and for itself, and is therefore to be considered divine and enduring and above the sphere of that which is produced. (quoted in Adorno 1990: 356; 1966: 349f)[20]

Adorno points out that what Hegel is describing here is affirmatively what Marx later would describe critically as fetishism. Hegel's observation that the state (represented here, *pars pro toto*, by its constitution) must appear as if it was not the artefact that everybody knows it to be, reappears in many disguises in many different, but related discourses: it is behind Renan's famous assertion that "one has to have forgotten" the many cruelties that were necessary for the nation, the great peacemaker that is so central to bourgeois political thought, to be built; or else, in Simone de Beauvoir's assertion that "being" a woman means "becoming" what one (supposedly) has been all along. When Hegel pointed to the daily reading of a particular newspaper as one of the reiterative acts that produce what looks like it has always been there,[21] the same can be said of Renan's "daily plebiscites" and Butler's daily acts of "performative reiteration" that produce the (real) illusion of sex. Marx's concept of "fetishism" is the tool to unpack all of the above.

It should be pointed out, however, that race and sex implications do not wilfully need to be inferred in the concept; they have been present there all along. The German philologist F. Max Mueller complained in a lecture of 1878 that "the very theory" of fetishism was at the time so widely debated in a whole range of discourses that it had itself become "a kind of scientific fetish" (Pettinger 1993: 90). Marx reflected the fetishism of fetishism in his own adoption of the concept. The word itself – related and similar in

meaning to "artefact," something that has been made, a product
– had in the Middle Ages referred to popular talismans, which
were heretical and illegal devices. The early Portuguese explorers
and colonialists employed the term to describe "the charms worn
by peoples encountered on the West African coast" (Pettinger
1993: 87), identifying the undesirable habits of savages at home
and in the colonies by referring to them with the same word. In
a text from 1704, a Dutch West Indies official, Willem Bosman,
reported that colonial subjects had massacred hogs after a hog
had eaten a snake, which happened to be the chief fetish of the
respective region (Pettinger 1993: 88). This enlightened gentleman
disapproved strongly of such uneconomic behaviour by which
"the real, commercial, value of things is obscured by a sentimental
respect of certain animals." By the middle of the nineteenth century,
"fetishism" had become increasingly racialised and denoted, in
the words of the anthropologist Edward B. Tyler, "the one-sided
logic of the barbarian" (Pettinger 1993: 84). But it did not escape
bourgeois scholarship that there was fetishism at home, too. Tyler
himself pointed to collecting "scarce postage stamps or queer
walking sticks" as the Englishman's own fetish. The point is,
however, that European fetishes were thought of as eccentricities
or anachronistic superstitions, whereas the mind of the savage was
constituted by fetishism. In 1888 the French psychologist Alfred
Binet introduced the concept of fetishism into the discourse on
sexuality. Binet referred to "degenerates who experienced intense
genital excitation from the contemplation of certain objects which
would leave any normal person completely unaffected" (Pettinger
1993: 85).[22] Thus throughout its evolution, from the heretic via
the savage to the sexual pervert, the concept of fetishism serves
bourgeois society (whether emerging or established) to denote what
it thinks it most definitely is not. The rhetorical power of Marx's
adoption of the term lies in its ironic inversion: in Marx, fetishism is
not the exception or the anachronism, but the truth and the essence
of modern bourgeois society. (The half-developed form of Marx's
concept, clearly revealing its origins, is evident in an article from
October 1842 in which Marx ridicules a debate in the Rhenish
Diet on a law concerning the theft of wood, conducted blatantly in

the interest of the aristocratic owners of the forests. Marx argues that the social and legal rights of human beings are sacrificed to the "wooden idols" [Marx 1975: 226]. In his conclusions, he turns the concept of the fetish against the provincial assembly, explicitly drawing on the colonial implications of the concept:

> The *savages of Cuba* held gold to be the *fetish of the Spaniards*. They held a celebration in its honours and then dumped it into the sea. Had the savages of Cuba attended the meeting of the Rhenish provincial estates, would they not have held the wood to be the fetish of the Rhinelanders? But they would have gathered from the following meeting that the Rhinelandish fetishism is to the service of animals, and the savages of Cuba would have dumped the rabbits into the sea in order to save the humans. [Marx 1975: 147])[23]

One commodity can stand in for other commodities only because it is a product of labour. The equivalent form represents the abstract labour that has "gone into it." The product of concrete labour is thereby reduced to being the form of appearance of a quantity of abstract labour, which assumes a somewhat higher form of realness: the abstraction becomes the essence, or the soul, of the concrete, from which it has been abstracted in the first place. It is on the basis of this "essentialism," as it were (not Marx's term), that "despite its buttoned-up appearance, the linen recognises in [the coat] a splendid, kindred soul, the soul of value" (Marx 1990: 143).

Marx draws another parallel: a king is a king only "because other men stand in a relation of subjects to him. They, on the other hand, imagine that they are subjects because he is king" (Marx 1990: 149). "King" is a social relation (actors say: "the king is always played by the others"). "King" is not the "being" (essence) of the person who is king, but it is the set of effects that constitute the relations between the king and the subjects. The normal behaviour of loyal subjects is that they reify, or essentialise, the kingness of the king and behave as if the king's kingness was the cause of their subjectness. Fetishism means (among other things) that a relational category is transfigured into an essential category: something that "really" consists in relations between people is presented as, and to some extent "really" becomes, an "essential," intrinsic and spontaneous characteristic of a thing, which in turn becomes the mere carrier of that essence.

At the very moment in history when the execution of the French king opened the door to a "society of equals," human groups came to be seen as formed by an irreversible "*diktat* of nature," which made "groups into fetishes, frozen into some intrinsic form of being" which was said to possess immutable, homogeneous qualities (Guillaumin 1995: 56, 63). The traditional idea of "the one great society of Man, ... subject to and contrasted with God" was replaced by the scientific conceptions of many different groups "scattered through time and space." Modern society created the individual as freed from estate and hierarchy (as well as from the means of subsistence) and placed him and her into the chains of somato-genetic determinism (Guillaumin 1995: 72). This argument, developed by Colette Guillaumin with both race and sex in mind, can help to ground historically the more generic critique of "essentialism" and "identity." Contemporary concepts of sexual, cultural, racial, ethnic, national or whatever such identity bear their eighteenth-century mark in assuming that social groups have an intrinsic essence and relate to other such groups only secondarily and accidentally, like Leibnizian monads: the ensemble of social relations is external to the essence of the group. History is outside essence, essence outside history. Whereas "black" skin colour had initially merely been the (arbitrary) sign of a particular social position (slavery), it was subsequently reinterpreted as the cause of that social relation (Guillaumin 1995: 142): initially, people in the areas where slaves could be made comfortably and with a healthy profit just happened to be black, later it appeared that they were slaves *because* they were black (at which point their black skin stood in for their racial essence which also coloured their souls). In what Guillaumin calls "endogenous determinism," the mark is more than just an (arbitrary) mark: it is an expression of the nature of the object. A particular nature is "directly productive of a social practice" and of social relations. Essence produces appearance without mediation and outside inflection; it is spontaneous nature. A social group is imagined to possess an invariant *substance* that is handed down through the generations. This essentialism, or "endodeterminism," is not an accidental case of "false consciousness." The point is that the individual is *really* made into a mere example of a category, a "class," imagined as a substantial entity possessing an essence that seems to determine spontaneously, from its own, the individual's inherent finality. The essence of the "class" is also the essence or identity of all that fall into it (although at the same time it never is).

The members of a modern race are an undifferentiated mass, an agglomeration of contemporaries juxtaposed in space, or, as journalists and politicians hunting immigrants love to put it, drops in an enormous tidal wave. All drops in a tidal wave are identical, and in their reducibility to a common abstract essence (water; race) they resemble the mass accumulation of commodities that constitutes capital. The monadic members of a race share their racial essence just like the modern masses of commodities share the quality of being carriers of value (the soul of the coat, in Marx's image). Furthermore, the racialised individual is characterised by the same precarious dialectic between identity (racial essence: obnoxious) and difference (individual appearance: sometimes acceptable or at least useful). This is what makes racism modern, a product typical of democratic and individualist society.[24] Guillaumin argues that "woman" refers to just such a "class" or category. Monique Wittig writes in the same spirit that while the declaration of colour has come to be considered discriminatory, the declaration of sex still goes unchallenged: one has widely stopped calling certain people "Negroes" but one continues calling certain people "Women" (Wittig 1992: 199f). Likewise, Connell writes:

> While homosexual behaviour of some kind may be universal, this does not automatically entail the existence of self-identified or publicly labelled "homosexuals". … "the homosexual" represents the modern definition of a new type of adult male. (Connell 1987: 147f)

This argument reflects Foucault's observation that, whereas "sodomy" had been a category of forbidden acts perpetrated by any human being as a sin that would or would not lead that person to the stake, the modern homosexual is a species that needs special treatment, involving experts ranging from social workers and psychiatrists to the concentration camp warden (Foucault 1979: 43).[25] The homosexual act counts not as an occasional sin but as expressive of the compulsive nature, the identity of the actor. The replacement of essence for sin may lead to more lenient or harsher treatment. Foucault and Mieli make virtually the same case that sex is an effect of social relations and practices, which come to be treated as an essence, a natural, transhistorical drive or urge. The fetishistic concept of sexuality lies at the pivot of the transformation of the family and the modern, normalising state and its racist practices. Within one and the same process, the automatic monster's (i.e. capital's) subsumption of the entire human life process normalises sexuality into sexual identities, "samenesses," a fetishistic process of negation and reduction.[26] The division of the social world into apparently autonomous spheres seems particularly crucial to this process: "the division of the public and domestic spheres," itself "a product of the expansion of marketised social relations and the liberal state," has "superimposed these increasingly polarized functions on traditional notions of gender relations" (Paige 2000: 15).[27]

The critique of essence-as-identity, and its underlying link to the historic process of "real subsumption," fundamental to otherwise rather different intellectual traditions, lies at the bottom also of Horkheimer's early critique of "sociology of knowledge" (as in Mannheim) which was a defining element in his formulation of the framework of critical theory:

> Marx correctly sought to do away with the conviction that there is some essence of being which pervades all epochs and societies and lends them their meaning. It was precisely this element of Hegelian philosophy that appeared to him to be an idealist delusion. Only human beings themselves – not the "essence" of humanity, but the real human beings in a definite historical moment, dependent upon each other and upon outer and inner nature – are the acting and suffering subjects of history. (Horkheimer 1993: 138f; 1981: 22)

But "the irrational ends of bourgeois society could hardly have been stabilized by other than effective irrational means" (Adorno 1990: 333).

MEN; THINGS

Sexuality, reduced to a crystallized social and intellectual essence, achieves the final spoliation of everyday life and that is its contribution to terrorism.
(Lefèbvre 1971: 172)

"If men no longer had to equate themselves with things, they would need neither a thing-like superstructure nor an invariant picture of themselves, after the model of things" (Adorno 1990: 95; 1966: 103). The "reduction of human labour to the abstract universal concept of average working hours" is "fundamentally akin to the principle of identification" (Adorno 1990: 146; 1966: 149): it makes "nonidentical individuals and performances become commensurable and identical." Just as "the concrete types of human labour are dissolved into abstract human labour as the creator of value," so also all "concrete peculiarities which distinguish one representative of the *genus homo sapiens* from another dissolve into the abstraction of man in general, man as a legal subject" (Pashukanis 1989: 113). In compensation for having become "slavishly dependent," the subject acquires under modern conditions a "rare gift," in Pashukanis's words: "a will, juridically constituted, which makes him absolutely free and equal to other owners of commodities like himself." Poor bourgeois subject: you think it unfair that not all individuals own equal numbers of slaves, factories, wives, acres, i-pods etc.? Don't despair; there is consolation: "everyone possesses *his own* body as the free tool of his will," as Fichte, expanding on Locke's conception of property, pointed out (Pashukanis 1989: 114). Fichte's notion that I own my own body as a tool also resonates with Descartes' concept of the thinking subject as radically separate from "his" (or her) body, and the fact that the owner of the tool can change this tool, make it fit better any given purpose or order, brings us back to de Beauvoir's central problem of the "becoming" of the subject, the problem of the human potential to transcend and reinvent – or rearticulate – the body, and the debate around Wittig, Butler and others that sprung from it.

Pashukanis describes a specific "legal fetishism" that complements commodity fetishism. He writes that "the social relations of production ...[on the one hand] appear as relations between things ... and on the other, as relations between the wills of autonomous entities equal to each other – of legal subjects" (1989: 117). While this is merely a restatement of the classic problem of free will and determination – in sociological language, agency and structure – Pashukanis points to the specifically capitalist form of what he calls the legal subject: legal subjectivity in the modern, bourgeois sense of the word is abstracted from every concrete claim, whereas in the feudal context, every right was a privilege.

> Only in commodity production ... does the general capacity to possess a right become distinguished from concrete legal claims. Only the continual reshuffling of values in the market creates the idea of a fixed bearer of such rights. (Pashukanis 1989: 118)

The abstraction from concrete claims is possible only through the everyday experience that the commodity-owner "changes roles instantaneously from claimant to debtor." The seller of a commodity, even if it is "only" labour-power, will be the buyer of another commodity in the next instant. The worker who spent the day in the factory may command the services of another wage-worker in the evening. This modern fluidity in the concrete makes possible and engenders the idea of the abstract, fixed, unalienable subject "as the bearer of every imaginable legal claim" (Pashukanis 1989: 118). It is *because* relationships are fluid that they are frozen solid, and only because of their frozenness (their "buttoned-up appearance") that they can make a claim to equality (their "universal soul"):

> The idea of the worth and in principle equal worth of the personality has a long history. It made the transition from Stoic philosophy to being employed by Roman jurists, went from there to the dogma of the Christian

church, and thence to the doctrine of natural law. ... But regardless of the various forms this idea may have assumed, it expresses nothing but the fact that, as soon as the products of labour are exchanged as commodities, the different concrete types of socially useful labour are deduced to labour in the abstract. In all other relations, people's dissimilarity (sexual or class-determined) is so conspicuously apparent in the course of history that one is amazed ... by the fact that, before Marx, no one had looked into the historical causes which produced this bias of natural law. For if, over the centuries, human thinking has returned with such persistence to the proposition that people are equal, and has elaborated this proposition in a thousand variations, then there must have been some objective reality behind it. (Pashukanis 1989: 152–3)

This reality is the exchange of commodities, for millennia an affair that barely affected most people but that in the modern period has come to constitute all of human society. But "Man is not only what he was and is, but equally what he can come to be" (Adorno 1990: 51; 1966: 61):

We cannot say what man is. Man today ... drags along with him as his social heritage the mutilations inflicted upon him over thousands of years. To decipher the human essence by the way it is now would sabotage its possibility. (Adorno 1990: 124; 1966: 130)

The reasonable form of society in which "men" no longer have "to equate themselves with things" will bring about that other modernity in which identity will be freed from the ice of identification: The remnants of a division of labour which the radical curtailment of working hours might leave in society would lose the horror of shaping the individuals throughout (Adorno 1990: 278f; 1966: 275).

In "The Essay as Form," Adorno referred to "the leisure of the child-like person" [die Muße des Kindlichen] as a defining feature of the essay, probably Adorno's most characteristic form of writing (Adorno 1991: 4; 1963: 11). Life in a reasonable society will be more like an essay than a treatise and will accommodate plenty of childlike leisure. However, as always, and an extra bit more clear-sighted than fellow theorists like Marcuse or Benjamin,

Adorno stops short of endorsing even the idea of "the leisure of the child-like person": in the crucial section 150 of *Minima Moralia*, Adorno warns that the advocacy of a readmission of the partial drives, an element of becoming childlike, is a crucial part of modernity *as it is*, and while the pluralism of the partial drives (as represented in Baudelaire's writings which for Adorno illustrate this issue) clearly has his sympathies, he warns that their embrace must not mean regression. The "idea of modernity," according to Baudelaire, contains the false promise that the self-destruction of "the monism of bourgeois reason" was modernity's hope. It produces, though, merely pluralism as a "many-coloured *fata morgana*," responding to the partial drives of the child. Likewise, the cult of "sensation," of immediate perception of the allegedly new (including the "craving for headlines" and other addictions), is merely a helpless response to the fact that capitalist modernity means monotony, identity and neurotic, compulsive repetition more than anything else. It effects the "decomposition of the subject" and "drains all firmness from characters." Ego-weakness, faithlessness and "pathic subservience to situations," though, will not beat the system (Adorno 1974, s.150).

Two complementary and indirectly related explanations for the emergence of the modern concept of sexual binarism are evident: one, more "macro" as it were, sees it as an effect, reflection or expression of the public/private divide, that is, the carving up of the social world into supposedly, but never actually, independent spheres, the other, more "micro," as an effect, reflection or expression of the imposition of near-exclusive genital sexuality, which in turn is part of the larger disciplining effort that created the modern subject. The domestication of the partial drives in the form of genital organisation of sexuality, capital's precarious insurance policy against its subjects' regression into childlike leisure, created the modern form of the idea that there are exactly two sexes, men and women, and that "being" one or the other organises and shapes every aspect of any individual human being. The trajectory to a reasonable form of society (or rather, a state of things after and beyond the fetishes of society, state and individual) would have to include the critique of the genital organisation of sexuality. The importance of homosexuality in this context is that it tends to be less strictly genitally organised for the obvious reason that it is not subordinated to what counts for society as the functional purpose of sexuality, procreation, although it can still, of course, be equally subordinated to social reproduction in a wider sense (i.e. beyond the reproduction of working bodies: hence legal-ideological phenomena such as gay marriage, etc.).

All aspects of modern bourgeois subjectivity are intrinsic aspects of one ensemble of social relations, the capitalist mode of production that can only be overcome *as* an ensemble. The society of identity has a belly (as it is still the old monster the Leviathan, in different clothes), and can always find reasons why some particular element of non-identity needs to be devoured. To the same extent to which the normal, banal, cool racism that is implicit in the nation-form does every now and again turn hot, the heterosexual world of two sexes may occasionally indulge in some gay-bashing, however respectable homosexuality-as-an-identity may have become. Because the non-identical is never completely accommodated in any identity, neither the homosexual nor the heterosexual is completely safe from rushes of gayness, the dissolution of "sexuality," just like no "historical compromise" and social-democratic national regime can ever completely eradicate rushes of proletarian-ness, the dissolution of class. All aspects of the capitalist regime remain precarious. The good news is that there is room for anti-politics, everywhere, always.

NOTES

1. "In marriage, Christianity transfigured the hierarchy of the sexes, the yoke that the male organization of property had put on the female character, as a union of hearts, thus assuaging the reminiscence of sexuality's better pre-patriarchal past" (Adorno and Horkheimer 1971: 96; 1997: 107; 2002: 83–4). Marriage was thus the legal expression of a kind of historical compromise between the sexes which has now become dispensable to some extent.
2. English (and hyphenation) in the original text
3. The actual quote reads: "to be a well-favoured man is the gift of fortune; but reading and writing comes by nature" (from *Much Ado*

About Nothing, III. 3; the line is delivered by Constable Dogberry, one of Shakespeare's great clown characters). The German translation quoted by Marx reads: "Ein gut aussehender Mann zu sein ist eine Gabe der Umstände, aber lesen und schreiben zu können kommt von Natur" (Marx 1993: 98); "favour" is used to mean "appearance" on several occasions in Shakespeare.

4. Mario Mieli lived as a student in London in 1970–1. He was an activist in the British Gay Liberation Front before he moved back to Italy and helped found the radical gay organisation *FUORI!* In 1977, his book *Homosexuality and Liberation* was published in Italian in Turin, and in 1980, in English in London. "Gay Communism," the concluding chapter, was also circulated as a separate booklet (nd, presumably from the late 1980s).

5. An interesting and in many ways powerful dialectic which is central to the topic of this book can be gleaned from the controversial background of this publication. This text was published in a journal of a section of the French *ultra-gauche*, which only a short time later embraced the Holocaust *négationnisme* of Faurisson. A useful discussion of this notorious *affaire* can be found in *La Banquise*, no. 2, 1983 ("le roman de nos origines," www.geocities.com/~johngray/roman17.htm). More recently, *Théorie Communiste*, no. 13 (www.theoriecommuniste.org/TC133.html) made an important contribution to an explanation of the catastrophic drift of a part of the French "ultra-left" into "Holocaust denial" and to defending petty reactionaries: the naïve notion (crucial to modern antisemitism) that an essentially human community is "vampirised" by capitalism into the "false community" of democratic (liberal, atomistic) society and that fighting democracy and liberal society, by any means and in whichever coalition is deemed necessary, should be a communist priority. It is evident that any ideology or movement that claims to liberate the true human community from being "vampirised" can be linked to this idea. (I am grateful for these references to Niels Turnbull.) The case of the French "ultra-left's" tipping over into reaction shows that the decisive difference between critical theory and French "ultra-leftism" is that the former is immunised against naïve, undialectical critiques of liberal democracy by a comprehensive theorisation of antisemitism.

6. Adorno is certainly not pretending to write from anything but a male, heterosexual perspective here; that is, his own.

7. The most programmatic statements on the question of "woman" in *Dialectic of Enlightenment* can be found in the last third of the "Juliette" chapter (Adorno and Horkheimer 1971: 96–107, 1997: 106–19, 2002: 83–93). Adorno and Horkheimer seem to refer

to women primarily "as the representatives of the possibility of exclusion understood as an *escape* from the all-inclusive system of power," their "potential exemption from the totality" (Hewitt 1992: 147). Although the condensed form of their argument relies on making "woman" a *chiffre*, again, despite itself, the notion that the marginalisation of women contains the potential of specific experience and insight, even a utopian element not accessible to those who are fully included/subjected/subjects, is the same that became crucial to modern feminism after de Beauvoir.

8. *Minima Moralia* also includes a number of comments on homosexuality that have been criticised as homophobic by Halle (1995) and Hewitt (1996). (I am grateful to Pr. S. for pointing me to this issue.) The rejection of a conception of socialism as rooted in the virility and fecundity of the proletariat is central to critical theory, which means that if elements of such "traditional," uncritical socialism can be found in critical theory, they must be interpreted and challenged as contrary to its main thrust. Halle and Hewitt make a strong case that Fromm's revision of Freudian theory, and the ways it was adapted by other members of the Institute for Social Research, was homophobic (namely in the conflation of narcissism and homosexuality, either of which are subsequently seen as conditions of Fascism); Adorno's formulation that "totalitarianism and homosexuality belong together" (1974, s. 24), which comes just before the sequence quoted above, indeed seems to reflect the Stalinist canard that Nazis are gay. The latter is of course itself a reflection of the right-wing idea that homosexuals are part of a conspiracy against the family and Western civilisation as well as the socialist tradition of rejecting "unproductive sexuality" (along with anything else that seems "unproductive") (see Hekma, Oosterhuis and Steakley 1995a; Oosterhuis 1995; Herzer 1995). The concept of the "failure" in Freud's notion that homosexuality is based in a "failure to adapt" to the heterosexual, oedipal norm should though, from the perspective of a negative dialectics, be read as an opportunity for emancipation, although, like all other aspects of the disintegration of the bourgeois subject, it can also lead to the opposite of emancipation, that is, to Fascism. It seems that Adorno did not recognise this particular dialectic although Hewitt (1996: 77–8) himself hints at the possibility to read narcissism through negative dialectics.

9. Krahl was one of Adorno's students and highly regarded by him (Claussen 2003: 397). Krahl died in an accident in January 1970, six months after Adorno.

10. Horkheimer and Adorno (2002) translate this as "denatures."

11. Unlike Connell, Mieli occasionally uses an ambivalent rhetoric that implies an underlying, original, trans-historical nature to which we might have recourse via "liberation": for example, in his suggestion to "give life back its human form and essence" (Mieli 1980: 116), or "to (re-)conquer our mysterious underlying being" (Mieli 1980: 119). His *explicit* position is, however, critical: "The struggle to liberate desire, the 'underneath,' is a struggle for the (re-)conquest of life", but this "is not a question of redeeming the noble savage (equally a bourgeois myth), but of releasing our aesthetic and communist potential, our desire for community and for pleasure that has grown latently over the millennia" (Mieli 1980: 169).

12. It is noteworthy that the editor of the English translation added (in 1980) that the gay movement failed to maintain and develop more radical politics such as those expressed by Mieli because it stuck to the concept of a biological sex underlying gender as the latter's "material base," failing to go beyond the (feminist) discussions of the time (Mieli 1980: 12). This is a strong hint that debates in the gay movement had already provided the critique of the sex/gender distinction (e.g. Butler 1990) in the late 1970s, a lead that it would be worthwhile exploring. The following formulation by the early Baudrillard (1981: 99) is also noteworthy: "No being is assigned by nature to a sex. Sexual ambivalence ... must be reduced, for as such it escapes genital organisation and the social order. ... [T]his irreducible reality [must be dispersed] into sexes that are full, distinct and opposed to one another. This structure leans on the alibi of biological organs ... [and] it is pegged to the grandiose cultural models whose function it is to separate the sexes in order to establish the absolute privilege of one over the other."

13. Consider also the following: "Given our original and underlying trans-sexuality, and recognising the polymorphous and 'perverse' disposition of the child to an eroticism that makes no exclusive distinction as to the sex of the object of its libidinal impulse, it is clear that each one of us has a hidden erotic attraction towards the sex that is not (or is scarcely) the focus of our conscious desire" (Mieli 1980: 122).

14. This aspect of Mieli's argument is paralleled by Foucault in the first volume of *History of Sexuality*, which was published roughly at the same time (Foucault 1979).

15. Wittig (more than Mieli) seems to presuppose an essential, ahistoric, non-gendered transsexual human being, which is dichotomised, subjected, sexed only in second place, by society. Butler uses Foucault's critique of 1970s Reichians to make the point that there is no human essence prior to history and society. The most

important point of critique she levels at Wittig would not apply to Mieli to the same extent: "Wittig's radical disjunction between straight and gay replicates the kind of disjunctive binarism that she herself characterizes as the divisive philosophical gesture of the straight mind. ... The ideal of a coherent heterosexuality that Wittig describes as the norm and standard of the heterosexual contract is an impossible ideal, a 'fetish,' as she herself points out" (Butler 1990: 122). The dialectic inherent in Wittig's as well as Mieli's positions (the real-abstract character of fetishised social relations) seems not to be on Butler's radar most of the time.

16. It was not, for example, until 1759 that anyone bothered to reproduce a detailed female skeleton in an anatomy book to illustrate its difference from the male (Laqueur 1992: 10). Until then anatomy books showed one basic structure for the human body – the "male."

17. Laqueur observed that "the erasure of female pleasure from medical accounts of conception took place roughly at the same time as the female body came to be understood no longer as a lesser version of the male's (a one-sex model) but as its incommensurable opposite (a two-sex model). ... Organs that had been seen as interior versions of what the male had outside – the vagina as penis, the uterus as scrotum – were by the eighteenth century construed as of an entirely different nature" (Laqueur 1992: viii).

18. This sums up some of Foucault's argument in the first volume of *History of Sexuality*.

19. A society based on a chain of ceaseless acts of "equivalent"-exchange of non-identical objects can allow subject–object–identity only as a philosophical idea, where it serves as a red herring, confusing those who look for a way out of the exchange totality. In reality there is no such identity.

20. This quote from Hegel is from the end of the section "Weltgeist und Naturgeschichte."

21. Hegel observed that "newspapers serve modern man [sic] as a substitute for morning prayers" (Anderson 1991: 35).

22. The term seems to play only a minor role in Freudian psychoanalysis. Freud discusses fetishism in chapter 2 of the first of the *Three Essays on Theory of Sexuality*, "Sexual Aberrations." Later, fetishism plays a role in the context of the theory of the fear of castration, laid out e.g. in chapter 8 of *An Outline of Psychoanalysis*. Further, there is an essay titled "Fetishism" from 1927.

23. The article as a whole is directed against the particularism not of bourgeois society, but of the provincial aristocracy who subvert and boycott the establishment of general, non-particular, rational law

and the modern (capitalist) nation-state. Marx attacks in this early text the Rhinelandish backwater (his home) for standing in the way of (bourgeois, Prussian) progress.

24. This case has been similarly argued by Etienne Balibar in several of his contributions.

25. That "homosexuality as we know it is a relatively modern institutional complex" was suggested as early as 1968 by Mary McIntosh, then, apparently simultaneously, by Michel Foucault and Jeffrey Weeks in 1977 (Gayle Rubin 1984: 276).

26. Mieli was influenced by Amadeo Bordiga and Jacques Camatte. Mieli took from Camatte's *Il Capitale totale* (1976) the Marxian concept of "real subsumption," an historical process where capital not only subsumes labour in the narrow sense of the word – those activities which are waged labour in capitalism – but also subsumes "the entire human life process" (Mieli 1980: 115). The concept of "real subsumption" is developed in a section of *Capital*, vol. I ("Results of the Immediate Process of Production"), which Marx did not include in the published text; it is published in Marx (1990) as an appendix, where "real subsumption" is defined on pp. 1034–8. In the published text of *Capital*, "real subsumption" is mentioned only once (Marx 1990: 645). Mieli also cites the *Grundrisse* (Marx 1973: 705f), where the concept refers to the processes by which capital subsumes Man's "general productive power ... the development of the social individual." "Real subsumption" leads to new and *specifically* capitalist forms and relations of production, and as such to the capitalist mode of production *sui generis* (Marx 1990: 1035). Capital assumes (apparently) a productive power of its own, which actually is the developed *social* productive power of labour.

27. "Rationality, instrumentality and impersonality" have only in the modern context become "masculine" qualities (Paige 2000: 14). Anthony Fletcher quotes an English publication from 1770 which states that a "new kind of animal, neither male nor female, a thing of neuter gender, lately started up among us ... it talks without meaning, it smiles without pleasantry, it eats without appetite, it rides without exercise, it wenches without passion" (Fletcher 1995: 320, quoted in Paige 2000: 14).

REFERENCES

Adorno, T. W. (1963) *Noten zur Literatur*, Frankfurt, Suhrkamp.
Adorno, T. W. (1964) "Sexualtabus und Recht heute," in *Eingriffe, Neun kritische Modelle*, Frankfurt, Suhrkamp.
Adorno, T. W. (1973) *Aesthetische Theorie*, Frankfurt, Suhrkamp.

Adorno, T. W. (1974) *Minima Moralia, Reflections from Damaged Life.* London, Verso.

Adorno, T. W. (1990) *Negative Dialectics*, London, Routledge.

Adorno, T. W. (1991) *Notes to Literature*, New York, Columbia University Press.

Adorno, T. W. (1994 [1951]) *Minima Moralia, Reflexionen aus dem beschädigten Leben*, Frankfurt, Suhrkamp.

Adorno, T. W. (1998) "Sexual Taboos and Law Today," in *Critical Models, Interventions and Catchwords*, New York, Columbia University Press.

Adorno, T. W. (2002) *Aesthetic Theory*, London, Continuum/Athlone.

Adorno, T. W. and Horkheimer, M. (1971) *Dialektik der Aufklärung, Philosophische Fragmente*, Frankfurt, Fischer.

Adorno, T. W. and Horkheimer, M. (1997) *Dialectic of Enlightenment*, London, Verso.

Adorno, T. W. and Horkheimer, M. (2002) *Dialectic of Enlightenment, Philosophical Fragments*, Stanford, CA, Stanford University Press.

Anderson, B. (1991) *Imagined Communities, Reflections on the Origin and Spread of Nationalism*, London, Verso.

Anon. (1983) "Le roman de nos origines," in *La Banquise*, no. 2, www. geocities.com/~johngray/roman17.htm.

Anon. (nd) "For a world without moral order" (no place indicated), www.geocities.com/CapitolHill/Lobby/3909/moral/. First published in French in *La Banquise*, no. 1, 1983, and in a different, apparently earlier, English translation in *Anarchy*, no. 38, Fall 1993; the French text, "Pour un monde sans morale," can be found at troploin0.free. fr/biblio/moral_fr/].

Balibar, E. (1994) *Masses, Classes, Ideas, Studies on Politics and Philosophy before and after Marx*, London, Routledge.

Balibar, E. and Wallerstein, I. (1991) *Race, Nation, Class*, London, Verso.

Baudrillard, J. (1981) *For a Critique of the Political Economy of the Sign*. New York, Telos Press.

Buck-Morss, S. (1977) *The Origin of Negative Dialectics, Theodor W. Adorno, Walter Benjamin, and the Frankfurt Institute*, New York, Harvester.

Butler, J. (1987) "Variations on sex and gender, Beauvoir, Wittig and Foucault," in S. Benhabib and D. Cornell (eds.), *Feminism as Critique*. Cambridge, Polity Press.

Butler, J. (1990) *Gender Trouble, Feminism and the Subversion of Identity*, London, Routledge.

Claussen, D. (2003) *Theodor W. Adorno, Ein letztes Genie*, Frankfurt, Fischer.

Connell, R. W. (1987) *Gender and Power, Society, the Person and Sexual Politics*, Stanford, CA, Stanford University Press.

Connell, R. W. (1995) "Democracies of pleasure: thoughts on the goals of radical sexual politics," in L. Nicholson, L.and S. Seidman (eds.), *Social Postmodernism, Beyond Identity Politics*, Cambridge, Cambridge University Press.

De Beauvoir, S. (1961) *The Second Sex*, London, Bantam.

Fletcher, A. (1999) *Gender, Sex & Subordination in England 1500–1800*, New Haven, CT and London, Yale University Press.

Foucault, M. (1979) *The History of Sexuality, Vol. I – An Introduction*, London, Penguin Books.

Guillaumin, C. (1995) *Racism, Sexism, Power and Ideology*, London, Routledge.

Halle, R. (1995) "Between Marxism and Psychoanalysis: Antifascism and Antihomosexuality in the Frankfurt School," in G. Hekma, H. Oosterhuis and J. Steakley. (eds.), *Gay Men and the Sexual History of the Political Left*, New York, Harrington Park Press/Haworth Press.

Hegel, G. W. F. (1991) *Elements of the Philosophy of Right*, Cambridge, Cambridge University Press.

Hekma, G., Oosterhuis, H. and Steakley, J. (eds.) (1995) *Gay Men and the Sexual History of the Political Left*, New York, Harrington Park Press/Haworth Press.

Hekma, G., Oosterhuis, H. and Steakley, J. (eds.) (1995a) "Leftist Sexual Politics and Homosexuality: A Historical Overview," in G. Hekma, H. Oosterhuis and J. Steakley (eds.), *Gay Men and the Sexual History of the Political Left*, New York, Harrington Park Press/Haworth Press.

Herdt, G. (1996) "Introduction: Third Sexes and Third Genders," in G. Herdt (ed.), *Third Sex, Third Gender, Beyond Sexual Dimorphism in Culture and History*, New York, Zone Books.

Herzer, M. (1995) "Communists, Social Democrats, and the homosexual movement in the Weimar Republic," in G. Hekma, H. Oosterhuis and J. Steakley (eds.), *Gay Men and the Sexual History of the Political Left*, New York, Harrington Park Press/Haworth Press.

Hewitt, A. (1992), "A Feminine Dialectic of Enlightenment? Horkheimer and Adorno Revisited," in *New German Critique*, no. 56, Special Issue on Theodor W. Adorno.

Hewitt, A. (1996) *Political Inversions, Homosexuality, Fascism, and the Modernist Imaginary*, Stanford, CA, Stanford University Press.

Horkheimer, M. (1981) "Ein neuer Ideologiebegriff?" in M. Horkheimer, *Sozialphilosophische Schriften*, Frankfurt, Fischer.

Horkheimer, M. (1988) "Kritische und Traditionelle Theorie," in *Gesammelte Werke,* vol. IV. Frankfurt, Fischer.

Horkheimer, M. (1993) *Between Philosophy and Social Science, Selected Early Writings.* Cambridge, MA, MIT Press.

Horkheimer, M. (1972 [1937]) "Traditional and Critical Theory," in *Critical Theory, Selected Essays,* New York, Continuum.

Karamazov, D. (1998) *The Poverty of Feminism,* London, Elephant Editions. First published in *La Guerre Sociale* (1977) as "Misère du feminisme."

Krahl, H. J. (1971) "Ontologie und Eros – zur spekulativen Deduktion der Homosexualität," in *Konstitution und Klassenkampf, Zur historischen Dialektik von bürgerlicher Emanzipation und proletarischer Revolution,* Frankfurt, Verlag Neue Kritik.

Laqueur, T. (1992) *Making Sex, Body and Gender from the Greeks to Freud,* Cambridge, MA, Harvard University Press.

Lefebvre, H. (1971) *Everyday Life in the Modern World,* London, Allen Lane, Penguin Books.

Marx, K. (1973) *Grundrisse,* London, Penguin Books.

Marx, K. (1975) "Debates on the Law of Thefts of Wood," in *MECW* 1, London, Lawrence & Wishart.

Marx, K. (1990) *Capital,* vol. 1. London. Penguin Books.

Marx, K. (1992) *Early Writings,* London, Penguin Books.

Marx, K. (1993) *Das Kapital,* vol. 1, *MEW 23.* Berlin, Dietz.

Mieli, M. (1980) *Homosexuality and Liberation, Elements of a Gay Critique,* London, Gay Men's Press.

Oosterhuis, H. (1995) "The 'Jews' of the Antifascist Left: Homosexuality and Socialist Resistance to Nazism," in G. Hekma, H. Oosterhuis, and J. Steakley. (eds.), *Gay Men and the Sexual History of the Political Left,* New York, Harrington Park Press/Haworth Press.

Paige, J. M. (2000) "Abstract Subjects: 'Class,' 'Race,' 'Gender,' and 'Modernity'." Draft, 3 January 2000, www.sscnet.ucla.edu/soc/groups/ccsa/paige.PDF.

Pashukanis, E. B. (1989) *Law & Marxism, A General Theory,* London, Pluto.

Pettinger, A. (1993) "Why Fetish?" in *New Formations,* no. 19.

Renan, E. (1990) "What is a Nation?" in H. K. Bhabha (ed.), *Nation and Narration,* London, Routledge.

Rubin, G. (1984) "Thinking Sex: Notes for a Radical Theory of the Politics of Sexuality," in C. Vance (ed.), *Pleasure and Danger, Exploring Female Sexuality,* London, Routledge.

Schmidt, A. (1971) *The Concept of Nature in Marx,* London, New Left Books.

Théorie Communiste (nd) "L'ultra gauche, le négationnisme, et le démocratisme radical," in *Théorie Communiste*, no. 13, www.theoriecommuniste.org/TC133.html.

Weeks, J. (1989) *Sexual Politics and Society, The Regulation of Sexuality since 1800*, London, Longman.

Wittig, M. (1992) *The Straight Mind and Other Essays*, New York, Harvester.

10

SOLIDARITY WITH THE FALL OF METAPHYSICS: NEGATIVITY AND HOPE

Fernando Matamoros *

> It is you, metaphysical entity of places,
> who lull children to sleep,
> it is you who people their dreams
>   Louis Aragon

INTRODUCTION

This chapter approaches certain digressions of the concept of metaphysics. With negativity as hope, it aims to go beyond the established truths of society. With the possibility of theory as political action for liberation, we try to rescue the dimensions of the *incomplete human*. We do not offer absolute answers, but rather multiple questions on metaphysics, beyond the academic, political and institutional character of authorised action. We do not stray into metaphysics in order to philosophically restore a mythical, academic or linguistic *origin* of the concept; on the contrary, we highlight the constitutive and practical moments of critical thought inside the concept itself: times of social struggles and words as constellations. We could say that, like *God*, *metaphysics* as a conceptual object is the geometric centre of the discordant and antagonistic time of contradictory and concurrent standpoints. In this sense, the social significances in the meaning of metaphysics are made up of external and internal realities. Indeed, the concept is mediated by human substances and class struggle, along with the ideas-essences of thoughts referring to the representations, signs and symbols of life's specific experiences and practices. Metaphysics covers a critical and reflexive moment of thought that thinks that which is thought, *physis*, what is real from the truth of experience and its sufferings. Paraphrasing Benjamin, the concept *is not empty or homogeneous*; it is mediated by what can be interpreted, what can be comprehended from experience through substance and essence: critical thought and praxis of the subject. Also, founded on what is thought, there is a moment which has become a reflection and possibility for critical and political thought on utopia and ontology, it is the *Metá*, what *is beyond* the comprehension which is determined by the concept, the non-identical and the non-truth, the encounter of the desired as a possibility of critique in the praxis of liberation.

I

It is difficult to question or formulate problems surrounding metaphysics, even more so when the intellectual and rational definitions of common materialism have qualified it as nonexistent, as speculations of ideas, intellectual moralities of a *God* without subjects. However, according to Adorno (2000: 1), if the concept of *metaphysics* and its paradigms are hard to understand, negative dialectics is manifested in the very existence of the identical of the nominalist concept, *physis*. We believe the order of the chapters in *Negative Dialectics* is not a matter of chance. Negativity, non-identity and metaphysics are the central mediations in the preoccupations of the philosophical (metaphysical) object in the context of the dialectical and identity-negating work expounded by Adorno.

II

In the Preface to the French translation of the courses on *Metaphysics, Concept and Problems* (Adorno 2000), Christophe David asserts that this concept is used by Adorno to trace the critique and negativity of the singular in the particular-identical, which characterises the rationality of power, which, in its turn, is protected by the objectivity of the non-identical, the negativity expressed in singularity. He also highlights the importance of the concept of metaphysics as a constellation of Adorno's experiences, war and death programmed on the basis of identity (*Auschwitz*), just as the 1951 reflections in *Minima Moralia. Reflections on a Damaged Life* is part of the metaphysical inflections inscribed in *Negative Dialectics*. These courses indicate the problems of ontological and dialectical reasoning surrounding the concept. In order to go politically beyond the nominalist conditioning of philosophy and sociology, David asserts that these courses on metaphysics are the centre of reflections and inflections, the very core of *Negative Dialectics*. It is no longer about Aristotle and his metaphysics, or about Hegel with his totality of the *Idea* and the *Being* as dialectical synthesis, but about stressing that at the heart of metaphysics can be found the times of *desire* and *knowledge* (experience and critique of the poverty or misery in the world), another possibility to see the *praxis* of *desire* in action and politics: *to save* the critique crushed by the concept of the existent (see chapter 1 of *Negative Dialectics*, "The Ontological Need"). It is worth stressing that this *constellation* in metaphysics or negativity as metaphysics is inscribed in Adorno's thought as rescue, salvation or *redemption* (Benjamin, *Thesis on the Philosophy of History*). Indeed, the "meditations on metaphysics" and culture in the third section of the last chapter of *Negative Dialectics* are not left to chance. The courses on metaphysics were a laboratory of reflection and of the salvation of non-identity, what David (2006) would call *Minima Metafísica*. So, recourse to metaphysics offers an opportunity to save and redeem the sufferings of the past; to think of the possibilities of metaphysics in our own discursive context of knowledge and dialectics, to update the revolution in constellation. It is a critique as *politics*, a possibility of saving critique by acting on the limits of the factual and concrete dimensions of the rationalised world of democracy and its freedom.

III

From *Mínima Moralia* (1951) to *Negative Dialectics* (1966), two years after his courses on *Metaphysics*, we find that the spirit of critique as the salvation of culture is the link between his analyses on the pain of the world. For Adorno, to save *culture* entails emancipating the metaphysics that makes it live as a human essence. Thus, his dialectical analysis of the ontology of the world, the first part of *Negative Dialectics*, emphasises the links, nexus, bridges of critical history that, although secularised, burst in on the crisis of the concept and the ontology of the Being. In other words, as we shall see, in the face of the concretisation of the *index veri* of horror rendered source of catastrophe (where all arbitrariness, corruption and putrefaction are born), metaphysical meditation forbids closing the idealisation of the teleological origin of the concept, for nothing, or almost nothing, is left of metaphysics in the history of the victorious. On the contrary, it is from the *minimum* of metaphysics that remains to us in the *damaged life* of the *Physis* made from pain that we can once again rebel. From what can be called life, the static of the media lie, war and death as extensions of a politics made secure without utopia, without God and without metaphysics in the real space of hegemony and power, Adorno's critical proposal offers us the possibility of thinking that which has been thought so as to act in a utopian way with what little is left of metaphysics and *ethics*. He incites us to act in order to transcend the sentence and violence of the concept, to scream the suffering that, in the end, is the condition of the realisation of truth in metaphysics: *To change the world*, to go beyond the science which is authorised by the concepts of *its* politics.

A Reflection with Our Gaze Turned to the Past

To approach the critique proposed by Adorno (2000) is to declare solidarity with metaphysics so as to save the critique of the concept itself from the perspective of the negativity and potentiality inscribed in the subjects. In the contemporary world, to emphasise the hopes dialectically negated and concealed in conceptualised reality means thinking beyond the conceptualisations of the movement teleologised by the thought of development and progress. In the dynamics of *believing* and the *Spirit of Utopia* (Bloch 2000) one can find metaphysics as critique, the possibility of going beyond the anthropological experiences which are known through the words of reification, identified and homogenised by the power of capital. We are names and condemnations of institutionalised discourses: woman–wife–role, homosexual–sick–degenerate, indigenous–backward–savage, developed or underdeveloped. But we are more than the designations, sentences and destinations announced in the extensions of domination; we contain social antagonisms and tensions, possibilities of breaking identities which are also non-identities. We are simultaneously object and subject under construction against the destiny and violence contained in words.

In the same deceitful form of what is named and presented as natural in *progress* and its different discursive modalities (development, civilisation, etc.), maybe we can reflect with "metaphysics" or "messianism" (see Adorno 1990; also Benjamin 1969) on the subjectivities of the desires of another world which is longed for and inscribed in history. It is hope as the critique of the reality imposed by the rationalisms and positivisms that reign in the objective–subjective certainties of social sciences and their statistics. As a methodology (not to say anti-methodology and *cross-current history*) we propose a vision that considers *constellation*, for it allows us to see that the experiences of the past, acting in our present, are dimensions which are mediated by social relations and class struggle. Just like words, the concepts and categories of social sciences are undergoing a crisis, they are mediated by the objectivity of the world and its contradictions. They contain not only struggle as the synthesis of power, but also the potentialities of confronting the condemnations contained in the announced destinations in the truth and myth of their reification.

How are we to reflect on the concepts and representations of identities from the perspective of the very centre of the configurations of culture, but with the dialectical constellations of metaphysics as rebelliousness and political action? Will the subjectivities of the past appear only in official history and its records as the establishment and legitimacy of the power of the myth of law and its truth, or do they contain the constellations of class struggle? Even within the essentials of the empirical created at the top of the pyramid of power (institutions and representations of truth), there are constructed "from the bottom and to the left" (as the Zapatistas in Mexico say), imaginary alternatives which are present in the struggles of social movements. It is unbearable to think that all that is intolerable in the universe in its evident destruction (devour or be devoured) will be reproduced in the religious, political, economic future, without rebellion. "Whoever hates what is destructive, must hate life along with it: only what is dead is allegory of what is living and undistorted ... The nihilistic antipathy in his words is not merely the psychological but also the material precondition of humanity as utopia" (Adorno 2006 s. 48).

Adorno never stopped wondering about the constellation which covers the experience and empirical ontology of the realism which has been vulgarised by science and philosophy. In order to answer, without concluding with the classifications of positivism and so as to walk acting, he urges us to reflect on the reasoning of the truths of everyday reality, and to stress the need for *solidarity with metaphysics* and thought (as an object linked to the subject faced with desire and change). His critical thought is not the repetition of Marxism, but an epistemological perspective of critical theory and social subjectivity, thought of as possibilities and potentialities of the past, in the same present reality which constitutes the subjects as negativity in the face of the positivist discourses of capitalist civilisation and identity, with its disastrous consequences in history from the sixteenth to the twenty-first centuries. The sum of the deaths of the *other* is disastrous in the exterminations of the original peoples of America, the Caribbean and Australia, and the slavery brought by colonisation, with its ethnocidal and genocidal consequences (Ferro 2003).

Starting from the regimes of truth and the subjectivised interior of the objectified exterior, each world constructs the meanings of the words of history in order to define borders which do not necessarily coincide with those of the objectivity of power. We must stress that words can asphyxiate a thought. The addition of an adjective changes the weight and consequences in its use, for example *non-organised, non-desired* genocide. When the extermination or disappearance of a culture is presented as an error or folly of isolated individuals (Hernán Cortés, Hitler or Pinochet, etc.), and not as something structured by the historical reasoning of a society which aims at exploiting or extending its domination, there is a loss of the subjectivities of class that constitute them as a society. In this sense, to accept or deny a word allows us to comprehend the antagonisms and paralysis of a thought. Marc Augé (1998:10, 12) asserts that all words, despite being domesticated, "conserve a savage background," contain *crisis*. As soon as they find themselves unrestricted, as soon as they warm up their wings in daylight and dreamlight, they once again imagine themselves in the "reigns of shadows" and in the carnivals and rituals of the imaginaries, reconfigured in social struggles. "It is you, metaphysical entity of places, who lull children to sleep, it is you who people their dreams" (Aragon 1971: 27). However, Augé says that, before enclosing the potentialities of a word, the professional "bird-catcher" of thought will first learn not to trust them, for "some bite." He practises in discovering their hidden nests at the bottom of the wild jungle, he anaesthetises them with other words in order to observe them and follow them up close, control their direction, see where they take refuge or free themselves from the strings which are organised by the sciences of what is defined in the dictionaries that catalogue and control them. Thus, we can highlight Adorno's assertion (2006 s. 43) that one must not feel *terrified* when faced with the verification of domesticated truths, for behind the classified and confirmed in subjectivity data there is always arbitrariness and, naturally, the fear of positivist arguments towards objectivity, the antagonisms in conserved subjects.

> What the truth might objectively be, remains difficult enough to discern, but when dealing with human beings one should not allow oneself to

be terrorized by this. There are criteria there, which seem satisfying at first. One of the most reliable is the reproach that an expression is "too subjective". If this is laid down with that indignation, which echoes with the furious harmony of all reasonable people, then one has reason to be satisfied with oneself for a couple of seconds. The concepts of what is subjective and what is objective have been completely inverted. Objective means the non-controversial side of the phenomenon [*Erscheinung*], its unquestioned imprint, taken as it is, the façade constructed out of classified data, therefore the subjective.

Faced with the facts and social determination of the domesticated past, everything seems normal and natural. In the images of the genesis of power, until pain as destiny and sentence, we continue to conform to the identification of repetition. In the *universitas literarum* (see Adorno 2000 s. 44) everything is an *a priori* amongst the communicating spirits, all celebrities of knowledge validate irrefutably the conceptions in the objectivity of the empirical. Before the force of such conformism, the positivist formalisation of habitual objectivity, we lose, we forget, we repress other interiorised aspects of the desire for life. Society and power chew us up and swallow us. "All bridging concepts, all connections and logical helping operations, which are not in the matter itself, all secondary consequences not suffused with the experience of the object, should fall away" (Adorno 2006 s. 44). In this sense, to think that which has been thought with the imaginaries and desires in the modern world demands distancing oneself from the empirical truths, interiorised in the subjects, manipulated and repeated by the media. Configured in the so-called *mass culture*, they are instrumentalised through the media by the ideology of *their postmodern* culture. In life itself, as anguish, in the pretension of seriousness in scientific judgements, we shall note that it is in their own territory where the prejudices of their empirical illusion disappear. As Adorno stressed (2006 s. 43), the calculations of positivism and the cultural industry are frustrated as their veiled objectivity advances. "In contrast to this, reason has fled completely into eyeless [*fensterlos*] idiosyncrasy, which the caprice of the power-brokers castigates as caprice, because they want the powerlessness of subjects, out of fear of the objectivity, which alone is sublated in these subjects."

So, from a Marxist perspective of the critique of political economy, Adorno, along with Marx, helps us think in the deconstruction of the *idea* of the totalitarian world of progress and capitalist accumulation.[1] He penetrates the concepts and representations of the philosophical discourses of the culture of the barbarian civilisation in order to go beyond that which exists as phenomenon and truth. The example of Western civilisation, a path and role model considered a necessary stage for developing countries, displays its fragility when the earth-world is portrayed – the destruction of the environment, racist and territorial wars, internal and external poverty linked to the internationalisation of capital and a reinforced individualism, which reduces the effectiveness of social and communitarian solidarity.

In his *Theses on Feuerbach*, Marx criticises the logical and idealist thought of Hegel (see Sohn-Rethel 1978: 14) and claims that materialist critique not only demands the comprehension of the world and its pre-constructed ideas, the culture of the commodity fetish, but also the creation, as the origin of philosophy and metaphysics, of the possibilities of a liberating praxis. "The philosophers have only *interpreted* the world in various ways; the point is to change it" (Marx 1976: 5). In this sense, Adorno's work is paradoxical, realist and utopian. We cannot find the negative signs of dreams outside the world, but, as with language, it is constructed in the specific social-historical conditions of the present catastrophe, it is unfinished for it is utopia – negative and creative in the world and outside it.

In order to highlight the irregularities and abnormalities of a discourse and its reification, we must approach the past or, rather, comprehend the past as accumulated possibilities of desires. In "On Language in General and on the Language of Humans" Walter Benjamin detects in language a dimension of the divine. It is the *medium* through which the spiritual essence is communicated as accumulation of experiences. It is a *guard* which stores the *hoping* against a myth made law. This constellation, which is in our body, language and hands as *power-to-do* (Holloway 2005), as negative potentiality for transformation, is also pointed out by Adorno:

> Becoming aware of the constellation in which a thing stands is tantamount to deciphering the constellation which, having come to be, it bears within it. The *chorismos* of without and within is historically qualified in turn. The history locked in the object can only be delivered by a knowledge mindful of the historic positional value of the object in its relation to other objects – by the actualization and concentration of something which is already known and is transformed by that knowledge. Cognition of the object in its constellation is cognition of the process stored in the object. As a constellation, theoretical thought circles the concept it would like to unseal, hoping that it may fly open like the lock of a well-guarded safe-deposit box: in response, not to a single key or a single number, but to a combination of numbers. (Adorno 1990: 163)

With constellation we can see that the concepts we live with are in crisis. In order to comprehend the fugitive images in the social significances of class struggle one would have to tear apart or *dynamite* the modern, reified and mythicised concepts, the words and their significance. To assist in their dismantling would allow us to understand that they form part of the conflicts with their dialectical components in historical moments. That is, we must ask ourselves if the events-occurrences submerged in the concepts of the writing made myth, or what is expressed in the sculptures and walls of history, did not exist previously in the traditions of language and conflict, in the cosmogonies created on the basis of specific geographies-spaces and histories of the past: myths that participate in the negative potentialities of the religious and political discourses and their constellations which re-signify history's *not-yet existent*, the *utopia, a* carpe diem *in a genuine present* (Bloch, 1986, vol. I: 306–13).

For his part, Marx (1970: 69) highlighted this permanent drive in the present: "It will be clear that it is not about drawing a straight line from the past to the future, but about bringing the ideas of the past to life. We will see that humanity will not engage in a new labour; it will rather consciously realise its old labour from the beginning." In other words, it is not romanticism for the conservation of the past, but above all the realisation of accumulated hopes in our new constellation. From Adorno's – but also Benjamin's – point of view, this, in practice, means that the critique of pre-bourgeois progress has no other value than as a fertiliser for the certainties of what is new.

It is worth stressing that the temporal question is neither a starting point for the origins nor, much less, the end of a straight line of human evolution; it is, rather, a movement. Therefore, we deal with the implicit change in that which is lived and thought in the inflections of time. So, we can ask ourselves why Adorno (1990: 408) ends his theoretical contributions in *Negative Dialectics* with the urgent need to think of solidarity with the fall of metaphysics as a possibility of politics and life-thought as an action of philosophy. Is there actually any point in thinking of the subjectivity of the *I* and the *we* from the perspective of metaphysics (what in rationalism would be called the speculation of the inexistent) in the paradigms of the stage of the social spectacle? Could it be that real-life alienation, organised in the hidden spaces of the postmodern industry of oblivion, is a brake on the negativities of another world? Would there be any point in thinking of the desires and aspirations emanating in the negation of the world as truth and lack, from the perspective of the concepts of culture and identity in the present? Why think on the basis of the multiple cultural representations of the current situation if they are nothing but a reflection of a genealogy of knowledge as power and domination? In order to try to answer these questions we must establish ourselves in space, like Thomas Mann in *The Magic Mountain* (1996) perhaps, for, when reading Adorno, a *desiratum* appears before the sick society. Questions emerge surrounding the desperate urgencies of *our* time against the time of capital. These questionings do not come from the *archives of history* or from the resignation inscribed in structuralist pessimism, not even from the present, dominated by the ontologies verified through empirical science. The contributions by Adorno and other critical theorists are situated beyond, in a utopia beyond the world of alienation, which makes it possible to break the experiences of the *being* normalised by the dominant philosophical discourses and the disciplinary institutions of identity that compares, hierarchises, homogenises and excludes (see Foucault 1977: 183). In order to become existent in the disciplinary structuring of power, this beyond must expand inside that which is yearned for as nonexistent in the positivity of the empirical (Adorno 1990: 408).

This desire infuses the work of Adorno with a *continuum* of metaphysics as an enormous heritage of messianic traditions which, paradoxically, being traditions and culture, conserve the images of the past as potentialities of change (see Echevarría 2001); they are the rays of history eclipsed by the culture of barbarism. Metaphysics, due to its own concept, does not allow itself to be caught in the classified and standardised context of traditions imprisoned by conformism. It is an expert in non-classified desires, it is situated outside that which is accepted as normal and good *or rational and demonstrable*. Each time it becomes manifest it is *satanised* and driven away from the existent. However, it must be stressed that this beyond should not be conceived and acted out as what is *absolute* and absolutely different from the real concreteness of orderly thinking, but as a legible constellation of existing hopes. If the concept of identity as something *absolute* is broken, metaphysics will appear from within it as movement and the possibility of change. "It lies in the definition of negative dialectics that it will not come to rest in itself, as if it were total. This is its form of hope" (Adorno 1990: 406).

Metaphysical Mediations and the Dialectics of Vertigo in Time

Every day we go out, we walk, we dream, asking ourselves about the wars and misery in the world. We hide behind the masks and guises of capital, behind our cars or in front of the television, which pushes us into the habit of repetition and boredom. Others among us rebel with our time of insubordination, asking questions which seek urgent answers to the evil continuity of *progress*. Our attempt to answer the initial interrogatives of the world's questioning will be centred in the metaphysics proposed by Adorno in the twelve years of reflection of his *Negative Dialectics*. The conclusions of this work place us before the need of a self-reflection of negative dialectics in order to think of solidarity with the fall of metaphysics in the chaotic and civilising terrain of the objective truths of the world (Adorno 1990: 405–8). When thinking through the social and cultural mediations of metaphysics (see the third section of "Meditations on Metaphysics" in *Negative Dialectics*: 361–408), we observe that the author's utopian inspiration is at the centre of what I *want* to think as the necessity of *doing* in the face of death. Adorno's negative dialectics is not only an expression of the historical influence of the catastrophes of progress and their totalitarian implications (Fascism and Stalinism). His metatheoretical reasoning on possibilities is also a breaking with resignation and oblivion, just as Benjamin tries to bring to a halt the "train" of modernity which leads to the destruction, humiliation and death of whoever goes against it.

The difficulty in understanding *Negative Dialectics* lies in the critique of the conceptualisations and structuring made reality. It evades us, it will not let itself be caught, it is outside and inside this world. Adorno insists on thinking the cultural categories and classifications of identity of scientific thought, regulating conflicts. He places himself not only in the same reality, but also in the *beyond* the existing path, in the figure of negativity as a constellation of hope, that which is hidden in abnormality and resistance against the hierarchies of value and structuring homogeneity.

It is a *yes* that is constantly concealed in the marvellous *no* against the everyday domestication of images. The no entails a yes; to be precise, various instances of yes, but they are rooted in the no to existing society, they are founded on a "grammar of negativity" (Holloway 2005: 218). It is not a *yes* which positively asserts the existent, but rather a Freudian or Lacanian de-negation of the deconstruction of the *no* in order to exist with a different and creatively acting *yes* of the transformation of the world. It is negativity which can change the world and its reasoning. It is a *yes* which is anchored in the *no* of the *gestus* of the action of dignity as a *mode* of life against death. At the end of the road, among the questions that have risen from the *no* to the *mathematical*, classificatory truths of the knowledge of human sciences (Foucault

1973: 347–55), the *yes* of dignity will appear, that which exists against the *punishment* and *surveillance* of what is inventoried as normal or pathological in individual suffering. In thinking of the language of anthropological everydayness as the *organon* of the world, Adorno does not accept the claims of superiority of an objective and ontological reasoning of the *being*. He rebels against the myth of truth and law as a repetitive goal; he denounces the torture and anguish of the world.

By avoiding classifications, Adorno opens up concepts, turning them into participants of the structural cracks that undermine the capitalist *system-world*. Is it in exceptions that we can free ourselves from the ruler that measures us in the *rule of the law* which determines our actions? We believe it is in the articulation of the truths established as economic rules and laws that we can epistemologically decentre discourses as rules of power and domination. It is a matter of answering the optimistic and militant questions of the future directed towards the *not-yet* of the *novum* posed by Bloch (1986, vol. I: 198–200). Indeed, returning to Marx, it is not a question of realising the abstract ideals of being and philosophy, but about liberating the oppressed intuitions of humanised (i.e. concrete) society.

Negative Dialectics allows us to break truths in their purest state, to update, through the perspective of crisis, a material class struggle of *refined spirituality* (Benjamin 1969: 255). It helps us question ourselves, in order to critically comprehend the over-determinations of the social contradictions which act in the breakings and possibilities of liberation. The discursive decentrings of the world can be found in the same legitimacies of the myths. In this sense, with Marx and beyond him, it is in the categories of political economy themselves, conceived as the reflection of that which has been thought, that we can find the possibilities of that which has been thought as the becoming of capital. As we have already insinuated, it is not about reading Marx in repetition, or Adorno in dogmatism, but in the articulation of critical theory, for example, the *Theses on Feuerbach* and the *Critique of Political Economy*. We speak of an interpretation of the world from the perspective of its own tragedy. It is the wager of *believing* in success (Goldmann 1985: 398). It is the existing possibility of the forgotten in the desire of the *not yet conscious* thought, accumulated in memory and acted out by entire generations for transformation (Bloch 1986, vol. I: 128–132). In the last instance, turning to science in order to make anti-science is perhaps the discovery of that which is enclosed by the classificatory categories which cover class struggle with standardisation and reification. To turn to knowledge would help bring this oblivion into the light, it would allow the reinforcement of memory with the creating genius of revolution, it would be the seed of the awakening of the world to a different morning.

> Science, in the materialist sense, is perhaps, above all, the discovery of the infinite recurrence of men's *false conscience* of their world and, more generally speaking, of the history they make without ever truly knowing the causes. (Moutot 2004: 35)

How can we think critically starting from the same dominant empirical thought of the structural determinations of the truth of the world spirit? Is there any point in continuing to ask oneself dialectically in-against-and-beyond nature made law and power, the exterior of the past printed on the interior of the objects and myths of what is static in the empirical truth of the real world?

We believe the questions and thoughts as coordinated, moving reflections and inflections are Adornian questions and proposals for the cultural action of identities. When Adorno dreams of throwing a bottle with a message of his philosophy of exile into the Californian sea (Holl 2001: 508), he is thinking about not losing his inflections on identity in repression or oblivion. In the shadows of everyday misery, the communication of *power-to-do* confronts, as pagan heroes, the determinations of the watchfulness and the scale of the gods, of the classifications of identity and its consequences. So, as Hans-Günter Holl (2001:506) asserts in the postface to the French edition of *Negative Dialectics*, we can think that Adorno's metaphorical writing lives in a constant state of *shock*, of tearing apart with the *World Spirit*, with the dominant philosophy which appears to be the most serious element in social sciences but is finally full of non-truths. The force of his reasoning lies precisely in this metaphysical and philosophical demand of thinking of the potentialities of that which is possible within the context of the impossibility of established truths. His thought destructures the construction process of capital's reifying advent as the possibilities of negative dialectics to break with the commercial establishments of truth and knowledge. These critical thoughts, which become deliria when faced with totalitarian truths, cannot liberate themselves alone. They must know how to wait, with their time of insubordination, resistance and strategy, for the possibilities of the inexistent, the beyond which is necessary so that one must not continue to live with the everyday, alienated pain of the commodity.

It is here and now, in the approach between theory, thought and reflection as *inflections*, and in praxis as the path of freedom, that we not only encounter the essence of Adorno's reasoning, but also that of the Frankfurt School (Páez Díaz de León 2001). We can say that the demand for knowledge is inscribed in the same claim for objectivity (*Réflexivité réflexe*) by Pierre Bourdieu (1999: 1391–2) in order to understand the pain of those excluded from the interior of *the world's misery*: to comprehend that at the bottom of behaviours lies the social structure that determines possibilities. The identities experienced in the concrete universal are not nationalised in a world without conflicts and transformations. Along with identification with the goal of being exploited, they are crisis and therefore rupture and capacity for negative action. Their construction entails change and a reinvention of the symbolic status in order to continue living.

Negativities and their individual possibilities are not elaborated in the solitude of identities, but rather in what must be thought in and beyond the law which moves us. It is in the *trans-individual* configuration of the past in the present that the variations of ethics and of the action of our wagers for the change of the *finite goods* and *terrestrial ills* (Marx) or of Goethe's *diabolical evil* (see Goldmann 1985: 397) are objectively determined. With the internalisation of faith and hope in the objective world, one day silence turns into the scream of I've had enough, I'm fed up – the *Ya basta!* of destiny and of the myth of law. At midday, men and women gather at the barricades of collective life struggling for dignity. At the end of the day, all cry in solitude bemoaning their impotence in the face of the powerful. The following day, exclamations with deep currents intertwine at dawn; and, in the morning, they take part in the confrontation, maybe death. There is a time when rebellion arises. Tomorrow, inevitably, from the catacombs must emerge what is now but an intuition, a metaphysical desire from beyond the lived moment, the *not-yet* as an accumulation of desires, frustrations and mistakes of the past. It is not only a complaint of accumulated neurosis, it is also a force of the subject struggling in the transformation of the world.

Although the essential motive for Adorno's critique is in the critiques of the culture of *barbarism* and the genocidal identity of capitalism as the *spirit of the world*, we stress that metaphysics must not be sought in another philosophy of aesthetics: the one that substitutes for the philosophy of the death of the other. Like Benjamin, we must search for it not in the metaphysical essentialities of capitalism and "the spirit," but rather in the combat between capitalism and the proletariat as social forces (see Traverso 2004: 174), spaces of labour where the subjectivity of the subject and its critical theory are constructed. In "Dying Today" (1990: 368–73), Adorno argues that one must question and go deep into the appearance of the culture of death, a reality covered with guilt and truth. If, as Adorno asserts (1990: 371) "since Auschwitz, fearing death means fearing worse than death," then what is left at the bottom of pleasure and the art of creation as negativity is metaphysics, which wants to exist as a possibility of changing the *essential* of the empirical, *a priori* concepts of truth and the identity of capital and its wars. If the relation of blindness that chains men is so powerful, then, dialectically, the imaginary part of breaking – from mysticism – that veil of writing also emerges from there, as in the Jewish tradition of the *Cabbala* (see Adorno 1990: 372; and Benjamin 1969: 263–4) and – as Benjamin would do in his "Theses on the philosophy of history" (1969: 253–64) – messianically go beyond the world and its desperation. This historic movement of desperation and its ideology is also socially conditioned by the itinerary of the knowledge of metaphysics, the sister in solidarity of philosophy at the fall of *its* humanity. What is still to come is neither homogeneous nor devoid of hope, *every second of the present into the future is the strait gate through which the Messiah might enter* (Benjamin 1969: 264).

Indeed, Adorno considered the catastrophe of Auschwitz to be the product of civilisation, of the rationality of capital and identities instrumentally led by progress and technique to the consequences of Fascism. To him, Nazism was not a passage inside democracy, it lived inside the democratic forms that brought it to life, it was reification as the life and death mask of the market. Just like Benjamin, Adorno considered *progress* to be civilisation's storm wind blowing towards catastrophe. However, his melancholic (sometimes romantic) and sombre gaze sought the anchor points of this society and its existence, the market of culture (technical reproduction), the industrial product (fetishised commodity) and consumption (as the only form of pleasure in life) in order to open our eyes onto a different future. He sought the *essence* inside the *essential* of what is lived in the universalist discourse.

Although Adorno appears sceptical in the face of the ontological thought of the spirit of the world, his social critique of philosophy allows us to rethink the symbolic effectiveness of discourse and knowledge; to go deep into the comprehension of the social causes of anguish and catastrophe. It deconstructs the concepts of the world in order to encounter, in the subsurface of our existence, the origins of the discourses and thunderbolts of history. When dissolving them with transgression, we break the mirror of the identity of pain into millions of particles: they are the "world of many worlds" of insubordination. With this epistemological rupture there appear innumerable illusions accumulated over time with metaphysics, of what apparently does not exist in the empirical world of the mystic definitions of the dictionary, of what is *difficult to comprehend* because it is in the mysterious myth of the beyond, of what is far from this world.

What is clear in Adorno's reflection on *vertigo* (1990: 31–3) is a painful struggle against ontological models. His reasoning slips away like the lines of the arts of resistance. In order to break the ice of the identity of knowledge, in order not to be tied down by the falsification of the scientific schools which devour each other in order to confirm and standardise traditional thought and common-sense habits, Adorno's heterodox reasoning refuses to be enclosed in classifications. His reasoning is compensated in the everyday torture at the fringes of capital's reproductive life.

If, to Adorno, the *vertigo* of the book of truth of the real world is the *index veri*, it is also the possibility of opening up the concept that encloses truths which are simultaneously non-truths. The *shock* of the inauguration of what is new is the negativity that is renewed with the past in the present that is covered up with the *same instance* of the reality of the non-truth: the non-truth of the *society-spectacle*. The advantage of vertigo, of the suffering of the existence of negativity in the shadows of the reality of the truth of the universalist spirit of the world, is that our *knowledge* is not satisfied with the objective, partial and provisional truths of the knowledge of power and its totalitarian dreams. One can perceive the vampire of fiction, that *Seigneur du monde*, feeding on the blood of the non-truth of the common visions which are everyday repetition and boredom. Mythologised in the empirical world, the rationality of truth is turned into the repetition of the *stupidity* of the image environments, the recognition of responsibility and the stimuli of labour in conscience. The inhibition of consciousness as the practice and will which constitute the *being* is transformed into the systemic reproduction of the reproductive truth of self-indulgent conformism (Roitman Ronsenmann 2004: 3).

However, the existence of the realities of constructed spectacles leaves a margin of movement for negativities towards freedom. Only those who hold on to the end as part of the struggle against reality, those who continue to deny the *secure* world of technical reproduction as self-satisfaction and postmodern nihilism, continue to wager like Pascal in order to win at the risk of losing. It is the starting point, the deployment of ethics as autonomous behaviour of the trans-individual, a "sweet certainty of the worst" (Benasayag and Charlton 1991), a risk of thinking that which is thought as the rupture of dominant thought.

Many scientists base themselves on surveys and inquiries to observe the existence of a society fallen sick with its postmodernity of the market and *its* freedom and, supposedly, they speak the truth: the seriousness of the object constructed in anthropological empiricism and coherent with the world. They do not seek another place. They do not scrutinise the paths of this desired place, inexistent in reality, utopia as a room of the imagination renovated with the soul. They only wish to diagnose, detect symptoms in order to cure society and its sufferers, propose solutions in the world of the market. In their agonised delirium, the dying of this sick society are thirsty for life. They tear apart the screens in order to open windows onto possibilities and release their souls into a new time. If Adorno's society of *vertigo* is a reality reified with the word and the un-differentiation of the scientific and philosophic mask, for Baudelaire (1970: 99) "life is a hospital where every patient is obsessed by the desire of changing beds. ... It always seems to me that I should be happy anywhere but where I am, and this question of moving is one that I am eternally discussing with my soul." We could say that those metaphysical moments of rupture are the desires inscribed in Tabucchi's *Little Misunderstandings of No Importance* (1989). More than resignations, they are the allegories of emancipation, the ghosts of life with the love of our times, those present in the *magic mountains* of life struggling against death. Paradoxically, these times are brief but, when multiplied, they are as big and volatile as the sighs and gazes of the world we live in: "the hour around you is as vast and solemn as space, a motionless unit of time which is not marked on the dial and is as light as a sigh, as quick as a glance" (1989: 70).

Our time is not a time autonomous of the past, or a straight line, but a carousel of events directly linked to our *what-to-do*. If our time were independent from the world of the ghosts of the past, it would be *nothing*, movement would have disappeared without the changes which are hoped and wished for every day. However, What is time? Thomas Mann asked (1996: 240, 340) in the *Magic Mountain*. They are inflections of time as movement and change; it is an occurring of time constructed by us as the eternity of duration directed towards another world; it is never backwards. Time is the hope of the change of reality in the face of death.

[It is] a secret – insubstantial and omnipotent. A prerequisite of the external world, a motion intermingled and fused with bodies existing and moving in space ... Time is active, by nature it is much like a verb, it both "ripens" and "brings forth". And what does it bring forth? Change! Now is not then, here is not there- for in both cases time lies in between. But since we measure time by a circular motion closed in on itself, we could just as easily say that its motion and change are rest and stagnation – for the then is constantly repeated in the now, the there in the here. ... Time is a gift of the gods to humankind, that we may use it, my good engineer, in the service of human progress. (Mann 1996: 240, 340)

Finally, along with Jacques Prévert (1968) in his poem *L'accent grave*, we can conjugate life's essential question with *to be* or *not to be* or *to be* what one *is not*, and reconfigure the time of being itself which does not want to *be* what it *is*. It also wants to *be* what it *is not*, everyday dialectical questions when we ask ourselves why we are what we do not wish to be: racist, sexist, arbitrary, aggressive, etc., subjectivities which are imposed and manipulated in the surveys of truth as totality. Discomforts which are embodied every day through neurosis which are often only expressed in the suicide of the social, in the confrontation of dreams with reality or the abandonment of the aspirations of the collective as well-being. Then, intuition protects itself with the shields of life; once again it *waits*, with the time of the arrow and the sword, for the right moment to break the chains of imprisonment.

In this sense – following in the poetic footsteps of Baudelaire (1970) – in metaphysics, inscribed in the present world (there exists no other), there will always be an assertion of distancing and exile towards another place: it does not matter which, but to live and dream one must always travel outside the world.[2] Just as those who go far into the desert in order to think the truth with subterranean subjectivity, one reflects upon the landscapes of the present with the past of hope, searches in the uncertainty of everyday life. In the trains travelling between Germany and France, Benjamin wrote *Paris, Capital of the 19th Century*

(1999), he sought the bridges of resistance with past centuries so as to think of the constellation which could save us from the painfully announced catastrophe. Finally, in those instants of the everyday life of terror, amplified by the totalitarianisms inscribed in institutions and in the words of identity, love slips into thought and establishes intelligence with the friendship and the goodness of a desired and more beautiful community.

Shadow and Movement of Metaphysics, the Gods and Negativity

Adorno's tragic reasoning in *Negative Dialectics* reflects the pain inflicted by the guilt of identity and racism with its consequences in war, destruction, ethnocide and genocide. Adorno returns to Marxism through the epistemological door of the relation between matter and thought. He goes deep into what is thought in order to decentre what is hidden in the fetishised thoughts of philosophy and capital. He realises the dangers that exist in the processes of rationalisation of that which is rationalised in concepts. With *negative dialectics*, he penetrates into those rationalisations of identity and identification in order to question himself as to the possibilities contained within the affirmative impossibilities of the rational empirical world.

As a negative pagan man, he realises it is better that the pain of the gods continues to exist in order to deny a real world suffering, lack, unemployment and hunger. However, it would seem that in secrecy and reserve, the gods, like the heroes of *Antiquity* or those who seek to resemble them in creative potential, come down to earth and materially blend in with men in order to recreate the world and the twinkling of the stars. They are the *barbarians* who in no moment of their present try to restore the world, just as before, chained down by the discipline of alertness and punishment (Foucault 1977:1 35–228). Just like the creative "gladiators" of Walter Benjamin in the struggle of their own desires (as a staging of the practices of pleasure), in their dreamy walk of freedom, everything is possible in *conflict* and *combat*. They parry blows with the shield of the time of the new, the rescue of the eternal return of the struggle of the heroes of capitalist modernism (see Weigel 1996). They even fly below the surface, in catacombs, in the cellars of those who are underneath, in order to confront reality and condemnation. They are capable of lifting mountains, dominating the forces of nature for the good of humanity, being more realistic in their search for the impossible, this not-yet which underlies the dreams of a tomorrow which will always be better. So, for example, in a "War of the Gods," Prometheus, Jesus Christ and Topiltzin-Quetzalcóatl[3] are dialectical significations of the gods transformed into *terrestrial promise*. They are part of the concrete and material man, they are critical points which prepare the constant conversion of the physical person into a visible conscience (mask) of collectivity as a need for change. They are part of the natural history of the conversion of nature into man through the sign of the word in the thought for action. From the autonomy of humanity as resistance and rupture, the defeated construct their time of rupture, they imagine another world, they revive in the communities that rebel and nurture their dreams and beliefs so as to expand their freedom. Inside their own *I*, which is a *we* (in the *trans-individual* sense), they question the same structural determinations. They look around, searching for a way to escape from the normalisations and naturalisations of the victorious.

Even with the mysticism that can cast desires away to the inexistent beyond, the political and religious culture of liberation in the same myths is still fertile ground for us to continue wondering about the *beyond* constructed in the present. To resign oneself to the realism of the factual world and its contingencies amounts to accepting the new myth of neo-liberal postmodernism as the organiser of oblivion surrounding class struggle. To yield before these mythical notions of the *end of history* and the ontology of the universal, unique reasoning of multitudes, without reference to class or relation with the past, would mean accepting that the darkness of power and its apology have managed to crush all hope of the subject. However, we see new cracks opening every day, deepening the crisis inside power. As Tischler points out (2005: 45–6), in order to continue constituting themselves as subjects, these "outlaw" men and women must reinforce the deep connections of the past generations with the present. That is, "configure a new constellation with the broken, but not deceased, time of revolutionaries," this messianic force of the past which acts profoundly and secretly as a heritage in the *War of the Gods* (Löwy 1996).

In all civilisations, the significations outlined in pagan gods are negative signs of what is missing (lack); hence they have been and are part of the cultural creating genius of the power-to-do in the actual moment of everydayness. Within them lies the utopia which gave birth to them. It is in the observation of the world and the permanent crisis of the concept that the possibilities of doing are constructed. In these multiple screams, rooted in the *no* to lack and the tendency towards the fetish, in the ethical and social convictions in the imaginary of another better world, other possible worlds continue to flourish thanks to the constellation of the memory of the past reactivated in resistances. Just like the sculptures Benjamin (1985: 51) finds in a dream of a scientific expedition to Mexican caves, the gods continue to be the *essence* as transcendence of power-to-do. Watching them, static in their representations, with men bowing before them, Benjamin perceives the significations of the movement of their heads from right to left in a sign of *rejection*. He observes that the dialectics of the *no* continues to manifest itself against the reverences to myths and their violence of the past in the present.

In the anthropological *being*, mediated by the culture of capital's universal discourses, can we think of the art of resistances and alternatives against capital, lines of escape from the category of beauty made law? Is negative thinking a resignation to the mythical condemnation of the laws and the gods, or is it the dignity of the time of resistance, the cornerstone of the gestures of the community creating its webs of movement and communication? It is not necessarily in mysticism that the possibilities of men transformed into gods and heroes arise (Christs–men–black and white, Prometheus–heroes, *quetzalcóatls–topiltzins*, etc.). The concept of culture is reconstructed as messianism and utopia in the same game of wagers and critiques mediated by the specific universality. It creates a space of innovation in order to rescue the traditional forms, not with the promise of conserving them as they are, but rather to save them from the disaster of power and the domination which repeats and reproduces the positiveness made truth in reality. It is memory which runs through the corners of the earth, syncretising in the conflict of local beliefs and traditions. It is in nature, in sunlight and moonlight and in the sacrifice of the gods to create the world, that the first people and their possibilities gave birth to hope. The small ones, the defeated ones, those who walk in the night, await the fall of the power of the sun so as to renovate, with the dreams of the night, the possibilities of the daydream of the morning.[4] Just like the myth of the giants from the past, they go beyond the limits of nature's power and inclemency. They confront it and struggle with their dreams awake, they construct the resistance and alternative with their time. They construct the pyramidal marvels of art and their worldview in order to control nature. They rise among ruins in order to make their surroundings possible.

Word, Time of Daydream and Movement

Can we metaphysically dream of a reality other than the apparent contradictions of the shadows of the world, or is metaphysics nothing but an irrational speculation of the inexistent divine? Will the alienated person simply be a reflection-subject among shadows, a node of power webs, or is it in obscurity and alienation itself where what de Certeau (1998) called the "invisible" emerges, the negativity of the *grand esprit*? In man himself and in metaphysical consciousness dwells that which is most elevated, sublime, beauty, art and creation; at the beginning it is invisible, unreachable by power's empirical rationality. Metaphysics is recreated in anonymous and autonomous spaces before linearity as the history of totalising development. However, it is in the dialectic mediation of the time of use value and the value of the word as negative critique that the specific world of present time is articulated. All the features of society contain the dimensions of culture, its relation with the land (fertility, the mother which gives fruit) and its pagan or *barbarian* gods (everywhere there appear new masked saints and local virgins who rebel against the universal truths of the planet's churches). We live, we suffer and we die through words and scriptures, in relation to a past and a present which are objectified in actions that are rationalised, specified and ritualised towards *specific goals*. In languages and their structures we can sift words related to time and space, dense territories of history and its permanence, density of *ancient* significations, concepts generated *outside* the mechanisms of capitalist production.

These are discordant times inside the essence of the critique of the material world. From there arises the word as subjectivity. It creates the cosmos and transforms it. On the one hand, critique is the raw material of the world which nature produces and reproduces and, on the other, it is critique which is born as the world's practice. So, from the original questions, we ask about the determinations of guilt and condemnation of the now of lack as the linear and homogeneous determination of truth. Naturally, even though the past and the dreams which shape constellations are lost in the factual dimensions of the realism of today's darkness, the memories of experiences cause the possibilities of the urgency of the time of praxis to re-emerge, in order to confront the present and its condemnation of the static character of the repeated history of "that is how it was, is and shall be." On the contrary, metaphysics is rupture as possibility, as a concept of crisis and class struggle. Indeed, the desires of metaphysics are the dreams of something else which does not exist in reality. The rationalities of the judgements passed on metaphysics continue to wish to bury it for, as a concept and as reality, it is an intellectual speculation of that which does not exist in reality. However, despite the empirical character of the sciences which negate it as a mundane possibility, it still constitutes an obstacle for dominant thought for it is part of the constellation of movements, a legible past in the history of the possibilities of thinking of a time with future, beyond the pain of everyday life.

So, time cannot be conceived without this movement of the metaphysics of rebellion, revolution, the desired change in re-creation. In order to become a configuration in a specific space it must extend over what it desires, over what lives loving and yearning for the inexistent. This is how, on the basis of the contemplation of desire, the world and the desires which encourage it are named and objectified as metaphysics. It is the opposite of the darkness of lived experience. It is the root of the experience of movement which denies life as a continuity of the moment; it is the discontinuity which causes belief in something else, *here and now*. In the instant of desire exists the insanity of the word of the night, forbidden and isolated from the daydreaming of another world in the real world of the everydayness of *then*. Thus, in the challenge of cultures and their identities there exists an irrevocable commitment with the past and the dreams which revitalised society's forms.

> My dream has granted it to me so clearly that I will always remember. Yes, I am overjoyed and filled with its warmth. My heart is beating strong and knows why. It beats not for purely physical reasons, the way fingernails grow on a corpse. It beats for human reasons and because my spirit is truly happy. The truth of my dream has refreshed me – better than port or ale, it courses through my veins like love and life, so that I may tear myself out of my dreaming sleep, which I know only too well can be fatal to my young life. ... Awake, awake! Open your eyes. Those are your limbs, your legs there in the snow. Pull yourself together and stand up! Look – good weather! (Mann, 1996: 487)

Time, Myth and Domination

In the very myth of the time of the powerful, of heroes, representations and images of the past, there exists the fallen blood of sacrifices: it is they and their blood that made-make-and-will-make the time of rebellion. Without them, time does not exist, it would be death as determination and destiny inscribed in rule and law. Paradoxically, this spontaneous manifestation of violence in myth contains specific dialectical dimensions. It is not a rebellion with means towards specific goals. In the beginning, everything is a manifestation of a no to law and its myth, be it against the force of nature or against the naturalisation of the social relations of domination. There are many examples in legends of heroes which cast light on the messianic and utopian manifestation of the courage and challenge of the ancestral pleasure of existing. They do not emerge as an expression of suicide before the impossible possibility of changing the world; they are born and die in order to re-emerge in the germination of the hope of offering people a promise of that which is *new*. As Mannheim points out (1966: 211), we can say that the possibilities of the social subject in its historical and symbolic configuration are not an artificial product; like the plant and its fruits they grow from the seed and its care. In fact, those who defy the powerful world of the objectivity of law incarnate in their body and soul what the community has looked for yesterday, today and tomorrow, the not-yet-existent of the desires of past and present struggles. Just like Jorge Luis Borges (1999), looking at the moon which has witnessed so many tears, the mere fact of seeing through the windows of the eyes is to think and cause the heartbeats which nurture the desires of perceiving another light among the shadows of the world. "There is such loneliness in that gold / The moon of the nights is not the moon / Whom the first Adam saw. The long centuries / Of human vigil have filled her / With ancient lament. Look at her. She is your mirror" (Borges 1999: 379)

Despite the reifying force of the myth of the commodity on social relations, questions and actions arise which express their opposition and coordinate the reinforcement of liberating potential. Faced with dominant universal discourses, multiple forms of resistance and negativity, accumulated in history's thunderbolts, appear. At the centre of such behaviours, linked to what is naturalised by the society of the spectacle, we observe that thought contains this desire-want, which is inscribed in the satisfaction of something the concept lacks. Those who deny the sentence imposed by the reason of law and rule as the instrumentalisation of violence (a just war towards avenging goals) express the *Ya Basta!* As Adorno and Benjamin claim, they have the subjective sovereignty – teleologically and politically – of no, a *de facto* possibility of the violence of the divine against the sacred violence which is organised by the powerful. As a vital need for life, they can reject the mythic violence which has founded law as condemnation. The distances created in time between the present and the nearest past are confirmed in the bridges of solidarity which unite the varied paths of resistance in movement. However, even with the barriers created by the powerful, the asphyxiating walls of shame between the North and the South, the totalities of the meaning of power are torn apart with the force of the movement of *vital necessity*. Desperately isolated, in a thousand resistances, the poor and miserable cause *totality* to explode.

So, to paraphrase Benjamin and Adorno, *negative dialectics* sees the fall of metaphysics and the avalanches of the barbaric civilisation through the eyes of an angel stunned by the human catastrophes. To fight for the impossible is to participate in the expansion of human solidarity, this constant desire for what is *new* confronted with the *repetition* of the immobile as universal dogma. It happens precisely because the life of humanity thinks of a possible place for the defeated, for what never occurs, but is potentially desired in the multiple representations of culture and identity, which are the negativity of the world and the force which liberates through the beauty of the inexistent. Subjectivity brings forward another art of living in order to create *what is new* as a vital and everyday necessity of the word solidarity.

We come face to face with the need to think of the mythical and sacred character of violence, the state and its philosophy. When reflecting with Adorno on the darkness of the world, there is a rejection of the violence of the universal discourse and the myth of law, making space for the moment of resistance, the need for revolutionary violence, always pointing to a way forward. In *For a Critique of Violence*, Benjamin (1986: 277) claims that in the real world of law, with its norms of power which erase the offence, there is an acquaintance with mythical violence, but not with the divinity of desire. In the moment of *now* of the powerful stick of law which crushes the divine forms of violence, the signs inscribed in subjectivity become sovereign. They call on freedom in order to survive in the world of discretionally administered violence in communication, the control and the surveillance of the myth of law and legalised violence.

A Question in the Movement of Despair

It must be stressed that Adorno's reasoning is not isolated, it is not the result of a *brilliant mind*. The critique in *Negative Dialectics* is part of a process of accumulation of many dramatic experiences, places of apocalypse and prophecies against all evil. However, if to say *no* encloses the want and desire for something else, it is also obscured in the painful stories reduced to smoke in identity's ovens. The immediate key to the reciprocal answers to the experienced world of identity and the negation of the Other, is to critically confront violence and the boredom of repetition by asking "What is justice and what is just?" The question arises in the very conceptual identity of the world, it is the birth of philosophy as a question and as painful knowledge, it is channelled towards the questioning of the *here and now* which is conjugated with a movement towards the *beyond*, in resistance and in rupture with multiple mirrors of the real world: the truth of justice which is the non-truth of justice in the immediacy of the world and of rupture.

When penetrating, from our interior, the *consciousness* of the illusory character of totality as identity and contradiction, we perceive guilt as a centre for thinking of domination but also as a starting point for its rupture, which is the negativity of the world and its forms. In the end, on the side of life, comes the confirmation that it is in the body itself that one detects the absence of what is desired in the vivid body as *landscape*. A critical gaze which is situated in the empirical world, leaving the past behind as a static yesterday, will only see a dialectics of the synthesis of power, of apparent subjectivity. It is also necessary to think distinctively the time of the homogeneous and power-empty present as a condensation of *non-presents* (Benjamin 1969: 260–3) for the previous, as an exception, reappears out of the footprints in the rubble of the established.

Naturally, metaphysics as despair originates in the world. It is not the path of suicide as pure and simple negation, the expression of the blockade of the movement's ideas. It must be seen as culture's starting point, as a possibility for the movement of human existence. Despite the force of the myth made violence, from the beginning culture and its social relations are the distorted question, the sigh of the oppressed weighed down by the force of nature made pain and lack, they are the beginning of the scream of hope in despair, the struggle and organisation for and towards a better world. In this moment of desire, the profound critique which underlies the statement born from the question will be constructing the subject in action. In the double reality of negativity, lack, hunger and pain will participate in a profound hermeneutics which questions, names and questions again in the culture of domination itself: what do I live for, to die in the sentence of the myth of right made power? No!, answer the repressed from *dignity* (Holloway 2005), they question, they smash the mirror into a thousand pieces in order to open the doors of the possible.

It is in the rupture with the violence of the new *ages* of *legitimate* and *just* wars that the resistances which give birth to that which is *new* emerge, breaking the vicious circle in order to participate in the questions of the past in the present. The significations and representations in a space and time which are alternative to crisis have been the starting point for a path of questionings, initiated with the reflection and negation which are inscribed in the lines of escape towards metaphysics. They are inflections or thunderbolts in history faced with the world of lack. If we ask ourselves about the heritage of the time of the past and its significations, the essential question is the beginning of exile from the world; it is the madness of the distancing of the abnormal in order to search for the divine of the dream of another world. The languid bodies of the repetitive reality of the misery of the world question, suffering, the desire of another world.

In order to respond and question *its* world, *apocalypse* as a configuration of desire is the stormy crisis of the millenary utopia announced in messianism as a prophecy, as *wait*. Questions distance themselves from evil in order to think of that same evil, they acquire consciousness of the desired good and of the movement made action. The distancing opens up perspectives in the face of the world, the movement and life against death break the preconceptions of the concluding truth of this is how it is and how it shall be, in order to think of the non-truth from within its own conclusions. In this sense, metaphysics with its *messianic wait* is not closed and static. It mobilises wills, it opens breaches so as not to live and walk in lack, but rather with other dreams, a constellation of inflections which allow for the configuration of a different future.

Critique is the struggles constituted in culture, the subjectivity and negation of a world of necessity made out of the death of the Other. At the moment of the fall of metaphysics, Adorno's reasoning and questions show solidarity towards critical dialectical thought. His anti-science is part of the rebellious, messianic reflections critical of violence. Between guilt and condemnation, oblivion and memory, he suffers the possibilities of causing the identities that have been manipulated and imposed by sciences and their culture to explode. To think of the desires and aspirations of messianic liberation and the redemption of history is to desire the intra-mundane utopia in order to tear apart the generic paintings of identity. *Certainty* is the violence of that which is divine and messianic as negativity before the world, that which will not lower itself to universal discourses and identities linked to power. In this sense, divine violence is autonomous and sovereign as to the absolute truths of power and domination. According to Benjamin (1986) the critique of violence is at the centre of the myth of violence, it is a sign and distinctive representation of dignity.

The messianic configurations of *waiting*, fragments of struggle, have been defeated many times by the force of power. However, many crucified Christs and statues-heroes are part of the metaphysics which brought them to life, they are part of the *no* and the question which bursts in the statement of another thing that brought them into existence.

Religion and Memory as Hope

Although societal figures are linked to the power of the myth and of the divine as contradiction, we must assert the existence of truths in life, as well as the dialectics of non-truths as autonomous resistances of movements. There is a secret appointment between the generations of the past and those of the present in the dialectical carnivals of everyday life. In the signifiers of language, in the constructions, in the artistic creations, in the poems of Benjaminian magic [*féerie*] one finds those secret indicators of the utopian capacities, a *star of redemption*, the gate through which the *Messiah* might enter (Benjamin 1969: 264). So, we could say that in the simplicities of language and of the poetic and metaphysic irrationality of the word we can find the lines of the imagination of what is possible, a rationality of what is different. It is a matter of the *no* implicit in literature and life's negative passions.[5] It is present in class antagonisms, it can explode like a volcano at any *moment*; it is expressed in the interstices of the missing time in the shifting hiding places of the darkness of lived experiences. It is the time of redemption of the *forgotten*, of the small, everyday moments of the history which has been accumulated by *those negated* in the *glory* of progress.

As Adorno suggests, from the perspective of Benjamin in fact, metaphysics in the heart of culture must allow us to penetrate the very concepts and representations of the myth of identity in order to highlight the irregular, the abnormal, that which does not fit into the identifications of the science of the *mundus intelligibilis*. If life is not only that which exists as despair, then, in the constellation, we re-encounter past paths, that which lives on and emerges in the dialectics of representations as desires of liberation against the lack inscribed in socio-technological mutations. They are the tensions found in Bloch's daydream, they are hope as a force which struggles in-against-and-beyond the myth of a *thing*, of the truth-appearance of the institutional as indestructible, as space and centre for reflection. So, we can say that negative thought as a constellation is utopia (confrontation), crisis and alternative. It distances itself in the context of the very political culture established as a subterranean struggle against the secret and disturbing weight of present everydayness as social synthesis in bodies and subjectivities.

Why do new magic-religious movements emerge at the moment of great transformations of the paradigms of the present? Why do social scientists worry about the emergence of new sects which are reconstructed in-and-with the old techniques of tradition and belief? What is the point of identifying, classifying and homogenising, as more or less religious, practices of believing in another world from the one which is known as institution and truth? In order to approach the comprehension of new forms of belief, we should mention that we are submerged in the myths of history and power in order to bear witness to the utopian tensions which intertwine inside religiousness and reality, the Marxist dialectic of the *opium of the people* and the *sigh* of liberation. If certain liberationist and rationalist movements explain religiousness univocally, from the perspective of the power which recuperates and captivates it, they do not see, they do not hear the sighs contained by the oppressed in an economic and historical context. They do not see that inside the myth of the violence of condemnation and guilt also lie the symbolic significations of the lamentation of those who live in misery.

Although the tragedy of *metaphysical indifference* is taking control of us, there is always the intuition that another possible world exists. It is true that in the real world we want truths and securities of the individualised, specific I. We grow more and more distant from each other, we do not know the world of love and solidarity as main gestures for the duration of the time of hope for life. However, there exists a potential certainty that something else exists, for it makes us question ourselves and spurs us into action every day. We cannot live without the dreams of another reality, we constantly move towards a desired not-yet. As Sábato says (2000:12): "There is something that does not fail and it is the conviction that – only – the values of the spirit [metaphysics as hope] can save us from this earthquake that threatens the human condition."

In some corner of our memory something gains control of us. Guilt and the condemnation of law are not the end of the road for man, rendered anonymous and imprisoned in power's labyrinths. This man is also the light of metaphysics projected onto the shadows of the reality of a starless night. With *Negative Dialectics* we can highlight the saturations of time. The desires and possibilities which are close to salvation are re-signified in the struggles of non-identity in the present. With the category of time created by rebelliousness, the past is re-actualised in the present and in the future. In the re-appropriation of the potentialities of the past in the presence-negativity of the negated, the constellation causes the explosion of the founding and law-administrating violence which also seeks to be re-actualised in today's world.

Thus, in the dialectics of the image, one must unite or deconstruct the meanings of heroic and messianic images in order to understand everyday experiences as socio-historical re-significations of the clashes with modernity. Starting from the historical assemblies of concepts and their representations with their future images, we must set out paradoxically to deconstruct those same forms in order to evidence, with metaphysics, the lines and fragments of what is possible. There is no law of cause and effect in the set of signifiers, for they correspond to social meanings inscribed in social tensions. Indeed, there is an interaction between the fields of the inside and the outside in the acting person. Importantly, one can take in the exterior and decode it from one's interior, and transfer this interior field out to the exterior in a new way. So, the subjectivity of the interior is an objectification of the exterior and it coincides in the critique of the culture which provides the basis for what is new.

In "Meditations on Metaphysics," Adorno asserts that what the spirit of the world of domination wanted to do as that which resembles it (subject-object), constantly moves with what is not recognised as culture and spirit. Metaphysics, considered to be the absolute evil, *hides* from domination; it does not wish to be part of the materialist world and of official philosophy. In this process of material, scientific circulation, akin to money and its power, Adornian metaphysics, with the aesthetic spirit before the world's ugliness, becomes once more the escape route in the face of the truth of money and the positive science which denies the human potential for transformation.

The critical spirit rebels like Prometheus. It does not accept social illness or condemnation as an absolute evil, or the resignation of the time of reality. It dreams of another world, another culture, another life lived in the time of critique, aesthetics and ethics as movement and change. One must not try to romantically trace back the time of the arts of conversion and social values, but rather see that constellations are in *our present*, that they act covertly in the movement of the resistances of the time of insubordination. As Borges (2003: 26) says in *Tlön, uqbar, orbis tertius*: "the present is indefinite, the future has no reality save as present hope, the past has no reality save as present memory," that is, according to us, the a-present of the time of the mirror which has been shattered into a thousand pieces as negation and redemption of hope and utopia.

* Translated by Anna-Maeve Holloway

NOTES

1. Karl Marx (1965) mentions in *Capital* (vol. III, ch. XXIV) that "the so-called primitive accumulation" of global capitalism flourished with blood in order to attain its goals of development and civilisation.
2. "'Tell me, my soul, poor chilly soul, how would you like to live in Lisbon? It must be warm there, and you would be as blissful as a lizard in the sun. ... You see it is a country after my own heart; a country entirely made of mineral and light, and with liquid to reflect them.' ... At last, my soul explodes! 'Anywhere! Just so it is out of the world!'" (Baudelaire 1970: 99–100)·
3. It is known that, during the colonial period and contemporary history, the myth of Quetzalcóatl, god of the four cardinal directions, reconstructed in Mexico cultural bridges, new images, thunderbolts against the capitalist sentence (Matamoros 2005: 40).
4. "The old ones tell the store of Yacoñooy, a small but brave and audacious warrior, who feared nothing, no matter how big and powerful it might seem. ... The sun laughed, confident of its power and strength, and ignored the little warrior that challenged him from the ground. Yacoñooy challenged him once again, saying: 'the strength of your light does not frighten me, my weapon is time, which ripens in my heart' and he drew his bow, pointing the arrow towards the very center of the arrogant sun. Once again the sun laughed, and tightened the meridian fire belt of its heat around the rebel, in order to make the small one even smaller. But Yacoñooy protected himself with his shield and resisted until midday began to give way to afternoon. The sun helplessly watched its strength diminish as time

passed, and the small rebel still stood there, protected and resisting beneath his shield, waiting for the time of the bow and the arrow". Subcomandante Marcos, in *La Jornada*, February 3, 2003.
5. On the labyrinths of *no* as the negation of the world, see Vila-Matas (2007).

REFERENCES

Adorno, T. W. (2000) *Metaphysics, Concept and Problems*. Stanford, CA, Stanford University Press.
Adorno, T. W. (2006) *Mínima Moralia. Reflections on a Damaged Life*, at www.marxists.org/reference/archive/adorno/1951/mm/ch01.htm (accessed 23 May 2008). (Also available as Adorno, T. W. *Mínima Moralia. Reflections on a Damaged Life*. London, Verso, 2005.)
Adorno, T. W. (1990) *Negative Dialectics*, London, Routledge.
Aragon, L. (1971) *Paris Peasant*, London, Jonathan Cape.
Augé, M. (1998) *Les formes de l'oubli*. París, Payot-Rivages (forthcoming in English; translation from Minnesota University Press).
Baudelaire, C. (1970) *Paris Spleen*, New York, New Directions Publishing.
Benasayag, M. and Charlton, E. (1991) *Cette douce certitude du pire*, Paris, La Découverte.
Benjamin, W. (1969) "Theses on the Philosophy of History", in *Illuminations*, New York, Schocken Books.
Benjamin, W. (1986) "Critique of Violence", in *Reflections*, New York, Harcourt.
Benjamin, W. (1985) *One-way Street and Other Writings*, London, Verso.
Benjamin, W. (1999) "Paris, Capital of the 19th Century", in *The Arcades Project*, London and Cambridge, MA, Belknap Press.
Bloch, E. (1986) *The Principle of Hope,* 3 vols. Oxford, Blackwell.
Bloch, E. (2000) *The Spirit of Utopia*, Stanford, CA, Stanford University Press.
Borges, J. L. (2003) "Tlön, Uqbar, Orbis Tertius", in *Ficciones*, Madrid, Alianza Editorial.
Borges, J. L. (2000) "The Moon", in *Selected Poems*, London, Penguin Classics.
Bourdieu, P. (1999) *La miseria del mundo*, México, Fondo de Cultura Económica.
Certeau, M. de (1998) *The Capture of Speech and Other Political Writings*, London, University of Minnesota Press.
David, C. (2006) Preface to *Métaphysique, concept et problèmes*, París, Payot.

Debord, G. (1999) *The Society of the Spectacle*, New York, Zone Books.

Echeverría, B. (2001) *Definición de la cultura*, México, Itaca.

Ferro, M. (2003) *Le livre noir du colonialisme. XVIème–XXIème siècle: de l'extermination à la repentance*, París, Hachette-Pluriel.

Foucault, M. (1973) *The Order of Things. An Archaeology of Human Sciences*, London, Vintage Books.

Foucault, M. (1977) *Discipline and Punish. The Birth of the Prison*, London, Penguin Books.

Goldmann, L. (1985) *El hombre y lo absolute*, España, Ediciones Península.

Holl, H-G. (2001) Postface in Adorno, *Dialectique négative*, Paris, Payot.

Holloway, J. (2005 [2002]) *Change the World without Taking Power. The Meaning of Revolution Today* (second edition, with Epilogue), London, Pluto Press.

Löwy, M. (1996) *The War of Gods: Religion and Politics in Latin America*, London, Verso.

Mann, T. (1996) *The Magic Mountain*, New York, Vintage Books.

Mannheim, K. (1966) *Ideology and Utopia*, London, Routledge.

Marcos, Subcomandante (2003) in *La Jornada* (México), February 3, 2003. www.jornada.unam.mx/2003/02/03/006n1pol.php?origen=index.html (accessed: 2 March 2007).

Marx, K. (1965) [1864–77] *Capital*, Moscow, Progress.

Marx, K. (1976) "Thesis on Feuerbach" in K. Marx and F. Engels, *Collected Works*, vol. V, London, Lawrence & Wishart.

Marx, K. and Ruge, Arnold (1970) *Los anales franco-alemanes*, Barcelona, Martínez Roca.

Matamoros, F. (2005) *Memoria y utopía en México. Imaginarios en la génesis del neozapatismo*, México, UV-BUAP.

Moutot, G. (2004) *Adorno: langage et reification*, Paris, Puf.

Páez Díaz de León, L. (ed.) (2001) *La escuela de Frankfurt, teoría crítica de la sociedad, ensayos y textos*, México, UNAM.

Prévert, J. (1968) *Paroles*, Paris, Livre de Poche.

Roitman Ronsenmann, M. (2004) *El pensamiento sistémico, los orígenes del social-conformismo*. México, Siglo XXI.

Sábato, E. (2000) *La resistencia*. Buenos Aires, Seix Barral.

Sohn-Rethel, A. (1978) *Intellectual and Manual Labour. A Critique of Epistemology*, London, Macmillan.

Tabucchi, A. (1989) *Little Misunderstandings of No Importance*, New York, New Directions Publishing Corporation.

Tischler Visquerra, S. (2005) *Memoria, tiempo y sujeto*, Guatemala, BUAP y E-G Editores.

Traverso, E. (2004) *Cosmópolis, figuras del exilio judeo-alemán*, México, UNAM-Fundación Cultural Eduardo Cohen.

Vila-Matas, E. (2007) *Bartleby & Co.*, New York, New Directions.

Weber, M. (1963) *Le savant et la politique*, Paris, UGE-Collection 10/18.

Weigel, S. (1996) *Body- and Image-Space: Re-Reading Walter Benjamin*, London, Routledge.

11

MIMESIS AND DISTANCE: ARTS AND THE SOCIAL IN ADORNO'S THOUGHT

José Manuel Martínez

Mimesis is the internal nature of the human being and his affinity with the exterior nature from which he comes. It is the spontaneous impulse and the previous reason by which the individual answers to nature with the inevitability of an echo, and he recognizes himself being a part of it; is the complicity with any one of the creatures, from where emanates the solidarity with any living being. Even more, mimesis gives a name to the innate tendency of any human being to abandon the self into nature, to debilitate the limits of the autonomous and rational Ego in order to pour the self in the medium, renounce one's own differentiated identity and render the self in the other than oneself.

Mimesis is the contrary of the identity principle because it is the contrary of domination.

However, mimesis is also the contrary of negativity. Irrational, mimesis does not know the finitude or the distance necessary for a critical attitude.

(Marta Tafalla 2003: 132–3)

INTRODUCTION

Against identifying reason and its violence, against totalitarianism, Adorno proposed three categories: negativity, mimesis and memory. Certainly, these three categories were always important in modern arts and literature and in their criticism, and they are also categories that intervene in the very organisation and production of any contemporary literary or artistic artefact. It is not so clear how these categories function in respect to social organisation and social critique. It is to the credit of the Frankfurt School, and particularly to Adorno and Horkheimer, that they amplified the ambit of application of the categories of cultural criticism, applying these categories to the interpretation of authoritarian society and politics. A corollary not always explicit is that artistic and cultural criticism today are criteria that can be applied to the criticism of the social and even to contemporary political action. This is, of course, the very opposite of what is often assumed by left activism, where avantgardism in the arts is judged in "political" terms, which may indeed be "authoritarian political" terms. So the question is a controversial one and is particularly difficult once we go a little further than the repudiation of the Nazi regime, as Adorno and Horkheimer did in *Dialectic of Enlightenment*, and attempt to apply the categories of mimesis and memory to a strategic consideration of contemporary conflicts.

The association between revolutionary avantgardism and modernism in the arts, both supposed to be extreme positions of negation of the given, is recurrent.[1] It is commonly supposed that a spontaneous relationship between both kinds of avantgardism exists. It is well known that Adorno was against this assumption. For him the most important is not the semantics of arts or politics, what they are saying, but the real or structural position in which the subjectivity really is in relation to the political acts or the new objects or actions in arts. Adorno was opposed to the aesthetics of Hegel (as also to his metaphysics), so he was not interested in the narrative aspects of the arts. He turned instead to Freud, Nietzsche or Marx in order to reveal and denounce the inverted terms of ideology.[2]

It may be said that the first principle that political and aesthetic radicalism share is negation. Negation establishes a distance with the given facts of the world. But is an appropriate critical distance a matter of taste? Is it a subjective one? Is it an expression of an objective negativity? Or is it perhaps an absolute negation? I will discount the last possibility on principle. An absolute negation re-establishes the terms of pure affirmative facts. Adorno and Horkheimer were very aware of this, that, if it were absolute, negation would re-establish the terms of mimetic relationships. The point is that absolute negation is not arguable, it is a mere matter of taste and implies in practice whimsical behaviour; but if questions of taste are inseparable from mimesis, then capricious attitudes have a place in rebellion, so a dialectic consideration is always necessary, even in the case of negation. It is not an easy question. I want to clarify the matter in this chapter.

Some mediations are necessary, of the kind that Marx, Freud and even Nietzsche studied theoretically and that can make possible distinctions between different mimetic positions. There are not different mimeses or different mimetic impulses: all mean copying, but in different subjective positions. Mediations are related to memory or memories. Subjective position is characterised as criticism by a certain distance, basically a temporal one, but also a behavioural one. Negation has to be determined negation (to put it in Hegelian terms), determined by means of criticism, distance, interpretation and, of course, memory as an organiser not only of the subject itself but of historical conflicts in general. Determined negations are organised in constellations, subjective constellations with objective meaning.

Negation, simple though it may seem, requires clarification, so I will be dedicating my first point to it. Mimesis is a concept that comes from Aristotle's *Poetics* and from Plato's *Republic* and was not absent from modern criticism in general, in particular Freud's explanation of artistic production or Nietzsche's critique of the phantom of Ego, the feeble Ego of the individuals in multitudes; the concept is also present in literary studies and was the centre of the work of Auerbach entitled exactly so, *Mimesis*, where mimesis is considered principally as the study of different forms of appreciation and representation of reality. It was also very important for all the contemporary Marxist realists – Lukács and Brecht, for instance.[3] However, Horkheimer and Adorno went further and I will be referring briefly to their concept of mimesis. A third point refers to memory, consciousness and autonomy, considering the last in contemporary works of art and contemporary literature and Adornian aesthetics. Memory is the most frequented point in the literature related to Nazism. Memory requires a careful treatment, even if short; it is necessary to clarify whether we consider memory as independent of mimesis when a complete and operational concept of negation as determined negation is given.

Negation itself, as an isolated category, can recede to a postmodern abandonment of all distinctive criticism. In order to have a kind of model of criticism, a model of the critical position of the productive subject, the critical receptors and the always new artistic negative objects, we need to go further than the negation of spiritual and totalitarian absolutes to the clarification of a possible contemporary autonomous position.

Finally, I shall concentrate on the work of art as an autonomous object.

I shall give to the aesthetic question of autonomy a treatment connected with the question of memory and mimesis in order to consider the problem of liberty referred to the past and to the present. We need an analytical model referable to particular futures in actual situations of conflict; I hope that the clarification of the meaning of mimesis and negation in the Frankfurt School will be a modest contribution to it.

I   NEGATIVITY AND NEGATION

In all the work of Adorno, philosophy has its principle outside itself, it is born as an answer (Tafalla 2003: 67), it is criticism, and it is a negation that expresses what imposed identity means for the subject, something negative, domination, or what amounts to the same thing, the surrendering of reason to will.

Given this alienated position of the principle of identity, negation is never absolute. As negation is nothing substantial in itself, we arrive at a concept of negation by means of dialectical negations itself. What is not negation?

a) Negation is not equal to the abolition of the principle of identity in logics or mathematics, or even in any language. The structure of languages contains negation as meaningful operation. A new logic of negation is irrelevant.

b) Negation is not the abolition of the real, but criticism of the real.

c) Negation is not the complete abolition of identity in psychological terms; negation is not a product of psychosis; psychosis is not the result of negation in philosophical terms. Identity from the point of view of the subject has a meaningful memory, what negation of identity pretends is the liberation of the subject in a context of imposition of identity, not the abolition of the real, including the memory of the subject and his personal integration as such.

d) Negation implies the criticism of the phantom of Ego (an unreal megalomaniac projection of the subject as an unlimited power) and the mimetic acts of the subject of the multitudes (Horkheimer and Adorno 1987).

e) Negation is not plain action.

f) Negation is not an unconditioned, simple expression of the self.

g) Negation has its own categorical imperative: the orientation of thinking and action in ways that never repeat Auschwitz (Adorno 1975: 365). Corollaries of this moral principle are possible. Repetition as in Freud is the symptom of infirmity. "The new" is necessary not only as fashion, but as a means of producing the new constellations and corollaries necessary for the historically relevant negations. These constellations and corollaries are not enunciable *a priori*; they depend on subjects and conflicts; in any time they are postulated or reformulated, again and again.

Negation is closely related to the Adornian concept of negative liberty (Adorno 1975); as complete liberty has not the possibility of being real in the real world, there remains only one possibility of liberty and it is individual, a liberty that is given by means of knowledge and memory, and that is developed by means of a critical behaviour. Saying "no" is evidently not conformist behaviour; the guiding idea is to put distances, not participate, be an exile. Distance and negation are as mirror aspects of the same, but what puts the distance is criticism. Critical distance puts the object and the subject as an opposition, in certain ways creates the subject's position itself. But negativity is a quality of the real, of domination; as identity is imposed on the subject, negativity is also a quality of the subject.

It is convenient at this point to defer for a little the exposition while going on to the analysis of mimesis. The articulation of these concepts is dialectic.

Perhaps it will be convenient now to anticipate the conclusions of this chapter, violating in this way the rules of the game of essay writing. It would be good for the reader to have always in mind the inverted relationship between culture and politics proposed throughout the chapter as the very contemporary pragmatic problem. I can say that the model of the free individual is not the agitator in a multitude; but if the model is not the activist but rather involved in cultural production and cultural criticism, we have a problem on the left. And we have a problem in the association between revolutionary and artistic avantgardes, and it is a major problem. Adorno obtained the idea of a free individual inspired in intellectuals such as Benjamin or Berg who were able to resist identification with society. The works of Kafka, Beckett or Schönberg have their law in themselves, they are free in this sense and in their model of interpretation of the real; there are no absolute models, but they show the subjective position sufficiently to be preparatory and necessary in the formation of the new critiques. This means that we have to ground the kind of liberty conceived in *Negative Dialectics* in the concept of the aesthetic artefacts given in the *Aesthetic Theory*. It is in the concept of aesthetic criticism, artistic mimesis and the memory of arts and society included in the new works of art that all the dialectic and negation in thought acquires a materialist autonomous character (Tafalla 2003: 102). I think that the conclusion anticipated here will be acceptable if the obstacle that the ambiguity of mimesis interposes is removed.

II

Mimesis as a Theoretical-artistic Concept

Vicente Gómez introduces the exploration of the concept much as Adorno did, saying that art is not an anticipation of a better praxis, but is above all the criticism of a praxis that is domination, a criticism of brutal auto-conservation in the real by means of mimesis (Gómez 1998: 106). Adorno emphasised the second aspect developed in *Aesthetic Theory*, that is that the work of art is a criticism by means of mimesis. Some propositions may clarify the question, as follows:

a) Only a specific form of subjective and negative behaviour in the arts is able to develop as the non-identical with domination. Contemporary art is really such only when it is free of the manipulated mimetic impulse. Contemporary art should be distinguished from magic or religious art, and even from modern bourgeois art. Contemporary art is negative art. We have only one word, art, but the concept is completely different. Contemporary art is conscious of ancient and bourgeois art, as philosophical critique is conscious of classic and modern philosophy. In both cases consciousness leads to critical distances.

b) The behaviour of contemporary artists is mimetic, but differs from classicism and in the last instance from Lukács, and socialist realism in general, in that the mimesis in contemporary art and literature and in the conceptual treatment of mimesis in Adorno, is a mimesis of something that is not a natural beautiful perfection or a moment in a glorious narrative; it is mimesis of the particular terrors and pains or a particular expression of negativity; but remember, it is not negativity as an absolute. What contemporary art shows are subjective positions that reveal rational ways of apprehension; it is productive of something more than shock; it produces conceptual thought after the shock.

c) In Adorno mimesis is not the image of a "not yet," but the "copy" of the very structure of the given and an expression of the subjectivity affected by the negativity of the world. Artistic mimesis gives knowledge.

d) Mimesis in Adorno does not have a hypnotic relationship with the audience, as in Brecht, but on the contrary mimesis itself breaks the complacency of the receptors and moves them further than catharsis. What contemporary works are doing by means of mimesis is more than putting in place and moving and purifying; rather, it promotes changes in the subjective position of the receptor. It is this new position that puts the subject in a place where new cognitive constellations can be produced.

Contemporary art denounces the mimetic impulse which ends in a contemplative auto-complacence and pseudo-enchantments. So mimesis in Adorno is simultaneously not about illusions and not a mere copy of the real or ideal conceptions of the real; on the contrary it gives the very perception, real perception, global and mimetic perception, of the real in its negativity; by means of mimesis, the receptor of the work of art can remake the work by himself in his criticism, he acquires the artistic position in relation to the perceived object that operates as a door to the other, to an other that is real although not defined but dialectically present in the free mimetic relation with the structure presented, suggested or even posed by the receptor.

Mimesis and Fragment

It is known that Adorno was opposed to the metaphysical tradition, the memory of which he obviously did not want to abolish, but to criticise, as any other contemporary cultural characteristic (Adorno 1975).[4] System is the representation in metaphysics of the domination and the administration principles in society. Mimesis is irreducible to system. Mimesis is always a particular "copy"; even platonic pre-modern artists failed in an impossible copy of an nonexistent ideal giving us particular portraits of individuals much more particular and fragmentary than in previous symbolic medieval art. What can we say about mimesis in philosophy? The answer is on the side of fragment. Adorno understood that philosophy was not independent of its linguistic or literary expressions. So an anti-systemic expression has to follow the criticism of the illusory systems of metaphysics itself. Fragments of criticism are mimetic in the sense that they are related to particular conflicts that are expressed in particular conceptual constellations that depend on the perception of a particular situation. Rationally controlled mimesis and critical behaviours are exactly what remain after the destruction of imposed identity in culture; or (and this is in parallel) what remains after the Hegelian system was broken and shown to be illusory by Marx, Nietzsche and Freud.

Fragments are new approaches; essay has in common with contemporary artistic representation the fact of being expressions of "the new." Horkheimer had recovered the fragmentary philosophical essays written by Montaigne (Horkheimer 1982) or Rousseau as models for approaching contemporary problems related with subjectivity, and so did Adorno, but his most direct models of thought were those of the contemporary Austrian school of music. Fragmentary variations in music are the model of the new philosophy, the only philosophy that can be honest (Adorno 1987: 117). In Mahler, after the symphonies that resembled the Hegelian system or romantic novels (remember Beethoven), variations are the force that stand opposed to the completion of works; particulars stand against closed musical experience and systematic thinking. Mahlerian music recovered in an original way the Nietzschean concept that says that the system and its unity without fissures – the appearance of reconciliation – are dishonest, wrote Adorno (1987: 91). The excellent book by Martin Jay entitled *Adorno* insists in this characteristic and is completely structured around it. Atonal philosophy precedes the part of the book devoted to "the fractured totality: Society and Psyche", and the last part consolidates the approach as centring in culture and criticism (1984).

III MEMORY AND AUTONOMY

As Marta Tafalla writes, negativity is the most evident category in a philosophy that does not want to be systemic or affirmative; mimesis, on the other hand, puts some order into philosophy by means of a dissonance, introducing the irrational and the impulsive particular, all the temptations of regression and dissolution. But the philosophy of Adorno has to have a centre of gravity in an even deeper principle. Against totalitarianism, negation exercises criticism and puts distance, resisting as much as a negative liberty can resist, while mimesis offers compassion and solidarity; but only memory has healing power, however limited (Tafalla 2003: 195). According to Tafalla, if all domination consists in the last instance in the oblivion of the dominated, memory is the only instance that can defeat it and create some justice. If that is true, then, any form of liberty has to rest on memory. Certainly in an administered world the question of autonomous behaviour is not a simple one, as Adorno shows in part III of *Negative Dialectics*, where, in model I, he posits its possibility in memory and mimesis when he states that the lethargic conscience of liberty is based on the unconscious reminiscence of an archaic impulse about a situation in which there was no firm Ego in charge of subjective actions and feeling (Adorno 2003:221).

Therefore, from mimesis as a particularly bodily experience we can hope to derive a kind of universality associated with rational compassion, the maxim about good living as living like a good animal and also the end of reprisals (Adorno 1975: 296); but memory expands the pragmatic responsibility of any human being with an imperative, that of making impossible any repetition of Auschwitz (1975: 365). But if the problem is how to find pragmatically some form of autonomy, moral obligation and mimetic freedom are unable to resolve the question of an autonomous subject. We know that only a conscious process of production and reproduction of society, transparent for the subjects and determined by them would be the condition for liberty (1975: 261). Have we any anticipation of a possible autonomous production? The answer is yes, and again it is in the artefact of art. Without making a comprehensive study of the *Aesthetic Theory* I draw the reader's attention to some notions offset out in this work. These have a greater complexity, but I hope that they may act as triggers for a major study of *Aesthetic Theory* in relation to *Negative Dialectics* and stimulate further appreciation of the subject of change.

As we have said, mimetic behaviour finds a refuge in the arts. The subject whose autonomy is variable opposes what is different to him by means of mimesis with it. Artistic imitation reacts against the bad rationality of a rationalist and administered world. Mimesis, as a non-conceptual affinity of that which comes from the subject with that which is distant from him, is a feature of art as knowledge, as *rational*, given that the imitative behaviour tends towards an object of knowledge, notwithstanding the categories of knowledge that interpose precisely in the knowledge of these distant experiences (Adorno 1983: 77).

However, the mimesis is exorcised by means of the technological practices involved in the process of art production, which relates it to all the productive and reproductive processes in society, and this leads us to a paradox: the blind object produced by the artists produces the higher knowledge. Arts do not lead to change in the world, an ontological one; arts only change the subjective position (Adorno 1983:153). But if this is so, why are contemporary artistic objects an enigma? A simple answer would be that the contemporary artistic artefact has a double character as commodity in classical capitalism. Even if Adorno obtained the idea from Marx, he generalised the criticism of the double character from economics to culture; from crisis to disaster analysis, after the failure of the Bolshevik and other revolutions.

Arts are enigmatic. As arts pursue reconciliation, they say more than is existent; but they are not absolutes. Their participation in a kind of absolute implies a hubris that requires punishment, Adorno tells us in the language of Greek tragedy. What exists is not autonomous according to the consciousness except when it is by itself and wants the other; the work of art is the language of these wills. The elements of the other are in reality; they are awaiting a new constellation in order to find their exact place, continues Adorno in cabalistic terms borrowed from Benjamin.

But new constellations implied in any new artefact are completely enigmatic before being re-constellated by means of criticism and become less enigmatic and more conceptual after the critique. Criticism is the act detonated by the artefacts of contemporary art, itself negative and mimetic; contemporary art has been called a mostly conceptual art, not only because of a direct relationship with meaning and loss of meaning but because it is closely related to criticism; sometimes it introduces the critique of the work into the work itself, as in the case of modernism. After negation and imitation, the works of art represent the translation of a paper that has to be translated again and again in an inter-subjective criticism. Memory is absolutely necessary in these inter-subjective practices if the well-known Adornian dictum is to be accomplished; finally, the theory of imitation should be transposed: it is the reality that has to imitate art.

Being autonomous finds a kind of prefiguration in the negative and mimetic contemporary artistic and literary artefacts. Imitation of arts means memory and negation of tradition, mimesis with contemporary conflicts, looking always for new constellations.

NOTES

1. A good work on the matter in relation to the arts and politics in the latter half of the twentieth century is Giunta (2001).
2. All Adorno's work is oriented towards an adoption of Hegelian perspectives without their systemic or metaphysical implications, particularly in politics and arts.
3. It is certainly not the case with Benjamin, who is mostly a Marxist surrealist. In any case it is not my purpose here to reproduce the debate on realism in German Marxist circles, in which Adorno and Bloch had an important place.
4. In particular Model II on Hegel.

REFERENCES

Adorno, T. W. (1975) *Dialéctica Negativa* Madrid, Taurus.

Adorno, T. W. (1987) *Mahler*, Barcelona, Península.

Giunta, A. (2001) *Vanguardia, internacionalismo y política, Arte Argentino en los años sesenta*, Buenos Aires, Paidos.

Gómez, V. (1998) *El pensamiento artístico de Theodor W. Adorno*, Madrid, Cátedra.

Horkheimer, M. (1982) *Historia, Metafísica y Escepticismo*, Alianza, Montaigne y la función del escepticismo.

Horkheimer, M. and Adorno, T. W. (1987) *Dialéctica del Iluminismo*, Buenos Aires, Sudamericana.
Jay, M. (1984) *Adorno*. Cambridge, MA, Harvard University Press.
Tafalla, M. (2003) Theodor W. Adorno, una filosofía de la memoria, Barcelona, Herder.

LIST OF CONTRIBUTORS

Werner Bonefeld is a Reader in the Department of Politics, University of York, UK.

Alberto Bonnet is Professor at the Universities of Quilmes and Buenos Aires, Argentina.

John Holloway is Professor at the Instituto de Ciencias Sociales y Humanidades, Benemérita Universidad Autónoma de Puebla, Mexico.

José Manuel Martínez is a Lecturer in Aesthetic Theory at the Universidad del Museo Social Argentino, Buenos Aires, Argentina.

Fernando Matamoros is Professor at the Instituto de Ciencias Sociales y Humanidades, Benemérita Universidad Autónoma de Puebla, Mexico.

Marcel Stoetzler is Simon Postdoctoral Fellow, Centre for Jewish Studies, University of Manchester, UK.

Sergio Tischler is Professor at the Instituto de Ciencias Sociales y Humanidades, Benemérita Universidad Autónoma de Puebla, Mexico

Adrian Wilding is an Associate Lecturer at the Open University, UK

Darij Zadnikar is Professor at the Faculty of Philosophy, University of Ljubljana, Slovenia

NAME INDEX

SUBJECT INDEX

15133033R00147

Printed in Great Britain
by Amazon.co.uk, Ltd.,
Marston Gate.